Extraordinary Praise for
One Hundred and Four Horses

"A moving account of one family's determination to save abandoned horses. . . . Heartwarming. . . . Retzlaff provides readers with an intimate look at the personalities of these animals, as well as the physical and spiritual connections between each horse and rider. . . . A poetic memoir for horse lovers and those interested in stories of triumph over adversity."
—*Kirkus Reviews*

"[A] plainspoken, heartfelt memoir . . . with midnight rescue runs, forced departures in a matter of hours, theft, and betrayal. Retzlaff is at her best in her loving descriptions of the horses' personalities, allowing the reader to get to know the animals as individuals. The Retzlaffs' deep feeling for their charges will appeal to animal lovers of all stripes. . . . The couple's story—a drastic example of standing up for those you love—showcases the seemingly small but deeply significant heroism of doing the right thing."
—*Booklist*

"Dramatic, emotionally charged."
—*Daily Mail* (U.K.)

"What a wonderful, beautifully written story, one that grabs you quickly and only speeds up as it spins along. *One Hundred and Four Horses* is a breathless adventure set against a fascinating and terrifying time and an incredible story of a family that decided to be brave, that decided that the lives of the animals they loved was worth risking their own. It makes you wonder what you would do in the same position, but it left me inspired, truly, to feel like I was going inside that chaotic time and racing right along with them to save the horses. And more important, Mandy Retzlaff brings all these horses to life in a very moving, visceral way. You will mourn and celebrate with her at every step along the way."
—*Conor Grennan, New York Times* bestselling author of *Little Princes*

One Hundred and Four Horses

One Hundred and Four Horses

A Memoir of Farm and Family, Africa and Exile

MANDY RETZLAFF

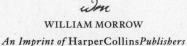

WILLIAM MORROW

An Imprint of HarperCollins*Publishers*

HarperCollins books may be purchased for educational, business, or sales promotional use. For information please e-mail the Special Markets Department at SPsales@harpercollins.com.

A hardcover edition of this book was published in 2013 by William Morrow, an imprint of HarperCollins Publishers.

FIRST WILLIAM MORROW PAPERBACK EDITION PUBLISHED 2014.

Library of Congress Cataloging-in-Publication Data has been applied for.

ISBN 978-0-06-220439-4

14 15 16 17 18 OV/RRD 10 9 8 7 6 5 4 3 2 1

*To all our beautiful horses, and especially to those
no longer with us—may their spirits run free*

Set a beggar on horseback, and he'll outride the devil.

—GERMAN PROVERB

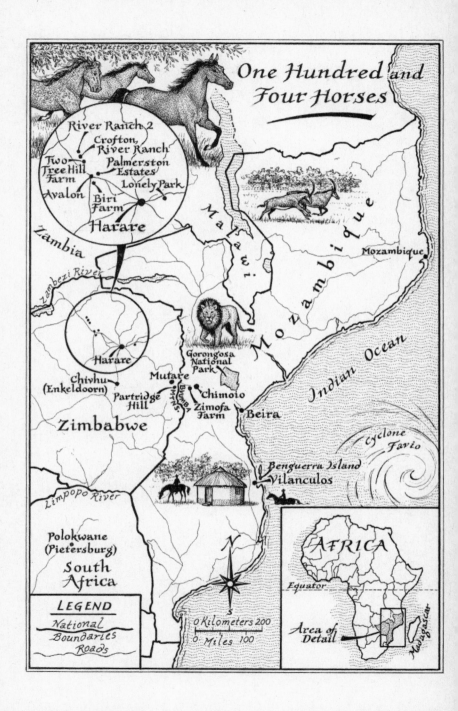

One Hundred and
Four Horses

2012 Hartman Maestro ©2013

River Ranch 2
Crofton,
River Ranch
Two
Tree Hill
Farm
Palmerston
Estates
Lonely Park
Avalon
Biri
Farm
Harare

Zambia

Zambezi River

Malawi

Mozambique

Harare

Chivhu
(Enkeldoorn)

Mutare

Partridge
Hill

Zimbabwe

Gorongosa
National
Park

Bvumba
Mts

Chimoio

Zimofa
Farm

Beira

Mozambique

Indian Ocean

Cyclone
Favio

Limpopo River

Benguerra Island
Vilanculos

Polokwane
(Pietersburg)
South
Africa

LEGEND
National
Boundaries
Roads

N

S

0 Kilometers 200
0 Miles 100

AFRICA

Equator

Area of
Detail

Madagascar

One Hundred and Four Horses

Prologue

THEY SET OUT as night was falling, but it is almost dawn and there has been no sign of my husband or our horses.

I stand on the wide veranda of the old colonial farmhouse, trying to make out shapes in the early-morning gloom. Before Pat left, he told me to get some sleep, but he has done this before—midnight missions to rustle our own horses off land we no longer own—and I know how it goes. Tonight, there is no way I can close my eyes. Whenever I do, all I see is images of the terrible things that might be happening, even now: my husband, so near to me, yet surrounded by men who might block the roads and build up barricades to stop him from getting out. Consumed by thoughts like that, I can do nothing but wait.

It is September 2002, and it has been only twelve hours since the Land Rover arrived at the gates of Biri Farm, our home in Zimbabwe, southern Africa, for the past nine months. Biri Farm stands ten kilometers across the veld from where I now stand, but it might as well be in another world.

Once the Land Rover was gone, Albert handed me a letter. We had, the letter said, only four hours to leave Biri Farm. If we dared to remain, we would lose everything: our horses, our worldly possessions, even our lives. By government decree, Biri Farm was no longer a safe haven.

Now I stand in the eerie chill before dawn, wondering what has taken my husband so long. The farmhouse behind me belongs to Nick Swanepoel, a good friend and neighbor. So far, his farm, Avalon, has been safe from the chaos spreading like cancer across our beautiful country of Zimbabwe. He has agreed to shelter us for the night, to take in our herd of horses until we can spirit them to a new home, and the farmhouse is piled high with all the boxes we managed to rescue from Biri. Somewhere in there, my mother is sleeping too, barely able to comprehend the madness that has become our lives.

There are ten kilometers between here and Biri Farm, but the mist is low and I can hardly see the end of the field in front of me. Pat should have been back by now. I shift nervously. All he had to do was get back onto Biri, rope up the horses, and lead them to the safety of Avalon. There was never any question, I knew, of leaving our horses behind. They are the horses of our friends, the horses of our neighbors, horses we have promised to protect. Some of them have been with us since the very beginning. Others joined us along the way. Many have already been driven from their own homes, attacked with spears or *pangas*— machetes—or abandoned on farms as their owners fled. They are our responsibility, and we are all that stands between them and long, drawn-out deaths from cruelty and neglect.

I hear movement behind me. Knowing that it is my mother, come out to make a fuss over her daughter—even though she is well into her seventies, she will always make a fuss—I turn around, preparing to tell her that everything is fine.

"Any sign?"

I shake my head.

"They won't be long," she promises, though she can hardly know. "It's a long trek with seventy horses."

I close my eyes. When I open them again, at last I sense movement. It seems only that there is something out there, yet everything around me is black. All the same, something tingles up and down my neck. I am certain now: there are different textures in the darkness.

"Mum?"

"What is it?"

"It's them . . ." I whisper.

Slowly, the shapes appear out of the darkness. At first they are like ghosts. It is only when I move forward, willing the ghosts to come to life, that those shapes begin to have definition. First a man, a groom, trailing a long rope behind him. Then a horse, bobbing contentedly forward, wearing a halter but no saddle. Then more horses alongside, each with a lead rope dangling from its halter. One, two, three, four, five . . . The procession continues into reaches of darkness I still cannot see.

"Is Pat with them?" asks my mother.

I cannot see my husband yet, but still I nod.

They weave along a track between fields of irrigated wheat, disappearing behind reefs of low gray mist and then coming back into sight. I know how many horses there will be, because I know them all by name. We have seventy-one now, but before long there will be more. Some days, the phone does not stop ringing. All across this once-proud nation, farms are being abandoned; farmers are fleeing, but in their wake are the animals they cannot take with them.

Then, at last, I see Pat. He is moving on the far side of the herd.

He is holding a lead rope in his hand—though, in truth, he does not even need that. The young mare he is leading, though a new addition to the herd, will do whatever he asks. The tallest and proudest of all our horses, she stands seventeen hands high, an aristocratic dun mare with beautiful black points and eyes that positively shimmer with keen intelligence. Shere Khan is the self-appointed queen of the herd, and like the queen that she is, she helps Pat guide the horses and grooms to safety.

There is an old German proverb, one I sometimes imagine Pat's great-grandfather might have used. *Set a beggar on horseback*, they used to say, *and he'll outride the devil*.

We have to outride the devil, that much is true—but watching the herd walk onto Avalon Farm, I wonder how long we can stay in the saddle.

"I see you're back," I say when Pat comes closer, not wanting to tell him how worried I've been.

"All of us."

Damn him, but he is almost grinning.

"Well?" I ask. "What now?"

Pat makes as if he is thinking about it. Behind him, the half-Arabian Grey and our daughter's mare, Deja Vu, are grazing the long grass, but even they must have some idea of what is going on all around us.

"We'll do what we always do," Pat says. "We'll make a plan."

TEN YEARS EARLIER

Chapter 1

I REMEMBER A place that was wild and filled with game. I remember a house with a giant mango tree in the garden and stables out back, where our horses grazed contentedly and waited to be ridden along dusty red tracks that wound their way into the bush. I remember picking up our children from school and driving home with the tsessebes—those powerful antelopes with chestnut hides, lunate horns, and strangely formed bodies—flocking into the trees alongside us. The farm was called River Ranch, the farmhouse Crofton. The farm's thick-forested hills and scrubby lowlands were held in the cradle of two rivers; its boundaries were patrolled by elephants tamed and trained to keep away poachers. Its soils held the promise of a new future, and on the day that my husband, Pat, and I took our children there for the very first time, in 1992, we thought it would be home forever.

That day, long ago and yet seemingly so near, we drove north on the Chinhoyi road, through fields of green wheat. Our car was laden with suitcases and packs, saddles and straps, and three squabbling children in the back. In the middle seat, our second son, Jay, was chattering animatedly about the game he might see. If there was one way of sparking the often taciturn Jay to life, it was to talk about the game he might track and hunt at our new home. The kudu, that large African antelope with its striped hide, huge horns, and powerful legs, that Pat and I had seen when we were first looking over the farm had been one of the things that propelled us to go to the auction and place a bid; this wild place was where we would spend our lives.

We followed the winding, dusty road and could soon see the farmhouse of Two Tree Hill, the farm that bordered our own, looming above us, with big workshops and a water tank in front. Farther on, we saw the glistening waters of the dam. A herd of the enormous black antelopes known as sable looked curiously at us, then turned and sped away through the wheat and into the cover of the thick bush. Behind us, the truck that was following jarred on patches of uneven road, but the four horses inside were content. This, after all, was to be a new home for them as well.

We reached the farmhouse early in the afternoon, when the midday sun was at its hottest. The building had a broad white facade and a simple roof of corrugated iron. Pat pulled the car around, into the shade of the mango tree, and, even before we had ground to a halt, the children tumbled out.

Paul, our eldest, was fourteen years old, big and broad and the perfect image of his father. Jay, just turned nine, had a mop of wild blond hair that almost hid his searching green eyes. Our youngest, Kate, was three years Jay's junior, a gorgeous girl who, surrounded by brothers and cousins, was growing up as tough as any of them and gave as good as she got.

"Is this it?" Kate asked.

"Your new home," I replied. "The farmhouse is called Crofton. What do you think?"

As Paul, Jay, and Kate inched forward to investigate, Pat and I turned our attention to the truck that had followed us onto the farm. Pat undid the latches and let down the ramp. Inside the truck, he ran his hands up and down the four horses' noses, promising them fresh air, clean water, and more grazing than they could wish for.

Frisky came first, her ears twitching inquisitively. An old skewbald mare, more than thirty years old, she barely needed leading. She simply followed the sound of Pat's voice. It was the same voice she had been hearing for twenty-two years, since the days when they would race antelopes together at Enkeldoorn (now called Chivhu), where Pat grew up. She was his very first horse, perhaps his very first friend, and I sometimes wondered which one of us was the real love of Pat's life.

After Frisky came her foal Mini, a bay mare with a wild temperament who had produced some very special foals. Once they were out, they turned to survey their new surroundings, while the other two horses, Sunny and Toffee, lingered in the shade of the horse trailer, unsure if they too should emerge.

While the children were looking up at the face of their new house, Pat ran his hands along Frisky's flank and listened to her responsive snort. His old friend took a few steps forward and dropped her head to start pulling the strange new grass between her teeth. When next she looked up, her nostrils twitched and she rolled her eyes.

This will do, she seemed to be saying. *If you say so, Patrick, this will do.*

When I look back now, moving to Crofton was a new beginning. Crofton was a place in which we wanted to invest the whole of our lives. We were to be surrounded by rugged, virgin bush, and we had set our sights on opening up and forging a productive farm, one that we might one day hand down to our children. It would be a place for the generations to come, and Pat and I would found it while our children had the most amazing childhood they could, running wild in our beautiful Zimbabwe.

I did not know that nine years later, our world here at Crofton would end.

I had met Pat in 1976, when he was studying at the University of Natal in Pietermaritzburg, South Africa. I had not met many Rhodesians before, having been born in Ghana and brought up in South Africa, but as soon as I met him I knew that he was the man for me. I had taken temporary work as a barmaid at a hotel popular with the university's students. Although I had never been to university myself, student life had become my life. My nights were filled with raucous laughter and parties, and I had become part of a big circle of friends, all of whom were studying at the university. Every year, the university held a fund-raiser they called Rag Day. On Rag Day, the students would build huge floats. Vast figures would be cast in plaster of paris, and garlands of flowers would cover trailers and cars. The students would climb on top of the floats and the procession would move along the streets of Pietermaritzburg, while we would all collect loose change for charities.

On Rag Day of 1976, I clambered onto one of the floats and headed off with the other students. As the floats lumbered along, we leaped on and off, proffering our tins, and the crowds in the street cheered wildly as each float passed by.

From somewhere in the crowd, I heard somebody calling my name. Standing pressed between two other students was a good friend from the university named Charlie Bender. He had caught sight of me on the float and was trying to attract my attention. When I spotted Charlie I waved back enthusiastically.

I did not notice Charlie's tall friend who was standing beside him. His name, I would later find out, was Patrick Hugo Retzlaff. It was much later in our relationship that I found out that Patrick had nudged Charlie and asked him who the waving girl was. When Charlie told him my name, Pat said, "Well, that is the girl I am going to marry. I have had a strange premonition."

Some months later, I was introduced to Pat for the first time. In the crowded hallway at a mutual friend's house party, we talked long into the night. As he told me about Rhodesia and his studies in animal science, he was, I decided, incredibly good-looking. Much taller than me, he had short-cropped hair and a fuzz of beard along the line of a firmly set jaw. At nineteen he was two years my junior. He had a delightful sense of humor that made me laugh out loud. As we parted ways that night, the party thinning out as dawn approached, he invited me to a birthday party the following week. I made no hesitation in saying yes and hurried out the door before he could change his mind.

On the day of the party, Pat picked me up at the hotel lobby. When he arrived, I was in my room upstairs, blow-drying my hair. I checked myself in the mirror—I had spent two years living in London and I considered myself something of a fashionista—and, when I was satisfied, went down to meet him.

The figure waiting in the lobby did not look like the tall champion I had met at the party. I stopped dead on the staircase and simply stared. It was Patrick Retzlaff, all right, but surely not the Patrick Retzlaff who had asked me out. His suit was at least three sizes too small and seemed to constrict him in all the wrong places. His feet, meanwhile, were showing through a pair of oversize, scuffed cowboy boots that had clearly seen better days. I looked at him in horror and my instinct was to slowly inch away, but Pat had already caught my eye. Perhaps I could feign illness. A migraine. Food poisoning. Anything to let him down gently. I did not know if I could be seen with a man who was so badly dressed.

My mind was wheeling, grappling to come up with some excuse, when suddenly there was a commotion in the bar on the opposite side of the hotel reception area. Pat and I turned to see what was going on. At the bar, a drunken and abusive man was bearing down upon a student much smaller and slighter than himself. There was a sickening crunch as the man's fist connected with the student's face.

Before I knew what was happening, Patrick—constricted by his ugly, ill-fitting suit—was barreling into the bar. In seconds, he had put himself between the student and the overbearing man. Lifting a big hand, strangled by the cuff of his suit coat, he pushed the drunk off. The drunk reeled back against the bar, and, beneath him, the student scrabbled out of the way.

When he had made sure the student was all right, Pat turned and made his way back out of the bar. His hand was dripping with blood, his palm a scarlet swirl where fragments of broken glass had raked across it. He didn't seem to notice until my eyes lingered on it, and when he did, he simply wiped himself clean up and down his suit.

Pat was wearing the biggest, broadest grin on his face.

"So," he said, "are we still going to that party?"

All thoughts of migraines and food poisoning had evaporated. Already, I knew that this was the man for me.

It was a wonderful birthday party, but more wonderful for letting me get to know Pat. We spent most of the night simply talking. Pat had come to South Africa on a scholarship, but his heart belonged in the old British colony of Rhodesia, and it was to Rhodesia that he planned to return, to take up a position on an agricultural research station. At the time, Rhodesia was more than a decade deep into a civil war. Following the British prime minister Harold Macmillan's famous "Wind of Change" speech in 1960, Britain had begun a process of granting independence to her African colonies—but by 1965, it had become clear that Britain would not grant Rhodesia her independence with anything other than a universal franchise. A policy like that would mean that every man and woman had exactly the same right to vote, irrespective of color or level of education, and this was deemed unacceptable by the Rhodesian government, which wished to preserve its present order, with fifty seats in parliament reserved for whites and fourteen for blacks. That system would have maintained a largely white parliament in direct contrast to the makeup of the country, in which only 10 percent of the population was white.

In 1965, Rhodesia's prime minister, Ian Smith, made a Unilateral Declaration of Independence; Rhodesia became independent, yet was not acknowledged as such by Britain. The UDI triggered the onset of the bitter bush war that had been raging ever since. I could not imagine what it was like to grow up in a country at war with itself, but for Pat it was all he had known. The Rhodesian army was locked in conflict with black insurgents led by a man named Robert Mugabe, among others, and a guerrilla war was being fought across the country. This was not war as I recognized it, but a succession of sudden conflicts, terror attacks, and violent reprisals, and many men on both sides of the divide were losing their lives. Rhodesia was in a state of stalemate, and as soon as he graduated from university, Pat would have to take up a gun and join the fray.

He told me all about that, but most of all, he told me about his horses.

I had never met a man as in love with horses and animals as Pat. He came from a long line of horse lovers. His maternal great-grandfather was the Baron Moritz Hermann August von Münchausen, an officer in the Prussian army who married an American heiress and built an enormous castle in Bokstadt, Germany. It was there that he founded a stable for breeding Thoroughbreds and became famous across Europe for producing champions. The most famous horse the baron had owned was named Hannibal, which he had bought for a great deal of money in those days, and whose skeleton, Pat told me, could still be seen in a Frankfurt museum.

Pat had inherited his family's ancestral love and skill with horses through his father, Godfrey, who had grown up in Tanzania and moved with his family to Rhodesia in 1965, just before UDI. In Rhodesia, Godfrey became the manager at a cattle ranch in the southwest of the country, and he would spend days in the saddle, riding around the eighty thousand acres of ranch. His favorite horse—and the one that, even into his old age, he would always vividly remember—was an Arabian stallion named Paul, after both his grandfather and his eldest son. Paul the stallion liked nothing more than to drink beer and would let nobody except Godfrey ride him. Over the years, many bets were placed on this, with cocksure young horsemen eager to prove their worth by climbing into the saddle—but Godfrey always won. With a little help from his friends, Paul, it seemed, could make his own beer money.

With family like that, it was only too clear that Pat would devote his life to horses—and, even on that very first night, I knew that it was so. And there was one horse in particular who had changed Pat's life, one horse who had been with him since he was a boy, one horse to whom he would always keep returning.

Her name, he told me, was Frisky.

In 1970, Rhodesia was five years into a bush war—but life, with all its loves, passions, and deaths, still went on. Pat was thirteen years old and on his way home from the school where he boarded. It was a year before his mother would tragically pass away from cancer, and he thought of nothing but running wild on the family farm. He had chickens and cattle of his very own, and would spend the holidays on horseback riding the farm horses, including his father's chestnut gelding, Bridle.

Pat reached the farm and was racing up to the farmhouse, dropping his school bags along the way, when he saw his mother and father standing out front. At first, he wondered if something was wrong. Perhaps something had happened to the cattle, which were his pet project, or the few chickens he still kept from an earlier obsession. Yet, when he reached his mother and father, they were smiling.

They did not welcome him home. That could wait. They simply told him to follow and led him to the back of the farmhouse.

Here, Bridle was in his paddock with two of the family's other horses. Pat ventured to greet his father's old horse, but, before he got there, he saw a new mare, a stranger come to the farm. She was small, fifteen hands high, a skewbald mare with beautiful markings and a willful look in her eyes. Pat stopped short, looking between his mother and father.

"Her name's Frisky," his mother told him. "Well, go on!"

Pat rushed over, stopping a few yards away from the horse to approach her more gently. She had already been tacked up. He put a hand on her muzzle and let her nibble at his hands. Her ears twitched as she became accustomed to this strange boy. Pat draped his arms around her, threw a look at his parents.

"She isn't saddled up for nothing," his father intoned.

His left foot went into Frisky's stirrup. Then, swinging his body over, his right found the stirrup on the opposite side. He lifted the reins in one hand, in the way he always rode, and started talking to her. It is a special moment, he knew, when a boy climbs into a horse's saddle for the very first time, even more special when it is his very first horse. Frisky walked slowly forward, to the edge of the paddock, where Pat looked down on his mother and father.

"Be careful with her," Pat's mother began. She had a tone that verged on the ominous, and Pat wondered if there was a story hidden here, something buried in Frisky's past of which he was not aware. He looked down at her, judged her to be ten or twelve years old. Hardly a foal, she must have had owners before, people who loved her like he knew he would.

"Well," his father said, "what are you waiting for?"

Pat brought her around. Across the farm, there were antelopes such as the tiny duiker or huge kudu to chase. He ran a hand through Frisky's mane. She, he knew, was going to love this.

Duiker on the left, kudu on the right. Frisky would rather chase the tiny duiker, but today she was happy to indulge Pat and they set off toward the kudu. Soon, the small herd scattered, and Pat and Frisky were through them, following a dirt track into the bush. The acacia trees were low here, and Frisky banked, first one way and then another. They were on the tail of some bushbuck when Pat ducked to avoid a low-hanging branch. He timed it badly, smashed into the bough. Beneath him, Frisky cantered on. Momentarily Pat grappled with the branch. Then, he fell. When he hit the ground, all the wind was expelled from his lungs. He lay there and heaved. Blackness came over him.

When Pat looked up, Frisky's face was all that he could see. She was standing over him, nosing forward, as if to make sure he was all right. When he began to stir, she walked away and turned slightly, presenting her saddle.

Get up, Pat, she seemed to be saying. *We haven't got time for lounging around. That bushbuck's already got away* . . .

When they reached home, Pat tried to hide the fact that he had fallen off—but his mother had already raised two other sons, and somehow she just knew. It was time, she told him as she dusted him down, for a story.

Frisky had once belonged to the relation of a local farmer, a gift for their young daughter. She had been the daughter's pride and joy, and she had spent long hours being ridden and groomed, doted on by all members of the family.

It was on a ride through the bush that tragedy had found Frisky.

Startled by some smaller creature shooting out of the bush, she had shied away and the girl in her saddle had been thrown. Like Pat had done, the girl lay in the dust; but unlike Pat, she would never get back up. Stricken with grief, the girl's parents could no longer look at Frisky. Their daughter's death hung heavy about them, and Frisky was a symbol of it. She would have to be sent away, or else destroyed.

Two weeks later, she arrived at Pat's father's farm.

"So you must be careful," Pat's mother concluded.

After the story, Pat did not stop to get changed. Instead, he went back to the paddock, where Frisky was waiting. He spent the night checking over her hooves and grooming her. Whatever happened in Frisky's old life, it was not her fault. In the years to come Pat would come off Frisky many times—a hole in the ground that she did not see, the assault of a low-hanging branch—but not once would he be thrown. All he ever had to do was remember the way she waited for him as he lay, winded, in the dust, and he knew: Frisky would look out for him just as much as he would look out for her.

That night in 1976, talking to this strange man in his ill-fitting and bloodstained suit, I was suddenly transported back to memories of my own childhood horse. I had longed for a horse like Frisky, one who would be my best friend and protector and in whose saddle I could lose myself for days at a time, but I was not as blessed as Pat. The horse I remembered was named Ticky. He was a fiery little piebald pony and threw me from the saddle more times than I can remember—but I loved him more than anything else.

I was eleven years old when Ticky entered my life. I was attending school in Johannesburg, and a new girl was enrolled in my class. Her name was Erica, and she lived on a small farm just outside the city, where her parents kept a whole herd of horses. When I was finally invited to stay with Erica for the weekend, it was a dream come true. We spent long hours brushing her horses' manes and combing their tails. We would both jump onto her horse and canter bareback for hours around the farm. Every time I returned home from Erica's, the only words that came out of my mouth had to do with horses.

On one of my weekends with Erica, we stopped fussing over her mare and watched as her father drove into the farmyard, pulling a horse trailer behind his truck. With a silent nod, he unloaded a small piebald gelding, perhaps only twelve hands high and with a very slight stature.

"His name," Erica's father told us, "is Ticky."

Ticky looked at us balefully, but Erica and I were not deterred. We circled him, trying to get close enough to brush his hair and comb his tail as we had the rest of Erica's horses, but he just stared at us with a malevolent twinkle in his eyes. Every time we came close, he swished his tail dismissively, shuffled away, and went back to grazing.

Nevertheless, I was obsessed.

When my father came to collect me, I squeezed his hand and begged him to ask Erica's father if Ticky was for sale. Unconvinced, my father suggested I should try to ride Ticky first, before we made any rash decisions. At last, a date was made, and I returned to Erica's farm, determined that Ticky should fall in love with me the same as I had fallen for him. Beautifully tacked up, Ticky awaited my arrival with that same baleful stare. All the same, I stroked his tangled mane and whispered sweet words to him. In reply, he bared his big yellow teeth, rolling his eyes.

Confident that as soon as we were riding we would form an unbreakable bond, I hoisted myself into the saddle, grinning at my father as I did so. Yet, before I could even grab the reins, Ticky took off, tearing down the driveway and out onto the open veld. In seconds, I had lost my balance, tumbled from the saddle, and landed flat on my back, all the wind knocked out of me.

By the time I looked up, Ticky was already headed for home. I trudged back alone. Once again, I hoisted myself into the saddle and, this time, was swift enough to snatch up the reins. I gave Ticky a gentle kick, and off we went.

Suddenly, Ticky put his head down and executed a buck. Unable to stop him, I soared through the air and landed, headfirst, on the road.

By the time the blurriness was fading, my father was standing over me. He looked down, his face swimming in and out of focus, and reached out to help me to my feet.

"Are you sure you want this horse?" he demanded, face creasing with anxiety. "It looks uncontrollable to me."

Dazedly, I nodded. There was no going back, no matter how wicked this little pony really was.

All these years later, listening to Pat talk about his own childhood horses, I wondered if Ticky might have been the sort of horse he would have liked: strong, willful, but intelligent beyond measure. My parents quickly learned to detest Ticky. I spent my nights protesting, declaring my unwavering love for the nasty little horse who would pin me against his stable wall, lunging for his bucket, but somehow I knew they could not be convinced. No matter how many times he bit, no matter how many times he kicked out, my resolve only hardened: Ticky was the horse for me. He was going to love me like I loved him, or the world would surely end.

One day, some months into my struggle with Ticky, we entered ourselves into the bending race at a local gymkhana (an equestrian meet). At Erica's farm, we cornered Ticky, fitted him with his bridle and saddle, and walked—or perhaps dragged—him to the club where the competition was to be held. As we approached, I could hear the cries of a huge crowd of excited children and eager parents and the neighing of all their horses.

I had already spent long hours brushing Ticky, and his coat gleamed in the morning sunlight. I was convinced: Today was going to be the day that Ticky would prove his true worth. Out there, on the track, we would come from behind to win, triumphant together; Ticky would know what we had achieved, and all of his nastiness would simply evaporate away.

At last, my name was called, and Ticky and I took our place along with six other riders. A red flag was waved, and Ticky and I were off.

We were not even halfway to the first bending pole when Ticky took flight. Making a dramatic turn, he charged at the fence, scattering spectators. Though we cleared it, somewhere in the air I lost my balance and toppled to the side, crashing down from Ticky's back.

Indignant, Ticky came to a stop, gave a kick of his hooves, and, without a look at where I lay, headed for home.

On the grass, I lay alone, my riding hat askew.

"That's it," I heard my father cry. "We are selling that damn horse!"

It was the last time I ever saw Ticky.

"I have to admit," I said to Pat, the sounds of the birthday party fading around us, "I haven't ridden since."

"Well, I suppose we'll have to do something about that."

He kissed me for the first time that night—and one week later, I packed my bags, said good-bye to my little room in the hotel, and moved in with Pat.

We were married in 1978.

In Rhodesia, the bush war still raged. The country's white farmers, isolated and not well protected, were targeted by the so-called freedom fighters. The rebels' guerrilla tactics of attacking suddenly and then disappearing into the bush kept army patrols busy across the country. All the same, there was only one place in the world that Pat had ever wanted to get married: the town of Enkeldoorn, close to his childhood farm, a place that occupied so many of his memories and thoughts. I had heard so much about the town and the land across which Pat and his beloved Frisky had cantered that I felt as if I knew it already; now, it was time for the formal introduction.

Pat's father's farm was every bit the paradise he had told me about on that very first night. After the service, the wedding party moved there in convoy, and, not for the first time, I noticed that many members of our party were carrying weapons, their eyes fixed on the horizons and intersecting roads. Rhodesia, I had to tell myself, may have looked perfect, but it was still a country at war.

At the farmhouse, we were met with a feast fit for a king. I stepped down from the car and felt a little kicking in my belly; our firstborn son was already well on the way. I wondered what he would have made of all this. Tables dressed in white damask cloths groaned under cured hams and other delights. Champagne flowed. The laborers of the farm had decked themselves out to join in the festivities and kept glasses full. My mind whirled, seeing these same men who watched the horizons with such steely eyes throwing back champagne and roaring with laughter. There was something about Rhodesians, I decided, that made them look at joy and disaster with the same eyes. It must have had to do with living under the shadow of war for so long and still preserving all that is good about life. I found it exhilarating, I found it absurd, I found it frightening and life-affirming all at once. In the years to follow, I would come to know this feeling by one simple word: *Rhodesian*. I felt the kicking again and the thought hit me: my son—he was going to be a Rhodesian as well.

It was time for the speeches. Happy under the effects of the champagne, Pat's father stood and made his way to the center table.

"When Pat first introduced me to . . ." He hesitated, seemed to be wetting his lips. "I'll start again," he continued. "When my son Pat first introduced me to . . ."

"Amanda!" somebody shouted.

"Amanda," Pat's father repeated. "Of course. When Pat first introduced me to *Aman*—"

In that instant, the wedding party fell silent. Pat's father's eyes fixed on some point in the middle distance, and, as one, the men at the party turned to follow his gaze. I stood. Out there, a vehicle moved, thick, choking black exhaust fumes behind it. It seemed to shimmer in the heat, banking along the same farm roads over which the wedding convoy had come. It was, it appeared, heading straight for us.

Nobody said a word. Nobody had to. All the men at the wedding simply stood and hurtled for their cars.

"What is it?" I asked.

Pat stood. "*Terrs . . .*"

Terrorists: the Rhodesian name for the black insurgents making war on the ruling government. The vehicles we had traveled in were all wheeling around, sending up flurries of dust, as men piled inside and checked their weapons. Pat ran to join his father's car, stopped, and hurried back to where I was standing.

"Here," he said, "take this."

I found a gun pressed into my hands. Though I took it, I had no idea how to hold it. Pat told me it was an LDP, a submachine gun that only Rhodesians ever wielded. After UDI there had been so many international sanctions against the country that importing almost anything had been impossible. This had given rise to industries in which Rhodesia had never before operated, and with the outbreak of guerrilla warfare in 1966, one of those boom industries had been in weaponry like this. The gun I was holding was nothing less than a Rhodesian imitation of the infamous Uzi.

"What do I do with it?"

"You just point and shoot," Pat said. He turned and began to lope after the other men. Then, absently, he looked over his shoulder. "But only at the *terrs*," he added. "Don't point it at us . . ."

I had never held a gun before—though, in the years to come, I would receive training in all kinds of weaponry, just as all Rhodesian women would, in case we too found ourselves caught up in war.

I was sitting, slumped over the bridal table with the submachine gun in my lap and an empty champagne glass in my hand, when the men returned. Looking up, I saw Pat striding back to the wedding table.

"Terrorists?"

Pat shook his head. "It was only a bus."

"Is this what life is going to be like?" I asked. "Too much drink, guns, chasing after terrorists through the bush . . ."

Pat could not have known what was in store for us twenty years from that day, when we would find ourselves having to leave the country I had come to love, but today he threw me a rakish grin and helped me to stand.

"Probably," he said.

I put down the gun. If this was the man I was going to love, I supposed I had better love his absurd, wild country as well.

"Then we'd better get on with the speeches."

Our first son, Paul, was born in Pietermaritzburg five months after the wedding. I was twenty-three years old, Pat twenty-one, and we were ready to start our family life together. As soon as Pat graduated from university we prepared to return to Rhodesia permanently and forge a life there. There was only one complication: like all men of fighting age, on his return Pat would be called up to join the army. Members of the South African government had tried to persuade him to remain and commit his new training in animal sciences to the nation in which he had studied, but Pat was Rhodesian at heart, and Rhodesians never die. His country needed him, and I followed him into a country at war. Pat enlisted in the army and was stationed at a barracks in the capital, Salisbury (now called Harare), while Paul and I lived close by.

In 1980, the bush war drew to a bitter, negotiated end. Robert Mugabe and his ZANU-PF party won a landslide election in March, and white Rhodesia began its transition into Zimbabwe. A sense of defeat hung over Pat and his compatriots, and across Rhodesia many families made preparations to leave and find some new corner of the world. For many, the thought of living in a country governed by one of the terrorists they had been fighting was too much to bear. Australia, South Africa, and Canada were richer countries for their leaving. Pat and I talked about finding a new life in Australia, somewhere for Paul and the brothers and sisters who might follow him, but I knew that, in his heart, Pat belonged in Rhodesia. And since Rhodesia was no more, Zimbabwe would have to do.

We sat together, late at night.

"I want him to have the life I had," Pat said, bouncing baby Paul on his knee. "I want the same sort of childhood for him. Somewhere he can ride with game, go wild in the bush, be surrounded by dogs and cattle and duiker and baboons. If he can have just ten years of a life like that, it has to be worth it, doesn't it?"

I looked at the way Paul gazed up at his father. That, I decided, was the life I wanted for my children as well. If they could look back on their childhoods with as much vivid nostalgia as Pat did his own, we would have given them the best possible start.

"What do you think, Paul? Do you want to be a Zimbabwean?"

Paul looked at me, then at his father. Stoutly, he nodded.

"The master has spoken," I said.

So Zimbabwean we were, and Zimbabwean we would stay.

It was those thoughts that returned to me as, twelve years later, we unloaded our packs at Crofton to begin our new lives. As I watched Pat swing into the elderly Frisky's saddle, and Kate and Jay tumble out of the barren house that would soon become our beloved home, I was thinking of the baby Paul, of those first days after Rhodesia became Zimbabwe, of the hopes and dreams Pat and I had shared long into the night. We had spent the last ten years living in various places across Zimbabwe—the agricultural research station where Pat first worked, the rugged farm Lonely Park, where Pat's brother kept one of the nation's biggest dairy herds—but the land around us was finally ours. It was a place we could mold, a place we could pour ourselves into and live until our lives were done. Ten years before, in one of our earliest homes, we had buried a baby, Nicholas, only a few weeks old when he died, and the feeling of leaving him behind was not one we wanted to live through again. Here, this new land on which we now stood, could be a place to put down roots, a place to live a good life and never leave anything behind again. It was scrubby, untamed, with low jagged hills crowned in bush and red earth that seemed impenetrable to the eye— but Pat brought Frisky around and, as he gazed into the distance, I knew already what he was thinking. Here, he would build barns; here, he would build workshops; here, the irrigation channels; here, the grading sheds for our tobacco. Behind him, Jay's eyes were on the hills. He listened for the sound of baboons and searched the shadows between the trees for antelope or signs of leopard. Kate reached up and wrapped one arm around a lower bough of the mango tree. She was scrabbling to pull herself up when Paul appeared behind her and gave her the lift that she needed.

In front of me, Frisky snorted softly. She turned her head against Pat's reins, as if all she wanted to do was look me in the eye. She too must have been considering the land. It dawned on me that this would be her final home, just as I wished it would be mine.

The land was ours. One day it would belong to our children, and our children's children. Our new life had finally begun.

Chapter 2

OPENING UP THE bush to set up a farm is like riding a horse; you cannot command the land to do your bidding—you can only ask it. Like a horse, the land has its own character. It can be willful. It can be defiant. But it can give great joy as well, unveiling its secrets for you as you come closer and learn to work together for a greater good.

As we gazed out over virgin bush, Pat and I shared a daunted look. The land was rugged, scrubby lowlands out of which grew the wild, rocky hills we called *koppies*. Though the farm was bordered by two rivers, one a perennial stream and the other flowing north into the great Zambezi, the soil on which we meant to farm was fertile yet difficult to handle, being very hard and compacted, the kind of land that was impossible to cultivate without heavy machinery and careful management. The thought of driving back the bush and seeing fields of green tobacco, acres of tomatoes, and the rich glow of Mexican marigolds was enough to buoy us for the moment, but there was no use denying it: this was land into which only somebody as determined as Pat would dare to pour his life. There is no doubt that my husband is the most determined and optimistic man I have ever met. Were he not that way, our lives today would be very different.

The land we had bought had been a farm once before, during the

Rhodesian tobacco boom of the early 1960s. For decades, though, no crops had been cultivated here; only cattle had roamed from river to river. In their fields, the mfuti trees with their long feathered leaves grew tall again, and the bush had crept down from the hillsides. For all its wildness, the farm was exactly what Pat had been dreaming of: a place where we might test ourselves like the first African pioneers, somewhere he could use all his years of study, a place we could shape and leave for our children.

All the history books had the same wisdom to share. It was not the pioneers who benefited from the years they did battle with the land; it was those who came after: their children.

"Where to begin?" I asked. Paul, Jay, and Kate gathered behind us.

"It begins," said Pat, "with tomatoes."

This land could not be tamed by Retzlaffs alone. In the days that followed, we hired more than 250 workers, who began to build their homes here, too. Never and his wife, Mai Never; our driver, Charles; our gardener, Oliver; and Kate's nanny, Celia—only once we were all together could we begin. Farms in Zimbabwe often had whole villages of workers living on the land, with their own farm schools and medical clinics, and our farm was to be no different. We would have a core of workers who lived here, and with the harvests, more would join us as seasonal contractors.

All over Crofton the rooms were dominated by big contour maps and plans Pat had drawn up: where best to build the grading sheds for some future crop of tobacco; how best the roads might run so that they were protected from natural erosion; how much of the land could be irrigated without resorting to building a dam. It was a broad, holistic approach to farming, a scheme Pat had been dreaming of since the first years of our marriage. To see it come to fruition was the culmination not only of a dream, but of decades of hard work.

Those first months were spent driving back the bush. It would take a man four days to carve a crater and fell one of the giant mfuti trees that flourished here, and four more to chop that tree into cords for shipping away. Even then the work was not done, for half the tree remained underground and would not truly leave the land until five or six seasons had passed.

Some days it was imperceptible, the farm changing as slowly as a glacier melts. Other days, the bush had visibly receded between dawn and dusk, and we would go to bed on a farm different from the one on which we had awakened. The children would go off to boarding school during the weeks and return for weekends to a farm that was never the same: only the same sheltering sky, the same herds of tsessebe, the same mother and father warning them about the dangers of the bush.

As the first yields of tomatoes were being harvested and packed into crates, Pat and I rode on horseback between the fields, with Frisky and the chestnut mare named Sunny. Tomatoes flourished on virgin land, and we knew how much they enriched the soil for different crops to come: tobacco, cotton, maize, and export vegetables and flowers.

Frisky whinnied softly underneath Pat.

"What next?" I began, watching the shadowed outlines of our workers move between the rows.

"I was thinking," Pat joked, "that I might get some turkeys . . ."

It is a curious feeling when your heart swells and sinks all at once.

Years ago, when we had been married barely a year, I had come to understand the particular nature of Pat's insanity, his desire to collect and hoard animals of just about every description. As Zimbabwe was being born out of the ruins of Rhodesia, Pat had worked at an agricultural research station called Grasslands, where company policy had been to slaughter the smallest lamb every time a sheep gave birth to triplets. Unwilling to accept this, Pat had taken to bringing them home, until our garden was heaving with his own private flock. While baby Paul crawled around the living room, he was surrounded by dozens of baby sheep, bleating out for their bottles. I became particularly skilled as a surrogate ewe, able to hold six bottles between my legs for the lambs to suckle while I fed another four out of my hands.

If this had been the limit of Pat's madness, perhaps I could have written it off as a strange idiosyncrasy. Soon, however, Pat found himself the proud recipient of a gaggle of turkeys as well—and, as turkeys are usually very bad mothers, he insisted that each turkey have its own cage in which to lay her eggs.

Pat, of course, had to go to work during the day, so the management of the Retzlaff menagerie invariably fell to me. One of the most important of my duties was to move the turkey cages each day, so that they were on fresh ground and could be exposed to the very best sun and shade, dependent on which each needed. Often, I felt as if I was being watched over by Frisky, who would immediately report on my work to her beloved Pat when he came home from work. Those two, I had begun to understand, were as thick as thieves.

After grueling days of feeding lambs and horses—not to mention our very young son—perhaps I could be forgiven for forgetting to move the turkey cages in accordance with Pat's regimen. One day, exhausted by the morning's efforts, I decided that the turkey cages would have to wait. That evening, while I was cooking supper, Pat came home and conducted his evening inspection of all his beloved animals, the toddler Paul perched happily on his shoulders. I was stooped over the pot, breathing in the beautiful aromas of lamb—not our own, I hasten to add—when I heard Pat's roar. In seconds, he appeared in the kitchen doorway, his face purpling in fury.

"What's wrong?" I asked, my thoughts turning to baby Paul.

Pat simply lifted an accusing finger.

"You," he said, "haven't moved a single turkey cage."

At Crofton, as he brought up the subject of turkeys again, I looked away, trying not to acknowledge Pat's wicked grin. I reined Sunny around, as if to make for home.

"This time," I said, "Jay and Kate can look after them."

In August the whole country would change color. These were the first stirrings of Zimbabwean spring. Across the farm, the msasa trees came into new leaf. Light pinks deepened into pinks and reds; reds softened into vivid mauves; mauves ebbed away, leaving a rich dark green in their wake. In the evenings we would ride from Crofton farmhouse and watch as the bush came alive in this new array of color.

On one particular morning, driving to pick up Paul at school, I was late. Even the traffic in the city of Harare seemed to know it, slowing down and jamming at every intersection I tried to drive through, as if deliberately trying to vex me. As I checked and rechecked the time, my only consolation was that Paul knew the kind of life we led too well; he wouldn't be expecting me to be right on schedule.

He was waiting at the bus stop in a scuffed-up school uniform when I arrived, at five feet tall an image of his father in miniature. Like his father, he scowled at me, but, like his father, he didn't mean it.

Also like his father, Paul loved all animals. My eye caught something squirming under the folds of his school blazer.

"His name's Fuzzy," Paul said, sliding into the front seat. The tiny head of a puppy, a Jack Russell crossed with a Maltese poodle, poked out of the top of his collar, inspected me with mischievous eyes, and then ducked back to wriggle against Paul's chest. "He's saying hello."

"Darling, where . . ."

I had taken off into traffic, my eyes flitting between the road and this ball of fur to whom Paul was now feeding the end of an ice cream cone from his pocket. From somewhere, horns blared. I looked up, managing to correct my course just in time.

"Remember when school gave me Imprevu?"

Actually, we had paid a fortune for Imprevu. She was a beautiful bay mare, extremely eager, responsive, and exciting to ride, and she would be ridden by Paul and Pat regularly after Frisky died. She had belonged to the riding school, but they were only too pleased to send her to Crofton and receive a princely payment in return.

"Well, it was the same thing. My teacher gave him to me."

"Just gave him to you?"

"He knows how much we like animals."

I had to smile.

"Look over your shoulder, Paul."

Paul looked over his shoulder, Fuzzy craning his neck the same way.

On the backseat sat a crate with two little Scotties peeking out. Each of them wore a perfect little tartan bow, and their tiny black eyes considered Fuzzy carefully.

"I've just picked them up," I said. "Aren't they adorable?"

"Mum!" Paul exclaimed. "You're *just* like Dad!"

"Don't start on that. Your father's much worse than me . . ."

Paul was fixated on the box of scrabbling pups. I had long been fascinated by Scotties. They looked perfectly adorable, with black eyes like the ones in the face of a teddy bear. Well, if Pat could go around collecting turkeys and horses and sheep, I had to be allowed a little indulgence of my own. Perhaps it was my husband's madness rubbing off on me.

Fuzzy made a spirited squirm out of Paul's arms and dropped into the backseat with the other pups.

"Have you told Dad?" asked Paul.

"Let's keep it quiet for a while." I grinned. "I've been promising him another Great Dane . . ."

Of all our children, Paul was the most eager to live a life in the saddle. Imprevu, the mare he had brought home from school, was similar to Frisky in many ways. She required an experienced hand and was ridden only by Paul and Pat. Paul experienced the same joy in saddling her up and exploring our farm as Pat had as a boy with Frisky.

Jay did not have the same passion for horses but loved the bush and spent his time roaming the farm with his best friend, Henry, hunting and birding—but I would often see Kate marveling at her father in Frisky's saddle, or Paul as he took off on Imprevu, kicking up dust as they cantered along the winding farm tracks. Soon, it would come time for her to learn to ride, and she would do it with the very same partner with whom Pat had spent those idyllic years of his own childhood.

When Kate was on Frisky's back, everything seemed to come together at Crofton. I would see her sitting in the saddle, her father just behind her, Kate's hands nestled inside his, with the reins folded up in between. She would tug and tease at the reins, and in return, Frisky would obey the simplest commands. Somehow, she seemed to know that this was Pat's daughter on her back, and she treated her with such kindness, such simple charity, that it pulled at my heartstrings to see it. In her old age, Frisky had lost the mischievous, flighty temperament of her earlier days—but there wasn't a thing she wouldn't do for Pat, or in turn for little Kate.

Kate took to riding like her father and elder brother before her. She was a natural, and soon she would join Paul and Pat at the local equestrian events and paper chases. Seeing her in Frisky's saddle, I often thought back to that cheeky little pony Ticky and how he had put me off horses when I was a girl. I wondered what I might have been like if I had had the same childhood as Pat, running wild on a Rhodesian farm with a beloved horse underneath me.

One morning, Pat and I saddled up Frisky and three other horses and set out with Jay and Kate to check the fences around the farm. The ride was long, and the sun was blistering overhead. As we approached the Munwa River, Jay reined in and gestured for Kate to do the same. They were looking, almost longingly, at the crystal waters. Jay gave me the same pleading look I'd seen before.

"Can we go for a swim?"

The horses, too, looked as if they needed a rest, so we dismounted and Pat held the reins of all the horses while I helped Jay and Kate undress.

As the children were preparing to run into the waters, Pat loosened his hold on the reins—but Frisky, covered in a sheen of glistening sweat, only looked nervously at the riverbank, refusing to go near. Pat and I exchanged a curious look and no sooner had we done so than Frisky released a desperate whinny and began to stamp her feet.

Pat, as he had done ever since he was a young boy, put his arms around Frisky, patting her neck and rubbing her flank, whispering to her so that she might calm down. Yet, no matter how much he consoled her, Frisky could not be calmed. As Jay and Kate scrambled out of their socks and headed for the water, she picked up her front hooves and smashed them back down. There was something desperate, almost pleading, rolling in the back of her throat.

I turned to Jay and Kate. They were almost at the water's edge. Only then did I see what Frisky had seen. The dark eyes of a crocodile glimmered menacingly, just above the surface of the water.

Yelling for Pat, I hurtled down to the riverbank and grabbed Jay and Kate to drag them back. From the water, the croc looked at us, shifting its malevolent eyes.

Back at Frisky's side, listening to her gather her composure, I shuddered.

"No swimming today," I said.

Terrified at what might have happened, we hastily turned the horses from the river to make the ride back home, but for days afterward I could not stop recalling the look of terror in Frisky's eyes: not that anything might happen to her, but that something terrible might befall one of our children. It is not for nothing that people say they can see keen intelligence shimmering in a horse's eyes. If I had never seen it before, Frisky was the one to teach me that lesson: the horse sees, the horse knows, the horse cares and remembers. We think we are their guardians, but sometimes—just sometimes—they turn out to be our guardians as well.

It was a lesson we would keep coming back to throughout our lives, for reasons none of us could begin to imagine then.

The lands were cleared, plowed, and treated. The irrigation pipes stretched for long kilometers from the rivers that encircled us. The grading sheds were ready, the curing barns waiting eagerly for their first crop; the tobacco seeds were germinating in the seedbeds, waiting to be transplanted to the land.

All we needed was the rain, but the rain wouldn't come.

Between 1993 and 1995 only fourteen inches of rain fell. The rivers disappeared, the game looked emaciated, and the waters in our neighboring Two Tree Hill Dam fell imperceptibly each day, until they were only a brown shimmer in the bottom of the basin, the dam wall standing high and exposed.

In those droughts, tomatoes were all that we had. The farm was telling us that she could do no more. They grew in the fields all year round, so all that year I was setting out after dark to sell them, running long circuits around Harare and, now, into the villages and townships, too. Along the way I could see other Zimbabweans selling tomatoes, maize, and bush fruits on the sides of the road. It did not come to this for us, but as I looked into the grading sheds and saw the poor, wilted leaves of tobacco we had managed to harvest, I wondered what we had done. Had we sacrificed our children's future by gambling on clouds in the sky?

Those skies were endless expanses of blue, cruel in their blank simplicity. Beneath them, Crofton baked. I walked along the narrow channels between the tomato vines, lifting leaves and cupping each green fruit in my hand, turning them gently to look for signs of infestation or disease. Along the edge of the field, Pat and Frisky followed one of the trails, calling out to workers in the opposite fields. Every time I saw a mottled leaf or serrated edge showing the telltale signs of some hungry insect, I called out. Pat turned to acknowledge me. When he did not hear, I shouted louder. Here, I said. *Here*, and *here*. In silent fury, he swung from the saddle. He wanted nothing more than to ignore me, to go back to wrestling with blighted tobacco in the fields or opening another stretch of bush in the deranged belief that the rains would shortly come. Instead, he strode over to lift the same leaves I had lifted, to see the early signs of disease. He exhaled, his face breaking into a muted grin as he realized how full of fire he had been, and called over one of our workers. In minutes they were there to spray the vines.

Opening up a farm, I constantly reminded him, was not only about driving back the bush. There were smaller, more insidious enemies to beat back as well.

"I'm sorry, Pat. There's nothing else for it. It really would be the kindest thing."

We stood in the garden of Crofton farmhouse. Dave, one of our local vets, crouched beside me. In front of us, the little foal Deja Vu, only recently born to Paul's mare Imprevu, lay with her head in ten-year-old Kate's lap.

"It's deep, Dave," I said, "but isn't there anything you could do?"

"With an injury like this, it's often better to put them to put them to sleep," Dave said.

Pat bristled. "No, David. Let's give her a chance and see."

As the vet said his good-byes, promising to come back if we needed him, Kate nuzzled Deja Vu. The little foal's eyes revolved in their orbits and fixed on her. For a moment, the foal seemed to want to stand. Then, realizing the pain in her leg was too great, she simply laid her head back down.

She had been in the paddock with her mother when she had become entangled in a length of wire fence. By the time her panic had roused the attention of a passing worker, she had struggled against the wire so much that it had tightened around her front leg, cutting her so that the bone was exposed. When Pat arrived, Deja Vu was in a weak, depleted state. Her mother stood guard over the trapped foal, and when Pat got near, it was to find the foal spent from her exertions, torn muscle glistening where the wire constricted her leg.

After cutting her free, Pat had carried the tiny foal into the garden at Crofton, where Kate attentively lay down with her. When I called for the vet, I already knew what he would say. Deja Vu, I thought as I put down the phone, didn't stand a chance.

Back in the garden, I saw Pat crouching over the ailing foal, dressing the wound.

"You wouldn't let him, would you, Dad?"

"Sometimes it *is* the kindest thing." Pat stroked the little foal's head. "But not this time, Kate. Not for this little thing . . ."

"What do we do for her?"

Pat was silent for only a second. "We don't give up on her," he said. "*You* don't give up on her, Kate. The bone isn't broken. She'll walk again. But the cut's deep. Her leg's torn up. She'll get infected. She'll get a fever. She'll need us. Need *you*."

Kate's eyes were open wide, but her arm lay along the length of Deja Vu's back. They both seemed so tiny together, shadowed by the mango tree.

"Dad," she whispered with a defiance I had never heard in her voice, "where do we start?"

I opened the cupboard at the top of the stairs. Two eyes glimmered out, a round, feathered face looming in the darkness.

I simply placed the folded sheets inside and closed the cupboard. This wasn't the first time that one of Jay's birds had found its way into one of the cupboards and decided to take up residence there. In fact, I was so used to seeing one of his hawks or owls lurking in some crevice at Crofton that I barely registered any surprise. Ours, you see, was not just a family home; it was positively a zoo as well, and Jay was in love with birds.

"It's your turn to take Jay out tonight," said Pat, tramping up the stairs behind me.

As I followed Pat into our bedroom, I caught sight of another pair of eyes, these hidden behind Jay's long blond mop, shining at me from the bottom of the stairs. It wasn't yet dark, and our thirteen-year-old son was already waiting. He had become a keen falconer since starting high school, and he plagued us incessantly to take him and his falcon, Buffy, out on night drives so that he could practice hunting with her. Buffy only hunted at night, and without this practice Jay was apt to become disgruntled, mischievous, and more taciturn than ever. And Pat or I had to go with them. But I really didn't want to go out tonight.

I snatched up a deck of cards.

"I'll play you for it."

When we were at loggerheads like this, sometimes there was nothing for it but to play a hand of cards. The one who pitched the high card would get to sleep in the warm comfort of our bed, while the loser would have to drive Jay and Buffy out into the bush to go hunting. Sensing no other way out, Pat nodded.

I cut the deck and cut it again. I passed it to Pat, who shuffled it in his big hands. He cut it, I recut it, he cut it again, then he fanned it out and offered it up.

"Just deal it," I said. The tension was unbearable.

Pat picked a card from the top of the deck: the seven of hearts. My hand hovered over the deck. I cut it again and lifted the top card.

The three of spades.

"Sorry, darling," Pat said.

Two hours later, I set out behind the wheel of our truck, swinging out of Crofton and up into the bush. The night was close around us, the stars hanging high above the mfuti and msasa. In the back of the truck, Jay stood upright, the falcon blinkered and leashed to his wrist. Eagerly, he urged me on.

I could never resent these midnight trips—Jay had never been a boy suited to school like his brother, and it was only out here in the bush that he had found real confidence—but I had been awake for eighteen hours already. At a high ridge Jay unleashed Buffy; she turned and dived in the headlights of the truck, her talons sinking into one of the tiny nightjars that made their home here.

Jay looked at me. "Let's go higher."

"Darling, aren't we finished yet?"

Jay frowned. "I think we should go higher."

This, I thought, must have been how Patrick's father used to feel.

Though Pat refused to admit it, Jay had certainly inherited his demanding stubbornness from the Retzlaff side of the family. As a boy, Pat had built up a flock of more than one thousand chickens. He had known every last one of them by name, kept meticulous records, and even co-opted several of his father's workers to oversee the chicken project while he was away at school. The young Patrick Retzlaff would run his father ragged, demanding feed and materials for the chickens at every available opportunity, and, over the years, cost the family a small fortune in the process.

Whenever Pat left for boarding school, the farm would breathe a sigh of relief not to be under his tyrannical chicken gaze for a few weeks. Yet, one day, they made a mistake that would haunt them for the rest of their lives. While Pat was away, they decided to slaughter a few chickens for the deep freeze, convinced that, upon his return, Pat would never know. The cook was dispatched with a large ax and selected a few of the plumpest specimens. Grisly business done, he returned with a brace of big birds for a banquet.

A few months later, Pat returned home for the school holidays and headed straight to the chicken house. In minutes, he had zoned in on the missing chickens and promptly thundered into the farmhouse to confront his father. The young Pat was so distraught that, at last, his father had to confess: son, he intoned with an air of genuine solemnity, they have been eaten.

It was the very last time that anybody touched any of Pat's chickens.

Tonight, at the wheel of the car, I opened my eyes, realizing too late I had fallen asleep. The moon hung, beached in a reef of cloud, above the line of the bush, and I was thankful I had not driven us both off the road.

"Darling, are we finished yet?"

"Just *once* more," Jay insisted, feeding a scrap of some suspicious meat to Buffy.

I could have sworn her eyes turned on me with a keen, knowing air.

"*Once* more," I insisted. I knew it would mean at least three more flights.

It was hours later when I drove the truck back into Crofton, heavy bags under my eyes. I roused Jay, who had fallen asleep, careful to avoid Buffy, who pierced me with her stare.

We were tramping past the stables where Frisky slept when I saw Pat striding out of the darkness between the barns. The tomatoes were packed, the trucks loaded, and he looked exhausted.

"Just an hour until you have to deliver these tomatoes, darling," he said.

I could have killed that man and his animal genes.

From Crofton's window I watched Kate. She had spent the morning doting on Deja Vu. The foal's leg was healing only slowly, for infection kept setting in, reopening the wound. Now, the wound was dressed and she was gamboling in the garden. Her scarred leg was stiff and she would always carry it heavily, but the sparkle in the young foal's eyes told me she did not mind, and the sparkle in my daughter's told me it had all been worth it.

As an exhausted Deja Vu settled in the garden to sleep, Kate sat in the shadow of the mango tree with her schoolwork spread around. Oliver, our gardener, kept calling to her from where he was working on the edges of the garden, and each time, Kate returned his call with a smile that, like Pat's, took over her face.

When I looked up next, her schoolwork was abandoned, loose pages caught up by the wind and only rescued from disappearing into the bush by Oliver's quickly flicking pitchfork. Now Kate was up in the leaves of the mango, hauling herself from branch to branch with the agility of any of the monkeys that made daring raids on Crofton to take the tree's fruit.

I remembered standing in this same place only days after we came to Crofton, watching as Paul and Jay swung from the same branches. That day, Kate stood beneath, marveling at her brothers, forbidden herself from following. Now she could climb faster and higher than they ever would. That was the thing about Kate: she saw what braveries her brothers could accomplish, and she always went one better.

In the highest branches, she stopped dead. Then, from the corner of Crofton, came Jay and his friend Henry, the son of a neighboring farmer. Both of them were holding their pellet guns.

In a sudden scramble of limbs, Kate jumped down from the tree just as Jay and Henry were disappearing into the first fringe of the bush. Quickly, she made to follow.

From the kitchen window, I watched her go. Jay, I knew, was going to be furious. I had seen her do this before. Jay and his friend were going to take potshots at birds in the bush, but it distressed Kate so much that she simply *had* to do something about.it. Rather than run and hide, she had taken to sabotaging their hunts by frightening off the birds they were stalking. She would clap her hands and sing loud songs—and it had been a long time since Jay had proudly brought back a feathery carcass to Crofton farmhouse.

Kate followed him from deepest gully to highest ridge, along winding game trails and farm tracks, down to the tall reeds on the shores of Two Tree Hill Dam and up along the rivers that held our home in their cradle. With every step that she took, she clapped her hands wildly, oblivious to her brother's orders, his threats, his pleading looks. Every time she clapped her hands, the birds on which Jay had trained his pellet gun took off, a chaos of flapping wings and cries of alarm.

In this way, Jay was deprived time and again of his kills. At dusk, he tramped back into Crofton, dejected, his pellet gun still full. When he threw it down in disgust, Kate clapped again.

"Don't worry, Jay. If Dad found you, you know what you'd have to do . . ."

Jay had been under strict orders ever since he unwrapped his prized pellet gun that he could shoot a bird only if he planned to eat it.

Jay looked at Kate.

"You're just jealous," he said, "that you can't shoot, too."

But when they lined up tin cans in the garden and took potshots at them, Kate won every time.

She took after her mother, you see.

In later years, Frisky began to wither. Pat had never known her true age, but the lines deepened in her face, she lost weight that she would never regain, and when she and Pat set out across the farm, driving what few cattle we had left into their crush for dipping or simply reliving the days of their youth, she lived up to her name less and less often. No longer was she frisky; now, she was stately, quiet, reserved. A gentle horse in her dotage, slowly winding down.

In 1998, she left the paddocks and moved into our garden. She liked to lie down on the grass, and Kate nestled contentedly between her legs, our daughter and our horse breathing in unison. She ate from our hands but was hidden away when guests came to Crofton. She was too old, now, skin and bones. Questions were asked when those who did not know her laid eyes on her: wouldn't her passing, they wondered, be considered a kindness?

It would not be the first time Pat had lifted his gun to shoot an old friend. Children on farms learn, very early on, that death is a part of life. Livestock are culled, poachers' dogs are shot, horses with tumors and disease might need their master's mercy. But, every evening, Pat went into our garden to put his arms around his oldest friend, and I knew he would not, could not do it. Frisky just grew older and older. Neither one of them would let go.

Pat was away from the farm on business when I stood in the kitchen window and saw Frisky lying in the shadow of the mango tree, her chest barely rising or falling. I left what I was doing and went out to see her. Kate and Jay followed, but instinctively they *knew* and hung at a distance. For the briefest moment, Frisky lifted her head, eyes rolling as if to search Pat out; then she laid her head down, and the only movement was the twitching of her nostrils. I sat with her for hours, her head in my lap, teasing her ears, whispering to her. I knew there was no coming back; her time had come. Her breathing grew low and ragged. It slowed. Then it was no more.

Kate and Jay sat with her for the longest time, but Pat would not be back until after dark. I was putting Kate to bed when I heard the telltale stutter of an engine that told me he had returned. I left Kate half tucked in and went to meet him as he climbed out of the car.

Hanging above us, in a frame of lantern light, Kate watched from behind the bedroom curtains. Perhaps she had that old childhood terror of seeing your parents crumple, revealing themselves as mere mortals. She was watching, but she did not want to see.

I told Pat that Frisky was gone and he did not breathe a word.

When he went to her, Oliver and some of the other workers were trying to lift her from where she had lain. One by one, Pat waved them away. And then, almost thirty years after she first came cantering into his life, Pat knelt down beside her and put his arms around her for the final time.

He did not come to bed until late that night. He laid Frisky in the ground himself, gave her to Crofton. It is what she would have wanted.

The morning after Frisky left us, I woke early to find that the bed beside me was empty. Reeling downstairs and out into the morning sun, I saw Pat and Kate tending to Deja Vu at the bottom of the garden. Her leg was healed now, and Kate led her gently up and down on a lead rope. Her dark eyes glimmered.

I went to Pat and put my hand in his.

"Are you okay?" I asked.

It is a terrible thing to lose a beloved horse. Pat had known Frisky longer than I had known him. They had grown together, changed together. She had taught him to ride, and she taught our children, too. And, as we rode out onto the farm that day, I had the inalienable feeling that she was still there, cantering alongside us. She would be here forever. She was part of Crofton now.

In a way, I felt as if Frisky had entrusted Pat to me. I would be with him for the rest of his life, while Frisky cantered on alone.

I did not mean to let her down.

Chapter 3

SOON AFTER WE came to Crofton, we drove over to the neighboring Two Tree Hill farm to see trucks being unloaded at the farmhouse on top of the hill. The new neighbors, it seemed, had finally arrived. Our lives—and the lives of our horses—were about to become richer than ever, as we welcomed long-lasting, genuine friends into our world.

We had heard that new managers were moving into Two Tree from the farm's owner, a successful South African farmer named Les De Jager. During the bush war, Les had fought with the PATU, the Police Anti-Terrorist Unit in South Africa, who were supporting the Rhodesian army. On patrol deep in virgin bush, he and his unit had set up camp along the banks of a river. That night, Les had an epiphany: this was the perfect site to build a dam wall, opening the river for the irrigation of all the untamed land that stretched around. When he closed his eyes, he could see it: the bush driven back, the land opened up with tobacco, soybeans, wheat, and more. It was an image so vivid that, when the bush war came to its conclusion, Les left his native South Africa and came here to see the dream fulfilled. Two Tree Hill now stood, testament to the nocturnal visions of a soldier too long away from home.

As we reached Two Tree, we saw a slim man, perhaps the same age as Pat, rolling up his sleeves and stepping into the back of one of his trucks. He had the most wonderful smile, vivid blue eyes, and curly blond hair. He moved into the darkness of the truck. He was out of sight for only a few moments before he reemerged, leading behind him a beautiful bay mare.

It was while he was turning to lead a second horse out of the box that he first saw us.

"You must be Pat and Mandy," he began. "My name's Charl. Charl Geldenhuys." He took a step back, his eye line almost level with Kate's. "And this must be . . ."

"Her name's Frisky," Pat cut in.

Charl stepped back, admiring the old mare that Pat and Kate were riding. Then he turned, ambling back to the horse he had already off-loaded.

"This is Lady Richmond," he said, laying his hands on her flank.

Charl, it transpired, had been the manager on Two Tree some years before. He had spent five years managing the farm before meeting and falling in love with the woman who was to be his wife, Tertia. They had been married in South Africa and spent two blissful years there, Tertia giving birth to a wonderful daughter, Resje, who was only a little younger than Kate. Charl had talked so nostalgically about his time on Two Tree that he had convinced Tertia to visit it as a holiday—and it was then that Tertia, a city girl at heart, had fallen in love with the wild, open spaces of Two Tree Hill. The farm, she saw, was a paradise, its wild places teeming with reedbuck, tsessebe, kudu, and sable. Charl could do nothing other than petition Les De Jager for his old job.

When Charl introduced us, I liked Tertia immediately: small, with dark hair and the most expressive brown eyes I had ever seen. Resje clung to her as she introduced herself. She had the same warm brown eyes as her mother and, we were to learn, had been born with a birthmark that covered almost all of her body. As a result, the brave little girl had to spend many months in hospitals across the course of her young life, and Tertia was the most devoted and caring mother.

Having managed Two Tree once before, Charl was familiar with its every hill and outcrop of bush, the bream in the dam, and the contours of the land. Tertia seemed to take to the country life with brave aplomb, playing the role of the perfect hostess. We began to spend many weekends with the Geldenhuyses at Two Tree farmhouse. Tertia would host lunches or preside over a braai (barbecue), and while we swapped stories long into the night, Pat and Charl would talk about the land, the game—and, most of all, their horses.

Charl was as avid a horseman as Pat, and countless were the days that were lost as they rode together, from one end of Two Tree to the farthest side of Crofton, taking in the sweeping bush and fields full of crops. As Frisky was to Pat, so was Lady Richmond to Charl—and when she came into foal, there could not have been a cause for a greater celebration on Two Tree.

Lady Richmond gave birth to a chestnut filly with a flaxen mane and a stately, self-assured look about her. The foal was so striking that Charl decided to name her Lady, after her mother. But in the first few hours after Lady was born, Charl knew that something was wrong. He had been around horses all his life, and instinct told him that this was bad. That night, Pat arrived at Two Tree to see for himself. In her paddock, Lady Richmond lay, weak and exhausted, seemingly not having recovered from giving birth. There was very little to say, for both men understood what had happened. In giving birth, Lady Richmond had torn herself inside; her foal, Lady, was strong and healthy, but Lady Richmond herself was rapidly fading away.

Come the morning, Lady Richmond's eyes were closed, her breathing shallow and ragged. Come the evening, she was gone, leaving behind her day-old foal.

Lady Richmond was buried on Two Tree, but her foal needed Charl and Tertia now. They would have to act as surrogates to the orphaned horse. Now, when Pat and I took the children to visit Two Tree farmhouse on a weekend, we would find Tertia and Resje sitting on the lawn with the dainty little foal greedily sucking on her bottle. Once she was full, Lady would race around the lawn, cutting circles around her adoptive family, kicking out with her hooves.

Watching the tiny creature hurtle around the garden, seeing how

Resje delighted in watching her tumble, I knew that our new neighbors were the very best kind of people: the kind who would reach out to a creature in need and step up to whatever challenge life threw at them. Without Charl and Tertia, Lady would have perished at her mother's side. Now, watching as Kate was allowed to hold out a bottle and let Lady suckle from its tip, I was reminded more than ever of the trust that our horses, and indeed all our animals, put in us. It was a thought that would come back to me time and again over the following years as, too often to mention, I would look into a helpless horse's eyes and, though I knew we did not truly have the means to help, promise them we would never let them go.

As the months and years passed, Pat and Charl sat up long into the nights, reminiscing and dreaming of the things they could do with this land. I had always known that my husband was a very specific kind of dreamer: the kind of man who could concoct an elaborate, wild scheme and actually see it to fruition. He had been that type ever since he was a boy, building great chicken empires or collecting his own herds of cattle, and I began to see now how our new life on Crofton was the natural conclusion. He and Charl would ride the boundaries and talk about which corners of bush might be conquered next. They would dream of new dams and roads, irrigation schemes so ambitious they might bring greenery to deserts. But most of all, they dreamed about their horses, and how they might breed something very special into their herds.

The opportunity for something a little special came soon after Lady was orphaned. When a fellow farmer was looking to transport one of his Arabian stallions to its new owners in Zambia, Charl agreed to provide a temporary home for the stallion on its journey north. This, Pat and Charl both agreed, was an opportunity too perfect to miss, a chance to add something of the Arabian's natural versatility into the bloodline on Two Tree. Arabian horses are one of the most recognizable of all horse breeds and date back almost five millennia, to when they were first bred by the Bedouin people on the Arabian peninsula. Selectively bred for the strength of the bond they develop with their riders, as well as their high spirits and endurance, Arabians have a distinctive head shape and high tail carriage—and the thought of letting this opportunity pass by was more than any avid horseman could bear.

The Arabian stallion, then, would not only be fed and watered during his stay at Two Tree; he would be catered to in other ways as well. The day after he arrived, Charl led him into the paddock where the mares were grazing and let nature run its course.

I had never seen Pat and Charl more delighted when the news came back about two months later: several of the Two Tree mares were coming into foal. A new dynasty was about to be born.

Almost a year later, the stallion long gone to his new home in Zambia, Two Tree was home to a fantastic new generation of half-Arabians. Grey was a silvery male, his half sister a bay whom Resje named Princess. As we stood in their paddock and fussed over them, we didn't know how well we'd get to know them over the years.

I would always look back on one particular moment in the lives of those foals.

Princess had grown to be a delightful little mare, the kind without any natural instinct to fear or mistrust humans. Most horses need gentle teaching on how to have their hind feet handled, to rein in that instinct to kick out at what they cannot see, but Princess loved being handled from the very start. She was gentle, she was patient, she delighted in having a saddle on her back and a girth fit around her—and, as she grew into adulthood, she loved nothing more than venturing out onto the farm, a rider in her saddle, to explore the bush.

The new horses of Two Tree had become as familiar to us as the horses of Crofton. One herd mingled with the other, so that soon I would more often find myself in the half-Arabian Grey's saddle than in the saddle of any other horse. When Frisky was still with us, she would nose around Princess, Grey, and a little foal named Fleur as if they were her very own offspring. So, as the Retzlaffs and Geldenhuyses became such strong friends, so too did our horses.

Frisky had been gentle and patient in teaching Kate to ride, and Princess was just as gentle and patient in teaching Charl and Tertia's daughter, Resje. Princess had developed into a beautiful horse, with the temperament of her Arabian sire and the stature of her dam, Chiquita. Now, when Pat and I took the children out on rides, we could see Charl and Resje following the same trails. Sometimes they were just small silhouettes on a distant contour, a fleeting glimpse between the fields of crops, Charl on another Arabian stallion named Outlaw or the silvery shimmer that was Grey, Resje trotting on Princess in his wake. Sometimes our rides converged, and we cantered with them alongside the herds of tsessebe.

There is one particular day that will forever stick in my mind. We had been riding down by the dam, and as the afternoon light waned we turned to follow the tracks up, out of the bush, and toward Crofton. We saw Charl long before he saw us, riding a trail deep between fields of tall wheat. Behind him, Resje sat proudly in Princess's saddle. As we got near, I could see her hands loose around the reins. Princess, so gentle and patient with her riders, simply followed Grey and Charl, seemingly pleased to be out in the fresh African air.

We called out to Charl, but we were too far away for him to hear us. In her saddle, Kate started waving her arms, as if to catch Resje's attention. Resje must have seen Kate, for she lifted one hand to wave back. Then she took hold of her reins and carried on riding. Soon the tracks would snake together, and we would meet Charl and Resje in a clearing of red dirt between the fields.

Suddenly, something changed. Princess, normally so sedate and calm, reared up. In the still afternoon air, we could hear her whinnying, even at this distance. She brought her two rear hooves up from the ground, scrabbled at the air, kicked and then bucked. In the saddle, Resje clung to the reins. The buck tore them from her hands. I saw her little hands grappling out to catch them again, but the reins flew free. She was about to fly out of the saddle when something caught her. She snapped, taut, in the air, and seemed to be snatched around Princess. Too late, I understood what had happened: one of her feet was caught in the stirrups; she could not be thrown free.

In panic, Princess crashed down and began to hurtle forward. Up ahead, Charl turned Grey to see the commotion—but it was too late. Princess cantered past, with Resje dangling beside her, one foot still in its stirrup, the whole of her body being dragged across the ground.

I looked at Pat. Pat looked at me. In that same second, he dug his heels into Frisky's flank and drove her on. Princess was cantering in our direction. Perhaps he could head her off before Charl.

Moments later, we took off too, cantering in Frisky's wake. Though Pat and Frisky surged ahead, we tried to keep up. For a moment, they disappeared over a ridge in the track, obscured by the undulating wheat. When we caught them again, they had reined down. Frisky was standing contentedly by, while Pat knelt at her side. When I got close, I could see Princess standing at a distance, seemingly calmed down. Pat was cradling Resje in his arms. She was battered, bruised, shaken beyond measure, but mercifully she did not appear to be seriously hurt.

Soon, Charl appeared through the maize. He brought Grey to a sudden halt and leaped out of the saddle.

"She's okay, Charl," Pat said, gently lifting Resje toward him. "What happened?"

"It wasn't her fault. Something came out of the bush, a duiker or a . . . I don't know. But it spooked Princess."

"We saw her buck."

Charl nodded, running a finger along Resje's brow.

"Thank God nothing's broken."

Princess, startled at whatever had hurtled out of the bush, had panicked, shying away. In the saddle, the reins had whipped from Resje's hands. Though she grappled out to take them again, it was too late. She flew up and out of the saddle, and would have crashed into the ground at Princess's flank had her foot not caught in the stirrup.

We accompanied Charl and Resje back to Two Tree farmhouse. I watched Resje, finally able to breathe again, following Tertia into the farmhouse and remembered vividly my weekends trying to climb into Ticky's saddle and stay there, my father's face swimming in and out of focus that afternoon at the gymkhana when Ticky had thrown me off and wandered, dispassionately, away.

That, I remembered now, was the last time I rode until Pat walked into my life, in his undersize suit and battered cowboy boots. A fright like the one Resje had had today was enough to drive somebody away from the riding life forever.

While Tertia tended to Resje, Charl led Princess back into her paddock, along with Grey and all the other horses of Two Tree. In the garden at the back of the house, Lady was aware that something had happened and turned in little circles, as if demanding attention.

That was the very last day that Resje ever rode. She loved horses and would always love horses, but the thought of being thrown from the saddle and snaring her foot in the stirrup would live with her forever.

At last, it was decided that Princess could not remain on Two Tree. The memory was too fresh, and though Resje would always love Lady, Grey, Fleur, and the other Two Tree horses, the thought of Princess spooked her. Like Frisky long ago, Princess would have to be sent to a new home, to find a new family to love her, without the shadow of that one terrible moment in her past.

Charl did not have to look far to find a new home for Princess. Les De Jager's son farmed at Ormeston, in the district of Lion's Den, and agreed to take Princess on board. As well as being a strong working mare, Princess had her Arabian ancestry, and with careful management might add a little of her Arabian strength and endurance to the bloodline in Lion's Den.

I will always remember the day that Princess walked up the ramp into Charl's truck and left Two Tree Hill farm. We thought we would not see her again—but the world has a strange way of subverting your expectations. Princess had left Two Tree, but she had not left our lives for long. When she returned, it was to be under the most terrible circumstances. More change was about to come to our beloved Zimbabwe, and devastation as well to the new world we had tried to create at Crofton and Two Tree.

Everything was about to change—for our families and our horses.

In the early evening dark, Pat sat outside Crofton, working through the books in which we inscribed the farm's history: its seasons and yields, our cropping loans, the details of the workers who had stayed with us through the years. His head was buried in the books when he heard footsteps, a soft knocking at the door. He looked up to see Charles, one of our drivers, approach.

"Boss?"

"Charles . . ."

"It's about tomorrow, boss."

Pat shuffled back. "What's tomorrow?"

"I was hoping we can use the tractor tomorrow. To take everybody to the voting."

"Voting?"

Charles nodded, and as Pat questioned him further, things began to stir in the back of his mind, half-forgotten conversations and fragments of news items. Only a few months before, in November 1999, Mugabe's government had published the draft of a new constitution, which would be ratified in an upcoming referendum. The draft constitution effectively rewrote the constitution first created when Zimbabwe achieved independence, through the Lancaster House Agreement of 1979. It would, it dawned on Pat as Charles continued to speak, give Mugabe the right to serve an unlimited time in office, and even the right to appoint his own successor. What hit even closer to home, however, was the idea that, under the rules of the new constitution, the government would be able to forcibly acquire lands, even those that the government itself had sold since independence, without the owners having any legal right to be compensated for their loss. There was still inequality in the way in which land was held in Zimbabwe, even these twenty years after the coming of independence and the end of old Rhodesia, and we had always known something had to change. Yet, we had bought our farm in good faith; its sale had been sanctioned by the very same government whose efforts now seemed to threaten to take it away. I had the horrible feeling that the land reform program, which was not being handled properly by the government, would now be used by Mugabe for his own political gain.

In the weeks and months to come, Pat and I would think long and hard about this moment. That we had not properly recognized the importance of the upcoming referendum would one day come to sadden us. Were we really living so separately, out here in the corner of Africa we had pioneered for ourselves, that we had blinded ourselves to the path our country was traveling?

After Pat had promised Charles the use of the farm vehicles to ship all our workers off to vote, he found me at the back of the farmhouse, wearily preparing crates of tomatoes.

"What is it?" I asked.

"Did you know," Pat began, "about this referendum?"

I knew about it, of course, but not in the same way as I knew about how low the water table was, or how weak our yields had been in the last harvest, or how quickly the bank interest was gathering on our cropping loan. The referendum was a thing that was happening somewhere *out there*. There were problems enough at Crofton to dominate the day.

"It's tomorrow," said Pat. "A whole new constitution."

When he put it like that, it seemed suddenly to loom a lot larger in my mind. Behind us, in the darkness, the horses nickered in their stalls.

Things had become increasingly unstable in Zimbabwe over the past several years. We had thought things might improve once our drought years were over, but instead they seemed to get worse. Mugabe had been supporting the war in the Democratic Republic of Congo, ostensibly sending troops to support the president there, but really hoping to be able to exploit the DRC's mineral deposits in return—and, in response, the World Bank and various European countries had suspended all funding with Zimbabwe and placed various embargoes upon us. All this contributed to an economy rife with unrest—but nothing more so than when the government, under pressure from the Zimbabwe National

Liberation War Veterans' Association, led by the aptly named Chenjerai "Hitler" Hunzvi, agreed to hand out massive payouts and pensions to all the association's fifty thousand members. The Zimbabwean dollar had plummeted in value; inflation had soared, with a loaf of bread leaping in price from seventy cents to more than ten dollars; and the first voices of political opposition had begun to be heard.

"Are you worried?" I asked.

A wind lifted the tobacco and ghosted across us, bringing on it a fragrant scent.

"Not yet," Pat whispered—but, as he turned back to the farmhouse, I wondered whether he believed it or not.

Chapter 4

THE REFERENDUM WAS lost.

The people had spoken. By a large margin, they rebutted Mugabe's attempts at consolidating his power. They told him, in no uncertain terms, that they did not approve of his attempts to forcibly acquire land that was legally held. They told him they did not approve of him staying in power for endless terms and appointing a natural successor, like any warlord of old. They put their trust, instead, in a newly formed political party, the Movement for Democratic Change, which had been formed in the trade unions and was led by a man named Morgan Tsvangirai. The MDC had been campaigning for a no vote in the referendum, and suddenly the people seemed to be able to voice their opposition to Mugabe.

But in the end, it was to mean nothing.

On the surface the outcome was good for farmers like Pat and me. Questions of government and land reform had simmered, just below the surface, ever since the bush war ended in 1980. We had spent our entire married life with those unanswered questions lying in wait, just like the crocodiles down at the river, and perhaps Mugabe's attempt at changing things was just another blip, just another one of those moments in which the crocodile surfaces to study the riverbank with cold, reptilian eyes.

It was only a few days, however, before we heard the first murmurs of discontent. The same War Veterans' Association that had compelled the government to give unprecedented monetary handouts to its fifty thousand members, crippling the economy, had suddenly been mobilized. We heard stories of its members—some claiming to be veterans of the bush war in which Pat too had fought, even though they could not have been born at the time—amassing on the farms of white landowners, beating drums, chanting slogans, and confronting farmers and their families on the very steps of their homes. Already, some farmers had abandoned their farms out of fear for their children.

Charl and Tertia had always had trouble with itinerant poachers, as they were at the edge of a resettlement area, a former commercial farm that had been bought for redistribution to landless peasants. But after the referendum was lost, they began to see more and more of these settlers moving through Two Tree. Charl confided in Pat that he had found a note, skewered on a stick outside their farmhouse, instructing him that they would have to leave, that Two Tree and all its neighboring farms would soon revert to their "rightful owners."

The referendum had been lost, but Mugabe could still exact his will.

It was early in the new millennium, and our oldest, Paul, had returned from studying at college in South Africa to help run the farm. We had been struggling at River Ranch, a hangover from the droughts that had plagued us in the 1990s as we fought to open up the farm, and instead of returning here, he and Pat had leased some land at a farm between us and the town of Chinhoyi, a place called Palmerston Estates, where we were growing yet more tomatoes. Jay, meanwhile, had taken up a hunting apprenticeship that took him all across the northwest region of Zimbabwe. Only Kate remained with us at Crofton, though often her brothers would return on the weekends to join her and run wild as they had done when they were small.

Soon after the referendum was lost, Jay returned to Crofton to spend the week with us. The whispers of what was happening on

Zimbabwe's farms had reached the hunting areas too, and Jay—who knew every inch of the land, in a way much deeper even than Pat and I did—was keen to know what was happening on our own farm. We told him of the settlers we had seen drifting through, the tension in the air on Two Tree, but it was not until Jay was about to leave us again that we had the first indication that we, as a family, were in the line of fire as well.

Jay and Pat had been talking with Charl about the problems he was having with war vets at Two Tree. There was a sudden influx of settlers on his land from the nearby resettlement areas. Poaching was also getting out of hand as they moved over with their hunting dogs. As the afternoon waned, Pat and Jay climbed back into the Land Rover to begin the slow crawl back to Crofton. Dusk was gathering, and the dying light set the bush to brilliant color: crimsons and reds burst through the wooded foliage; the red dirt tracks looked like licks of flames between fields of tall wheat.

Then, a gunshot cleaved the silence.

Pat and Jay immediately recognized the sound for what it was. A crack, like concentrated thunder, had split the air. Instinctively, Pat slammed his foot on the gas pedal. The Land Rover slewed wildly in the dust. Pat craned to look through the back windshield—but all about, the farm seemed still. He wrestled with the wheel, brought the Land Rover back into line, and, with his foot still pressed hard to the floor, thundered back toward Crofton.

In the back, Jay reached instinctively for the shotgun hidden underneath the seat. He ducked at the window, the gun tight to his chest, keen eyes surveying the bushy koppie all around, in case he might see some figure lurking in the brush. Pat was proud to see how Jay reacted, so suddenly and so decisively. His months of training in Zimbabwe's hunting areas seemed to have given him even more steel.

At the farmhouse, Kate and I were waiting. When the Land Rover appeared, kicking up clods of earth, we knew that something was wrong. Pat wrenched the vehicle around, and he and Jay tumbled out, their faces lined in a strange mixture of bewilderment and fury.

"What happened?" I asked.

Already, Jay was on his hands and knees, running his hands along the doors and rims of the Land Rover, as if searching for a tick in one of the horses' flanks.

He looked up, eyes screwed shut as he squinted back the way they had come.

"Somebody shot at us," Jay breathed.

I looked at Pat. "Shot at you?"

"From somewhere up in the bush."

I fell silent.

I breathed and said, "They're already here, aren't they?"

Without words, Pat nodded. Finally, he said, "There could be *war vets*"—he said it with a strange lilt, because really they were not war veterans at all, only thugs in Mugabe's employ—"all over the farm and we just wouldn't know it."

"What's happening here, Mum?" Jay had some of his father's grit in his voice. It was a shock to understand, in that moment, how grown-up my second son had become.

I didn't know how to respond, how to explain. There was so much to think about—how our nation had come to this, how we had found ourselves in such a perilous position, how we had walked blindly— even willingly—into such a confrontation. Issues of land reform in Britain's old colonies were complex and often evoked great passions, as our neighbors in Kenya could testify to only too well. In the 1960s, they had gone through their own process of reform. In Zimbabwe, the interests of landowners had been protected in 1979 by the Lancaster House Agreement, which paved the way for the end of the bush war and Rhodesia's transition to Zimbabwe. The agreement protected the rights of those who had owned, or been given, lands under the old government for ten years, guaranteeing that their land could be acquired by the government only on a willing seller, willing buyer basis—and that, even in those circumstances, adequate compensation would be paid. On top of this, before any farms were purchased or land bought to be opened up for agriculture, the government had the right to veto the sale, or else provide a certificate declaring it had "no objection" to the sale. It was in this climate that we had become the owners of our farm. We owned the land legally and legitimately. Yet, now, as I watched Jay run his hands across the bullet hole scored into the Land Rover, I felt a terrible foreboding: all of the old guarantees on which we had built our lives, to which we had pledged our children's futures, were already gone.

That night, we returned to Two Tree for dinner. In the farmhouse, Tertia poured us drinks. Like me, she didn't seem to want to hear the conversation flowing at the other end of the table.

"It won't come to that," Pat said, his voice unfaltering. "It would be the end if they did. Agriculture's all this country has . . ."

He had said the same as we rode to Two Tree, our eyes on the hills for fear of more shots. Zimbabwe was not a country rich in mineral resources like so many other nations in Africa. Our only real resource was the land itself: rich and verdant and fertile for farming. It was not for nothing that we were called the "breadbasket of Africa." Ours was a country that did not go hungry, and one that could afford to pour grain and other crops into its neighboring nations. Without agriculture, we were nothing. The country's economy was already in tatters; the idea that the government would exacerbate that by systematically destroying the agriculture on which it depended seemed, to Pat, absolute nonsense.

The way Charl was looking at Pat, I could tell he did not feel the same.

"It's just not the way Mugabe's thinking. Mugabe doesn't think about the economy. It's as if he still thinks there's a war. He isn't thinking about five, ten years . . . He isn't thinking about next year, even. He's"—Charl paused, as if weighing up the thought—"thinking about *votes*," he concluded. "It isn't even money. It's power."

If the reports we had heard were even fractionally true, Charl had a point. It wasn't only the farms held by white landowners that were being targeted. Since the referendum was lost, thugs and soldiers in the government's employ had stepped up their tactics against members of the MDC—and, perhaps more important, against those members of the electorate who had dared to voice opposition by voting with the MDC in the referendum. There was a parliamentary election on the horizon, too, and with the support the populace had shown for the MDC in the referendum, we expected the MDC to claim a record number of seats. The fact that Mugabe and his ZANU-PF government were reacting with such aggression could easily have been, as Charl contended, a deeply political move.

"It still doesn't make sense," Pat returned. "The economy *is* politics. The economy *is* the votes. If they ruin agriculture, they ruin it all. They're not stupid. They have to see that."

Lay waste to the economy, Pat argued, and they laid waste to their chances of winning even a single seat in the next election. It was, he said, 1960s politicking—but we were living, now, at the dawn of the twenty-first century. To Pat, it was too preposterous to believe.

"It's worse than that," Charl added. "It's . . . personal insult. He can't understand why he lost. He still thinks he's the liberator, the proud black hope . . . How could a country he saved not vote with him?" He paused. "He has to blame somebody for that. Why not us?"

As Charl and Pat became more deeply embroiled in their discussion of Mugabe's strategy—if it was anything so clearly thought-out as a *strategy*—Tertia fussed around Resje and cupped a hand around her swollen belly. It would only be a few short weeks until her son, Charl-Emil, would be born. I could see it etched onto her face: she wanted him born into the Two Tree of three, four years ago, not into the place of constant apprehension that Two Tree was about to become.

I kept my eyes fixed on her face, heard Charl and Pat's heated debate fade in and out, and felt the first twinge of a very real fear.

A few days later, before he returned to the hunting area to continue his apprenticeship, Jay reported seeing strangers in the bush. Saddling up

Imprevu, Pat set out to investigate what Jay had seen: in the hills above the farm, where the bush was dense and men might remain hidden for days, huts made out of sticks had been hastily erected. Rings of black earth marked the places where campfires had been built, and the bush was thinned where men with *pangas* had taken to the trees. Pat and Imprevu made long circuits of the farm, moving in tightening circles, trying to scout out where the men were coming to settle and from which vantage points they could spy on our house.

I was glad to see Jay returning to his apprenticeship, and happier still when Kate could go back to school for the week. Though Paul and Jay had often been away at school for a term at a time, Kate was boarding during the weeks and returning to Crofton for her weekends—but, now, any time that she could spend away relieved a great welter of fear. Home had always been a place of safety for our children, a place to come and hide away from the world, but now it was beginning to feel as if they were better off staying far away. On Palmerston Estates, the situation was no better. Paul reported the same scraggly grass huts growing up near the railway crossing, with groups of people gathering around them, often drunk, seemingly stoned, raising their fists and chanting every time he rode along one of the winding farm tracks.

One morning, Pat, Kate, and I were eating breakfast in the Crofton dining room. The bright sun of early morning filtered through the curtains, and, as I helped Kate to eggs from a pan, Pat stood up to draw back the curtains.

On the grounds outside, twenty men were gathered, twenty strangers outside our gate.

If they did not look violent, if they were not drunk or stoned like the men we had been hearing about, they still inspired fear. Quickly, Pat pulled the curtains back into place. But it was too late; Kate had already seen.

Looking back, I believe that the only reason I did not panic was that I was thinking about Kate. For weeks now I had been making her do drills in how to respond if the war vets ever came to Crofton. She hated the drills—perhaps hated me for it too—but at least she was prepared.

There was a hallway inside Crofton, a place with narrow walls that Jay and Kate had often made a game of shimmying up, one foot braced on either wall like mountaineers scaling a sheer crevasse. If they got to the top of the passage, they could reach an attic crawl space there. It was in this hole that Kate was to hide should the worst ever happen. I turned to tell her to go, but before I could hustle her away, Pat was already striding out the farmhouse door.

Hanging back, I watched as Pat approached the men. This was not a baying horde of the type we had heard about. Pat stood, only yards away from them, and asked them what they were doing on the farm.

"It isn't what we want to do, boss," one of the men finally said. He shrugged, almost apologetically, and refused to meet Pat's eyes. "But we've been told not to leave. They told us to make some noise. Shout a lot, cause some trouble . . ."

I ushered Kate back into the farmhouse, where she could not see. Outside, Pat continued to talk to the men. When, at last, he turned to come back inside, his face was set hard. I remembered how he had looked, all those years ago, as he walked into the brawl in the hotel bar, decked out in his ill-fitting suit and shoddy cowboy boots.

"Well?" I asked.

"Well," was all he could reply.

It took some hours for the men to dissipate that day—but dissipate they did. Once they were gone, we ventured back out of the farmhouse. Their trails were clearly visible, as they had cut a path away from the farmhouse and back into the bush. Where they had come from, we did not know; why they were here was only too plain.

We were at Two Tree farmhouse with Charl and Tertia when we heard the news that the first white farmer had died. Charl and Tertia had had their own experience with war vets settling around their farmhouse— and though that crowd, like ours, had dissipated without violence, it had propelled Charl to thinking about their future. Tertia had just given birth to their son, baby Charl-Emil, and foremost in Charl's mind was how he might protect his wife and children. Some farmers had already sent their families away, anticipating worse to come, and at Two Tree that day Charl admitted that he was thinking of doing the same—not just for his family, but for his horses as well.

Lady, Fleur, Grey, and the rest were loose in their paddock when we walked through the farm. Lady hurtled over as we approached, responding to the quiet burr of Charl's voice. There was only one other animal that responded to him in the same way, an eland brought to Two Tree during the droughts. Em was perhaps the tamest of all wild creatures I had ever known. Fifty inches tall at her shoulder, with the eland's two distinctive spiral horns, she seemed to have fallen in love with Charl. Whenever he was out on the farm, Em would somehow know where he was and canter over. Tertia was of the opinion that Charl was a little bit in love with the eland, too. She had caught him, more than once, with Em's head lying contentedly on his shoulder, Charl rubbing her gently between the eyes— and whenever Tertia approached, Em would come to attention and push her aside, as if to say: *Charl is mine; this is my time with him now.*

"Where would you send them to?" I asked, my hands pressed against Grey's flank.

"Do you know Rob Flanagan?"

I nodded. Rob Flanagan was a mutual friend, a horseman who also farmed outside Chinhoyi, about thirty kilometers away. A polo player, he belonged to the same club where we would often go to watch matches. Charl had run into him only recently, at a farmer's meeting in Chinhoyi. So far, Rob's farm had not been affected by the roaming bands of war vets—and Charl, mindful that Two Tree was so close to the resettlement area, had begun to wonder: might there be room with Rob for some of his horses, if the worse came to the worst?

"There's too many of them," Charl said, looking into the distant bush where the war vets had begun to assemble their traditional huts. "And . . ."

Charl had cause to worry for his horses, for in the past, he had not spared the animals belonging to the men who came poaching on Two Tree land. Often, having chased the poachers away, he found himself compelled to shoot their dogs. It was a grisly business, for it was not the dogs' fault that they were being used to kill game, but there was often no other choice. The idea of these men returning to Two Tree in force and meting out their revenge was all too easy to imagine.

"There's nothing to say they'd be safer with Rob Flanagan," Pat interjected. "He's a farmer, just like the rest of us."

Charl nodded, one hand cupped around Lady's muzzle.

Back inside, Tertia poured us drinks. As we settled down, casting our minds around for something to talk about other than the land invasions, the telephone began to ring. Wearily, Charl stood and went into the hallway.

In the living room, we could barely hear the muted whisper of Charl's conversation. Yet, when he placed the phone back in the cradle and came through, his face was an ashen gray, his eyes wide and empty.

Wordlessly, he crossed the room to turn on the television. Channels whirled by until Charl finally found CNN.

He stood back.

"It's Dave Stevens," he said.

Dave Stevens was a farmer in the Macheke area of Zimbabwe, to the east of Harare. Up on the screen, we saw pictures of five of Dave's neighbors and friends. Their faces were purpled and swollen. Some looked disfigured, their eyes sealed shut where they had been beaten. Others had lacerations across the sides of their faces. One's nose looked dark and out of joint.

There was no picture of Dave, and there never would be again.

"They killed him," Charl said. "Came onto his farm, dragged him into their van, beat him, and then shot him in the face at point-blank range, near the police station."

We sat, transfixed, staring at the screen, trying to make sense of the words that poured out. Dave Stevens and his wife, Maria, and their four small children, it transpired, had had war vets squatting on their land since soon after the defeat of Mugabe's referendum. The day before, they had surrounded his home, chanting and beating drums, drunk and stoned, demanding he come out to face them. For Dave, there was no way out. The squatters snatched him and drove him to the town of Muhrewa. It was his final journey.

I reached across the sofa to take Pat's hand. Both of us, I knew, were thinking the same thing: this could have been us. It was only by some strange grace that this had happened on Dave Stevens's farm and not on our own.

The pictures of five bludgeoned farmers, Dave's neighbors who were beaten but spared death after coming to his assistance, came back on the screen. Unable to watch any longer, Charl reached out and turned the television off.

Was this what was coming to us, our families, our animals, if we remained in the homes to which we had dedicated our lives? Though the image faded to black, for days to come it was still there when I closed my eyes.

Those were weeks that tested our resolve. Crofton was our home, and Two Tree a place so dear to Charl that he had brought his young wife and children back to grow up in its splendor. It was the only land our horses had ever known. Yet the longer we remained, the tighter the noose seemed to become. We hated to think about leaving, but the thought began to creep into our minds. Yet this option was not so easy, not with so many animals, pets and livestock, depending upon us. We could not ditch everything and flee in a matter of minutes. To do so would mean abandoning horses like Deja Vu, Grey, and Lady, horses we had come to care deeply about.

Something had to be done. If we could not yet leave, we could at least send some of our beloved horses to safety. Charl's plan was to be put into action.

The following week, I stood at the foot of the Two Tree Hill homestead road, Deja Vu at my side, watching as Pat maneuvered a truck into place. Beyond him, Charl stood at the gates to the paddock, drawing Pat around. Pat edged the truck into position, climbed out of the cab, and opened up the back. There was room inside for six of the Two Tree horses. I did not know how Charl had picked who would stay and who would go. I did not want to ask. They were going to Rob Flanagan's, though whether that would keep them safe for long none of us could say. We only knew that it was a gamble worth taking.

Leaving Deja Vu tied to the fence, I helped Charl lead the horses out of the paddock. First came Lady, needing no other coaxing than Charl's voice to lead her up the ramp and into the darkness of the truck. After her came the chestnut mare Fleur and, after that, the big bay gelding Duke and his sisters, Duchess and Marquess.

As they drove off and the truck shrank in the distance, I hoisted myself onto Deja Vu and gazed at the other Two Tree horses left standing in the paddock. The silvery half-Arabian Grey's eyes seemed to be fixed on the truck while, around him, the remaining members of the herd grazed on in ignorant bliss.

It was only looking at Grey that I wondered if the horses, too, knew how suddenly our old world was falling apart.

Chapter 5

IT CAME, AS we had known that it would, in August of 2001.

Since the first stirrings of trouble across Two Tree and Crofton, Pat, Kate, and I had been spending more and more time staying with Paul at Palmerston Estates about a half-hour drive away. It had become a second home, one in which we might breathe more easily than in the tense atmosphere of Crofton. Early in the morning, as the first pale lights of dawn were just beginning to touch the Palmerston tomatoes, I pushed open the door to the room where Kate had been sleeping and stirred her. Urging her to get up, I dropped down into the kitchen to make us all a cup of tea.

Kate had not yet risen when I heard the first crackles coming across the radio sitting in the corner. Perhaps I was too distracted by rattling china cups and the hissing of the kettle to really acknowledge the fragments of words coming through the handset, but suddenly I recognized the voice. The china cup slipped out of my hand. I turned around.

The voice on the high-frequency radio belonged to Charl.

Wearily kneading her eyes, Kate appeared in the kitchen doorway, her eyes also drawn toward the spitting voice.

"Find your dad," I said.

Kate, the possibilities just dawning on her face, hurried away in search of Pat. Alone in the kitchen, I went to the radio and gently fiddled with the frequency, dreading the moment that the words would leap into real distinction. As I teased with the controller, I felt them come up behind me: Kate, with her father looming behind.

At once, Charl's voice leaped out of the radio, clear and free of static.

"We're surrounded," he said, broadcasting the words, not knowing who might hear. "Two Tree farmhouse is surrounded."

Images flickered across the backs of my closed eyes: Tertia holding Charl-Emil, barely a year old, trying to pretend that nothing was wrong; Resje, rushed into some back room, knowing too well what was happening but too afraid to voice it. I could picture the men at the gates, Charl's pained fumbling with the radio.

Pat pulled the radio to his lips.

"Get out of there, Charl," he urged. "Put Tertia and the children in the car and just"—he paused, as pictures of Two Tree flooded him—"drive through them, if you have to, Charl. But, whatever you do, get off the farm . . ."

"It's too late for that, Pat," Charl said—and, as the last word bled through, I heard utter despair in his voice.

We stayed by the radio as Charl reported the growing horde at the gates. Through the static, I could almost hear the chanting and shouting, the flare of an engine.

I looked up. Pat had an old, familiar look in his eyes, the kind a young man once had as he put himself in the path of a violent drunk at a hotel bar.

"Pat . . ." I said.

"Well," he began. "We can't just sit here, can we?"

He was across the kitchen by the time I could reply. Behind him, Charl's voice still rasped out of the radio. In the doorway, he pulled on his boots.

"Where do you think you're . . ." I asked.

I reached out and took hold of his arm. For a second, Pat was still. Then, the door was open and he was striding out. I followed him.

"What do you want me to do, Mandy?" Pat began. "We can't just . . ."

At that moment, Kate reappeared behind us, dressed and ready for school. She stood, framed between us, looking from one to the other. It was a strange imitation of the normal life we had been living only a short time ago.

"You can't," I breathed.

I looked into Pat's eyes and knew he was, finally, thinking the same things that I was: how Dave Stevens's neighbors had rushed to his aid, only to be abducted and savagely beaten, lucky to escape with their lives; how there would be no police rushing to Two Tree's defense today; how we had a daughter and two sons who needed us.

Something seemed to soften in Pat.

"But we can't do nothing . . ."

Back inside the farmhouse, the telephone started to ring. For a heartbeat, Pat and I simply stared at it. In the passageway outside, Kate slumped nervously against the banister rail. I could see the shadow of her brother Paul fall across her as he came through the door and she began to tell him what was going on.

I snatched up the handset, but it was another halting moment before I could bring myself to answer.

"Yes?"

"Mandy?"

There was a flood of relief, for this was not the terrible call I had been expecting. The voice on the other end of the line belonged to Carol Johnson. Carol and her husband, P.C., lived on Anchorage Farm outside Chinhoyi, and her son Andy was our son Paul's closest friend.

"Mandy," Carol breathed into the phone, "where are you?"

At last, I understood. The news had crackled across the radio that Two Tree and River Ranch were among the new wave of farms besieged by war vets, and she thought we were there.

"Carol, we're on Palmerston . . ."

Her relief was palpable.

Before I could go on, Pat looked up at me, waving his hand wildly to catch my attention. He was hunched over the radio, trying to discern the voices amid the crackle coming out of the speaker. I said a fevered good-bye to Carol and hung up.

Tertia's voice was coming down the line.

The first shots had been fired on Two Tree Hill. From the kitchen window, Tertia had seen one of the war vets lift a gun and shoot their pet Boerboel down. The dog now lay, spread-eagled, on the dirt before their home, its life pumping out of the wound in its side. Though Charl forced his way out to cradle it back to safety, he did not get far; another shot rang out, this time meant for him, and he beat a hasty retreat.

Tertia's voice was unnaturally calm, but behind it I knew she had to be afraid. As she put the radio down, she was carrying Charl-Emil and hustling Resje into a back room of the farmhouse and locking it down. She was, I knew, preparing them to die.

For the next moments, we sat in impotent silence.

"Is that it?" Pat uttered.

The radio was dead. No longer would we hear Tertia's frightened breathing, Charl's reports. No longer would we hear the chanting of the crowd crackling in the background.

Through his fingers, Pat looked up at me.

"You *can't*," I said. "What use would it be, Pat? We're not even armed . . ."

At once, he stood.

"Well," he said, "I can't just sit here."

He strode through the kitchen, past Kate and Paul in the hallway, snatching up the keys to our truck.

"Dad . . ."

He stalled, looked at Kate. Her eyes expressed the thoughts she dared not voice: that somewhere, even now, our neighbors and friends were injured or worse. All the same, she remained silent. Perhaps it was only that, if she did not say it, it need not be true.

"Mum's going to take you to school," Pat said, running his big hand along the line of her cheek. "Paul, you stay here, get on the radio as soon as anything happens." He paused, looking at me down the long hallway.

"What about you, Dad?" Paul said.

"I'm going to find Les," Pat said—and, with that, he was gone.

Out on the road, Pat found a number of farmers, and together they drove up toward the Lion's Den–Mhangura road to Two Tree Hill. On the horizon, dust clouds were kicked up by a convoy of cars that had turned off the road and were on their way to Two Tree and Crofton. Pat pulled over at the side of the road on the Two Tree Hill turnoff; he and a few farmers stayed and watched, ready to respond if the call came.

The radio had frothed with rumors and news from all the other local farmers, and for a little while it had been difficult to separate one from the other, as across the district farmers rushed to spread information. Now, from the edge of the road, Pat could tell that one particular rumor had been correct: there was a convoy of cars heading for Two Tree, ostensibly police going in to help.

It was three hours later when Pat saw the dust cloud returning, and the same convoy drove off Two Tree, careening onto the main road and heading back for Chinhoyi.

A lone car came along the dirt track. Before it was near, Pat could easily recognize it. As it approached, he flagged it down.

Charl sat in the driver's seat, with Tertia beside him, Charl-Emil on her lap. In the back sat Resje, her face webbed with the trails of her tears. She kept her head buried in her shoulder as Charl wound down the window.

"We thought . . ." began Pat.

Charl nodded, the sentence left unfinished.

"What happened, Charl?"

The convoy of cars that had burst onto Two Tree, through the baying horde, had not been the police riding to Charl and Tertia's defense. In those cars had been the local member of parliament, Minister Ignatious Chombo; two party officials, Peter Chanetsa, who was the governor of Mashonaland West, and Philip Chiyangwa, a cousin of Mugabe's; a truckload of police officers; and a Zimbabwean state television film crew.

Seeing the new arrivals from Two Tree's shuttered windows, perhaps believing the police uniforms to be a sign that order was about to be restored, Charl, Tertia, and the children had stumbled, broken figures, out of the doors of their home. Before them, the crowd was stilled, the chanting dimmed.

"But they hadn't come to help us," Charl breathed. "Not to end it . . ."

Minister Chombo was perched upon one of the farm trailers when Charl and Tertia emerged. From on high, he summoned them to his side. In front of the now attentive mob, Minister Chombo had declared Charl and Tertia to be the guilty parties. They had, he proclaimed, shot their own dog. They had, he proclaimed, stolen land that rightfully belonged to the people of Zimbabwe. As he went on, Tertia broke in, trying to defend herself and her family, spilling out the truth for all to hear, but she was roundly cut down. Minister Chombo's knowing gaze fell upon her. She would, he told her, be permitted to leave Two Tree with her life, and with the lives of her children and husband—but only if they left that instant and never returned.

Behind the wheel of the car now, Charl was grim-faced. He and Pat locked eyes. Neither of them wanted to say what they were thinking— Two Tree was gone, and there would never be any going back.

Charl and Tertia had been planning on taking a trip to South Africa, where they first met, and after being driven off Two Tree they accelerated their plans. For their sake, Pat and I were glad to see them go. They would be gone for a mere three weeks, but we dared not think of how different Zimbabwe would be upon their return.

The *jambanja* at Two Tree was only the start of a fierce crusade against the forty-five farms in the area. In the days that followed, the mobs moved onto the farms of our friends and neighbors, systematically driving families from their homes. It soon became apparent that this was more orchestrated than the other farm invasions that had been unfolding since the death of Mugabe's referendum. Most of the local black population in our district worked on the farms being attacked—and so, faced with a short-age of troops to carry out their invasions, the government released 7,500 prisoners from incarceration, with the express intention of using them in systematic violence against white-owned farms and supporters of the MDC. As the mobs spread and the farms fell, so too did the stories and rumors begin to take hold of our community. Some farmers, having aban-doned their homes, took to the skies, flying over the farming areas in little biplanes. What they reported was enough to make our hearts break. Photographs began to seep out: pictures of farm dogs shot to pieces and beaten with sticks; horses who had been doused with gasoline and put to the torch; cattle and other livestock hamstrung, speared, and axed.

Even so, nothing could prepare us for what we would find on the day we went back to Two Tree and Crofton.

As quickly as the mobs came, they moved on.

A few weeks after the looting had stopped, I received a call from the Commercial Farmers' Union, telling us that the crowds were gone and that, though we must be careful, it was now safe to return to Crofton and assess the damages. On Palmerston, Pat and I woke early and sat silently at breakfast. The day ahead loomed long and large. Neither of us wanted to know what we might find.

We drove north from Palmerston, stopping at Anchorage Farm to collect Carol Johnson on the way. Though I was glad she was there, not even Carol's joie de vivre could distract us from the day ahead. We banked left off the highway, into familiar fields of grain. The same sun beat down, and the same wind moved over the fields, but nothing was the same or ever would be again.

We reached Two Tree first. From a distance we could see the farm-house sitting on the hill above. Pat nosed the truck around to climb the track to the farm gates. As I looked up at the facade of the house, I remem-bered the snatches we heard across the radio: the shots fired, Tertia tak-ing the children deep into the house to lock the doors and wait for death. What had happened on that day hung across Two Tree like a pall.

"It's the work of the Antichrist," Carol whispered, stepping out of the car beside me.

Unlike Carol, I had never believed strongly in gods and hells, but perhaps she was right.

Only half a building loomed above us. The rest was gone, gutted. All that remained was a shell. Two Tree's farmhouse no longer had a roof, any windows, any window frames. We began to cross the yard, making for the open maw of the house, but momentarily I was distracted by a stirring of movement in the corner of my eye. As Pat and Carol ventured through the blackness of the missing doorway, I felt myself drawn to the shell of a motorcycle propped against the far side of the yard. Tied to the chassis with string, three tiny puppies huddled together. I bent down, reached out my hand.

They were the only farm pets we were to find living on Two Tree that day.

At the side of the house, we found the stains where Charl's Boerboel had been shot dead. As Carol took photographs of the nothingness left behind, Pat and I drifted on. And there, behind the house in the dam paddock, we caught sight of Grey, the half-Arabian.

His eyes rolled when he saw us, as if to say: *Where have you been?* Pat approached gently, in case he had been spooked by the mob, but all seemed well. After the pictures we had seen of other farm horses doused in gas and set alight, we could hardly understand. Pat looked over each of the Two Tree horses in turn, but none had been hamstrung or axed. After making certain that they had access to water and good grazing, we gathered again outside the farmhouse.

"Let's get it done," said Pat.

Collecting the puppies, we climbed back in the truck to make the solemn drive to Crofton. Along the way, we looked down on the dam, its waters as clear and glittering as they had always been.

Even up close, Crofton was unrecognizable. We climbed out of the truck beneath the same mango tree under which Kate had climbed out all those years ago, but the tree itself was the only familiar thing to which we could cling.

This was not a home. All that was left of Crofton was the walls, and even these were soon to be pillaged, our old lives torn down brick by brick to build the huts of settlers out in the bush. Everything else had been ruined, ransacked, or stolen. As Pat went to find Deja Vu, Imprevu, Toffee, and the rest, Carol and I dared to venture through the empty doorway. No roof hung over our heads. No windows sat in the walls.

With the stark memory of the way the Geldenhuyses' pets had been butchered, Carol and I moved from room to empty room, calling out for our old housecat, Kitty. Our voices echoed in empty chambers; our footsteps resounded dully from bare floors. The cold light of day spilled in through the place where our roof used to be, illuminating nothing: only Carol and me, standing in the place that had once been a home.

I heard a metallic ring and looked down to see a single object skittering across the naked stone. When it settled, I saw a napkin ring with a single word etched into it: *Kate*. I lifted it and marveled at it in the intruding light. It was all that was left.

At the window of what had once been our kitchen, I stopped. Looking through a frame of ragged brick, I saw my son Paul's old white car overturned and destroyed by fire. I think it was the waste that made me choke. If these "war vets" had stolen the car, perhaps I could have understood. That they hated us enough for such wanton destruction, I could barely comprehend. I wandered from one room to the next, my fingers trailing the places where my beloved family photographs had once hung. I heard the ghosts of the children's voices and the spirits of dogs barking as they played on the lawn.

At last, I found the place where our shelves had once stood, lined with albums of old photographs. Only days before, a trunk had sat in front, filled to the brim with bundles of Paul's and Jay's and Kate's school reports and the letters they had so regularly sent home from school. Now, in front of my feet, there was nothing. Every photo, every keepsake, every piece of our lives had been taken.

From outside, I heard Pat calling my name. For a moment, I was in a daze. I held the napkin ring close to my heart.

Carol and I followed the sounds of Pat's voice, retracing our steps through the barren halls. There, outside, Pat crouched over the mangled mess that was all that was left of Kitty. A shotgun had opened her side. Spent cartridges littered the garden.

Beyond Pat, two of our domestic workers stood, heads bowed. Our cook, Future, and our gardener, Oliver, could not meet my eyes.

"They slaughtered all the chickens," Pat said, lifting Kitty from the ground. "Stripped the gardens, too. The lemon trees . . ."

At this, Oliver finally looked up. He opened his lips to speak, but the words seemed to stick in his throat. In the end, Pat had to explain.

"They took them off," he began. "Rounded up all the laborers and dragged them to their *pungwe* . . ."

I had heard stories of the same. If the war vets could not coerce a farm's labor force into joining them—and more often than not, they could not; Mugabe had not foreseen how loyal farm workers would remain to their farms—they would, instead, corral them and force them into meetings where they would be made to dance and sing songs for days, without food or sleep. Looking at Oliver and Future now, I could see that they had done all that they could; their eyes burned with fear and exhaustion.

"Boss," Oliver tentatively began. "I turned out the horses, boss."

Pat was still crouching over what was left of Kitty, but now his eyes revolved to look at Oliver. For the first time, mirroring Pat's own expression, the corners of Oliver's lips twitched.

"Where?"

We followed Oliver along the trail that dipped down behind Crofton, in the opposite direction from Two Tree.

"There," said Oliver.

On the edge of the field stood Deja Vu. Her head was hanging low to graze, but as we stood and watched her, she lifted her eyes to return the gaze.

I took two faltering steps, but Deja Vu must have sensed the urgency in the way that I moved, and her ears turned, as if sensing danger. After that, I moved more cautiously. When we reached her, Pat ran his hands up and down her flanks, checking her for injuries.

"They didn't touch her," he said, almost bewildered.

There had been horrific brutalities against horses on farms we had heard about, but Deja Vu appeared untouched. Farm horses were not being butchered for meat, the fate of so much livestock lost in the land invasions, but only for sport, to incite and inspire hate in the farmers. I knew what the men who had come onto Crofton were capable of—the evidence was spread, in blood red, across the steps of our home; the only reason they had not done the same to Deja Vu, it seemed, was that she had been cut loose and was too difficult to catch.

"Bring a halter."

Oliver had managed to save some of our horse gear as well, and he rushed to come back with a halter in hand. After Pat had fitted it to Deja Vu, we led her back to the ruined farm. Horses know the world by sight much more than they do smell and sound, and there seemed to be confusion in her eyes. She considered what had become of Crofton and seemed to have little idea where she was.

In the stables, some of our other horse gear had survived. Pat watered Deja Vu and, certain now that she was in good health, saddled her up.

"Imprevu and the rest have to be out there."

Pat and Deja Vu disappeared along the trails, while Oliver, Carol, and I remained at Crofton, trying to see if anything could be salvaged from our old life. Carol's ride arrived to take her back to Anchorage farm. She hugged me tight, knowing that their days on their beautiful farm were numbered, and I could feel her despair. Pat returned an hour later, followed by Paul's horse Imprevu, wearing a halter and lead rope. Like her daughter, Imprevu did not seem to have sustained any injuries during the attack.

"She was down by the dam. The others are there, too . . ."

Though Imprevu rarely took to a rider that was not our son, we saddled her up, and, somehow, she let me onto her back and nuzzled my hand reassuringly. Together, Pat and I returned to the bush path, taking with us more lead ropes and halters to fit the horses.

We found our other horses grazing along the edge of the trail, the bush climbing high on one side of them, with the glittering waters of the dam hanging in the distance behind. They did not spook or scatter at our approach. I urged Imprevu forward and we rode past them, while Pat reined Deja Vu down in front. With the horses corralled like that, we climbed down to fit halters and led them in procession back to Crofton, where Oliver could look after them until we could move them on.

"Come on," said Pat. "There's nothing here for us now."

Back at Palmerston, Paul was waiting. As we climbed out of the car, I did not know how I would tell him of all the things we had seen. I hoped he would never have to see them.

"It's coming here, too, isn't it, Pat?" I said. "There's nowhere it isn't coming."

Pat looked at me, but he did not want to reply.

Chapter 6

I WAS IN the office at Palmerston Estates when I knew that something was wrong. Perhaps Pat was too engrossed in his work to notice, but through the walls I heard the rumbling of a car engine. When I looked up, I could see a black car winding its way up the farm track.

In front of the farmhouse, the car ground to a halt. The engine died. A single figure emerged, quickly joined by three more men. The driver was dressed in the uniform of the Zimbabwean Air Force. He held himself at the side of the car for a second; then he turned, and his eyes fell on mine through the window.

He strode toward us, and the three other men approached in his wake. The one closest to him, sinewy and lean, was dressed in a slick suit, and I felt certain that he belonged to the CIO, the Central Intelligence Organisation—nothing less, I knew, than Mugabe's secret police.

My eyes flitted between Pat, his head still buried in his work, and the advancing figures.

I decided to step out of the door.

In front of the farmhouse, the four men enveloped me in a broad semicircle. It was the driver who spoke first, his shoulders rising and falling beneath the big pads of his air force uniform.

"We'll need to see the maps," he began.

Silence lingered between us. I tried to see, in the corner of my eye, where the farm workers were, but all around me was stillness. Paul was somewhere on the farm, but I had no idea where. There was only me and, in the office, Pat, obliviously hunkered over his books.

"Maps?" I ventured.

The CIO man shuffled from foot to foot, but it was the air force officer's eyes that remained fixed on my own.

"Where," he said, "are the borders of the farm?"

"It isn't my farm," I began.

At this, the air force officer's eyes seemed to glow. "No, it is *not*—"

"We're *leasing* it," I interjected, knowing what that strange inflection in his voice meant. "We don't have maps."

After a few chilling moments, the air force officer broke away and paced around the farmhouse yard, looking out over the fields.

"What are you irrigating here?"

My reply stuck in my throat. I knew exactly why he was asking the question; he was weighing the farm up, thinking about what might be done with Palmerston Estates once it was his.

"Tomatoes," I finally breathed. "Paprika."

"You do well with tomatoes and paprika."

He had a withering look in his eyes, and I understood, at last: I was a mouse in a trap, and he was playing with me. He began to ask more questions about our work on the farm: the extent of our irrigation system; how we rotated the crops; what our labor was like and how much turnover we made each season. They seemed to stand closer to me now, the semicircle closing in to trap me. Unable to answer their flurry of questions, I risked a glance back, over my shoulder, at the farmhouse and the office inside.

I didn't seem to have any other choice.

As soon as I told them I would take them to Pat, they seemed to lighten. Even so, as I led them to the office, I registered the looks they shared and had the unshakeable feeling that even though it was they who were following me, it was I who was walking into danger.

In the office, Pat was waiting. As I pushed through the door, he acknowledged me with a mutter, a gentle exhalation of breath. I hovered there, knowing it could not last.

He looked up. I have often imagined what it must have looked like to him, me standing there, dwarfed by four of Mugabe's men. He seemed to take it in with one sweeping look. He barely moved.

I thought I could see every muscle and sinew in his body tense, up and down his arms, his face, his neck.

He was opening his lips to speak when the air force officer pushed bodily past me. In three strides he had crossed the room. Trapped in his seat, Pat froze—but it was not in fear. I saw him level his hands on the desk, his fingers straining. After all these years, I knew the signs: he was trying to restrain himself.

"Where," the air force officer barked, "are the boundaries of the farm?"

Pat breathed, long and slow.

"Why," he began, "would you need to know that?"

"I know your kind," the air force officer went on. "You think because you sit on this land, because you have your house and your crops, that it's *yours*. You don't dare think who this land really belongs to." He stopped. "Tell me, who do you think owns this land?"

"We lease it from—"

"This land," the air force officer uttered, lifting his forefinger to stab it at Pat's chest, "belonged to my forefathers—"

In an instant, Pat's grip on the desk disappeared. He threw himself up and out of his seat. The only thing separating him from the officer was the desk. His face grew purple.

He brought his hand up, curling it into a fist. In the office, everything seemed to slow. I took a step forward, opening my mouth to cry out, but I was too late. Pat brought his closed fist down on the desk with a reverberating thud. I thought I could hear the bones in his hand crunch.

"We've had enough," Pat thundered, his voice hoarse with rage. "Had enough of you, everyone like you . . ."

On the other side of the desk, the air force officer seemed to back off. I saw it all written on Pat's face: the day he and Jay had been shot at from high in the bush; Dave Stevens and all the other terrorized farmers whose stories we had seen and heard; the images of butchered family pets, of horses doused in gas and set alight. It poured out of him. He had been holding it in too long.

"Don't you understand?" Pat seethed. "Are you really too blind to see what you're doing to this country?" He checked himself, fixed his eyes on the officer. "To *my* country?" he went on. "I'm sick of being treated like this. *We*—all of us—are sick of being treated like this."

The men around me closed ranks. Pat lifted his closed fist, and, in the doorway, I could barely catch a breath. I tried to catch his eye, to plead with him to stop. Once, I had loved him for this, his fire, his willingness to walk into a fight when he could just as easily have walked away. Now there were no words to stop him. Cold fear gripped my stomach. I understood now: We were going to die. Our names and bloodied pictures would be seen across the nation in the evening news and, like those murdered farmers who had gone before us, we would leave our children to face this new, corrupted world alone. Paul and Jay and Kate would have to pick up the phone and hear the world-shattering news: their parents were gone, and never coming back.

At the desk in front of Pat, the air force officer turned around. If I had any resolve left, it evaporated. My body gave up. Now stuck between the three other men, I crumpled to the ground, my legs refusing to function. I lay there between them and felt the first flush of warmth between my legs. I did not move as the pool spread around me, soaking me and everything I wore.

I did not fully understand when the footsteps marched past me. I lay prostrate, eyes half-closed, body curled up, as the air force officer stepped over me and out of the office. One after another, his henchmen followed, until only the CIO officer was left. As he departed, he crouched at my side, his big, expressive eyes level with mine.

"You must watch your husband," he said. "Otherwise, he will be no more."

Whether he meant it as warning or threat, I did not know. He stepped over me, and then only Pat and I remained.

I was still lying there when I heard the engine of the black car gunning, turning tightly around in the farmhouse yard. Then, slowly, the rumble of the engine faded.

It took long moments for the strength to return to my legs. I stood, feeling like a newborn foal who doesn't quite trust her own limbs.

Pat was still at the desk, his fists still closed. A new fire surged through me, and I threw myself across the room, my own fists clenched. I hurled those fists at him, but he only stood there, unflinching.

"You risked our lives!" I cried. "We might have . . ."

His hands closed around my own, stopping me from striking any more blows. I looked into his unrepentant eyes, called him every name under the sun, cursed him and raved.

"What would you have had me do, Mandy? Just walk away? Let happen here what happened at Crofton?"

I could hold myself back no longer. Uncontrollable tears began to flow. They poured out of me and I couldn't stop.

Pat released his hold on me, and I stumbled back. He said nothing more, just gazed, unrepentant, in the direction the departing men had taken.

"We have to leave," I said. "For Paul . . . For Kate . . ."

At last, Pat nodded, but his face was as sad as I'd ever seen it.

The Commercial Farmers' Union had an office in Chinhoyi, and it was to them that we found ourselves turning. We were not the only ones. Thousands of the nation's farmers subscribed to the union, and in the past months, its responsibilities had swollen. The CFU had taken up the cause of finding temporary homes for farmers, as well as facilitating their flight from the country if the farmers decided to leave, but the union's resources were thin, and it didn't have sufficient staff for such widespread chaos.

Nevertheless, there was good news for us here. There was a property here in Chinhoyi itself that might suit our needs, a "safehouse" donated to the cause by a wealthy English businessman who was out of the country and sympathetic to the plight of Zimbabwean farmers and their families. What the union staff described to us seemed almost too good to be true: on the outskirts of town, a house big enough for Pat, Kate, and me on one floor, and another for Charl, Tertia, Resje, and baby Charl-Emil on their return from South Africa. There was good security, tennis courts, and even a swimming pool in which we could relax and pretend we were not living there against our wishes. We would be able to stay there for three months, or until other evicted farmers needed it, more than enough time to order our lives and, in true Zimbabwean fashion, to "make a plan." As the union people told me about it, I felt myself flushed with a new feeling of optimism. For the time being, Pat, Kate, and I would be safe.

We moved into the safehouse the very next day. Settling in was surreal. It was a town house on the edge of Chinhoyi, with private gates and gardens, very secluded and secure. Behind the gates of the grounds, it might have been any moment in Zimbabwe's long history. Here, we were cocooned from the world, cocooned even from the rest of Chinhoyi, whose streets still swirled with rumors of what was happening on local farms. It was easy, here, to forget.

We spent the first days organizing ourselves and beginning to make the plans from which we might put our fragmented lives in order. On the third day, a huge truck arrived at the gates and the driver opened up to reveal a great mound of household furniture piled up within. It was a gift from old friends of ours, the Pearces. Like us, they had experienced hostilities on their farm, and they had decided to leave while they still had a choice; now, they were bound for Australia with high hopes of beginning a new life out there, and their furniture was a parting gift. As we unloaded it and tried each piece in different corners of our new home, I was overwhelmed. There were, I knew, still good things happening in the world.

I had expected Paul to move into the safehouse with us, but the events on Palmerston Estates had taken a greater toll on our elder son than I had imagined. On the night we abandoned Palmerston, he had confided that he would not be joining us in whichever new home we could find. Like countless others, he had decided to leave and was making plans to travel to England and find work there. There were big Zimbabwean communities in London, communities that had swollen since the land invasions began, and the idea that Paul would be joining them was both painful and a blessed relief. I did not like the idea of our family fracturing, but I knew exactly how much Paul had inherited from his father, and I felt sick at the thought of him standing up to another invasion. Perhaps, if the country lurched from bad to worse, it was for the best that Paul was not here.

Even so, our new temporary home would be busy. Charl and Tertia were soon to return from South Africa, and I looked forward to their arrival like nothing else. It was only in these past few weeks, with the clarity of mind that comes with staring death directly in the face, that I realized how much our neighbors truly meant to us. At night, I closed my eyes and images of the attacks on Two Tree and Palmerston flashed through my mind—and I could not find the words to express how fortunate I felt that we had come through it unscathed.

On the day that they returned, Pat and I watched the car come through the safehouse gates and into the yard. For a moment we faced one another across the safehouse garden. Then, at last, we rushed over. Pat clasped Charl's hand in his own, and, though few words were said, we were overjoyed to have them back. I threw my arms around Tertia and held her tight, Charl-Emil pressed between us and gazing up at us with his big brown eyes. Resje hung back quietly, her small hand pressed into Tertia's. I pulled back. Tertia's smile was wider than ever, but I could sense the strain in her eyes. It was, I knew, taking enormous strength to do this, but Tertia would not show it in front of her children.

I took her around the safehouse, pointing out the swimming pool, the tennis court, the little parlor where I had taken to making soap to keep myself busy and occupy my mind.

"Not bad for refugees," she said with a grin, laying her hand softly on my back.

. . . .

Once we had shown the Geldenhuyses around the safehouse, we gathered for an early evening meal.

"Have you been back, Mandy?"

Charl had been wanting to ask the question all night. My eyes darted at Tertia's, and hers at Resje and Charl-Emil. It was time, it seemed, for them to be put to bed.

"Crofton was ruined. Two Tree too," I said. "They were just shells. Photographs, furniture, window frames—it was all gone."

"What about the horses, Pat?" Charl interjected.

At last, we could relate some good news.

"They hadn't been touched," Pat began. "They were roaming free at Crofton, some of them down by the dam. Grey and the rest were still up on Two Tree. Not a scratch on them. The workers had cut them loose."

Leaving our workers behind had caused us great concern, especially when we knew how Mugabe's thugs treated any workers who remained loyal to their farms. That they were still on Crofton and Two Tree was both a relief and a worry, but at least they had been there to tend to our horses. We sat in silence, imagining what it must have been like, the horses spooked and running down the farm trails while the mobs moved into the farmhouses.

"They can't stay there," Charl said.

Pat weighed the idea up. Since we had settled in the safehouse his thoughts had been heading in the same direction as Charl's. Deja Vu, Imprevu, and the rest could look after themselves for a time—there was plentiful grazing, and water was not scarce—but they could not be left to go wild. The horses had been fortunate once, escaping the attacks wrought against our other animals, but to risk them again would have been foolish.

"Charl's right," Pat began.

Before he could say anything else, Tertia cut him off. "Then what?" Her eyes drifted up, as if she could see Resje and Charl-Emil sleeping in the rooms above. "Go back onto Two Tree?" Her voice faltered. "How?"

"Under cover of night," said Pat. "And as quickly as possible."

. . . .

With so many animals left behind on the terrorized farms, the SPCA—Zimbabwe's Society for the Prevention of Cruelty to Animals—found itself at the forefront of a crusade to rescue domestic pets from the looted farms. Officers of the SPCA had special dispensation, and often police escorts, that allowed them to enter occupied territory and coax out a family's beloved animals. In this way, a multitude of house cats and farm dogs had been brought to safety, not a few by Meryl Harrison, a doughty and stalwart SPCA officer who, time and again, risked her own personal safety for the betterment of the animals in her care. Yet the SPCA had dispensation to go onto occupied farms to remove the livestock only under extreme circumstances. So if we were to rescue the Two Tree and Crofton horses, we would have to do it ourselves.

As Pat and Charl steered a farm truck out of the gates of the safehouse that morning, I will admit to a faint stirring of unease in the pit of my stomach—but perhaps I was grateful that I would not have to see Charl's anguish when he saw what had become of their home.

It was quiet as they turned from the Chinhoyi road into fields where Charl had once sown and reaped soybeans and wheat. Pat and Charl were not alone—they pushed the vehicle carefully past the eyes of settlers who watched them from the sides of the road. Voices did not cry out. Weapons were not raised. Pat looked at Charl and saw his eyes glassy and glazed. He said nothing, but simply stared ahead, as memories of his last day on Two Tree flashed through his mind.

He did not flinch as they drove along the farm track and the ruin that had once been Two Tree's farmhouse appeared on the hill. He simply kept his eyes on the track, and the truck rolled past the empty shell, past the gutted barns, on past the fringes of Two Tree Dam, and out toward Crofton.

Deja Vu, Imprevu, and the rest were waiting to be rounded up, and even Imprevu seemed not to complain as Pat led her up the ramp into the back of the truck. Once they were secured, Charl pulled the truck around and nosed back along the trail, leaving the remains of Crofton behind. Some of the bricks had been taken from the wall to build more shacks in the bush. Soon, the farmhouse we had spent all those years in would be gone forever, like a mountain eroded by time.

With our horses loaded up, Pat and Charl returned the way they had come. Once they had gone past the dam, they banked left, up the hill toward what was left of Two Tree Hill.

Charl pressed his foot to the brake and brought the truck to a grinding halt. In the back, the horses shifted awkwardly. A single snort split the silence.

"What is it?" asked Pat.

Charl said nothing, only kicked open the door of the cab and swung out of his seat. Guardedly, Pat followed.

His eyes were on the ridges around him, seeking figures in the bush. Certain that this was what Charl had seen, and remembering the day he and Jay had been shot at along these very same tracks, he followed Charl along the banks of the path.

There, lying at Charl's feet, was the body of a dead antelope. A terrible wound had been opened in its side, and a mass of flies billowed out on a cloud of sour, meaty scent.

Pat stood at a distance, but Charl grew close, crouched, and turned the dead antelope's head. Two distinctive spiral horns protruded from its forehead, marking it as an eland.

Charl looked up.

"Em," he said.

Now Pat recognized her, too. In death she looked like any of the other game that had been slaughtered across Two Tree, so much of it, it seemed, not even out of a necessity for finding meat to butcher, but just for the thrill of the killing.

"Come on," said Charl, eyes lifting to Two Tree farmhouse sitting above. "Let's get this finished."

He was about to climb back into the truck when Pat stalled him.

"What about Em?"

Charl's eyes said it all: there was no helping her now; there was still time, though, to do something about Grey and the rest of his horses.

They rumbled the truck up the hill and into the yard where, weeks before, the mob had raged. In silence, they stepped out. The building still stood above them, its empty windows like sightless eyes.

At the back of the farmhouse, the horses were waiting.

Some were grazing nearby, in the paddocks in which they had always lived, but others seemed to have jumped the fences and begun to roam. A brown mare with dark points lingered between two of the enormous barn buildings, while a chestnut gelding seemed to spook at Charl's sudden appearance and trotted off, disappearing into shadow. Pat and Charl pushed to the fences to inspect them further, but a sudden movement from behind startled them, and they turned to see a slight, dark mare shifting in the shadows of the ruin.

"Where's Grey?" Charl began.

Pat scoured the paddock, but the silvery half-Arabian gelding was nowhere to be seen.

"They didn't . . ."

Pat did not want Charl to finish the question and sharply shook his head. "They didn't touch the other horses, Charl. Why would they harm Grey?"

They scoured Two Tree, rounding the other horses back into the paddock as they did so. The sun disappeared behind a fleeting cloud, spreading a gray pall across the farm. When at last they had ridden from one end of the grounds to another, there was Grey, standing alone and bereft, hugging the walls of one of the farm buildings. As they approached he seemed diminished, somehow, a shadow of the horse he had been only a few weeks gone.

Charl called out for him, and Grey turned, his ears revolving. Softly, he blew through his nostrils.

By the time Charl got near, he understood what was wrong. Somehow, Grey had been confined. Against one side, the barn building rose; against the other, farm equipment precluded him from easing his way out. The grass around his hooves was grazed to the quick, and the trough at which he had been drinking was dry as the earth.

He was visibly malnourished, his withers thin and ragged. As Charl spoke to him, his eyes lifted. He pushed awkwardly forward and nuzzled Charl's shoulder, listening to his words of reconciliation.

There was anger in Charl's eyes then, that it had come to this.

Once Grey had been coaxed out into the open and fitted with a halter, it became clear that malnourishment was only the beginning of his troubles. Every time he placed his right foreleg down, his body lurched and, cringing, he lifted his hoof again. Between two tall barns, on the way to the waiting truck, Charl eased him to a halt. Careful not to startle him, he crouched and lifted his ailing foreleg.

There was no injury to speak of, no mark where some war vet had taken to him with a *panga* or spear. Yet Grey's hoof seemed beyond repair. The flesh hung, thin and loose, around his lower leg, separated almost entirely from his hoof. Grey cringed when Charl's fingers brushed softly around the tender area, but Charl ran his other hand firmly across the underside of Grey's flank, assuring him that everything was all right. Pat, too, tried to fix him with a look, wordlessly imploring the poor horse to be still.

"He can't walk on this," said Charl.

The hoof, Pat saw, was almost hanging off, connected only by bone and thin strips of Grey's hide.

"We should get out of here," said Pat.

Yet Charl remained crouched at Grey's side, studying his damaged hoof: Grey, who had been born and raised on this very farm; Grey, on whose back he had ridden; Grey, who now might be lame for the rest of his days, whose eyes a lesser horseman might cover while he pressed a gun to his temple and shot.

Charl gently placed Grey's hoof back on the ground, but as soon as the wretched-looking gelding put any weight on it, his body started to shake.

"I don't think he can walk, Pat. We should have come sooner."

"Sooner?" Pat returned. "Don't you remember what it was like here?"

Pat and Charl coaxed Grey forward, but each time he put the damaged hoof to the ground his head lifted and he drew back, eyes rolling in pain. With one hand on his bare flank, Charl ushered him on. He came forward tentatively, refusing to put weight on his damaged hoof. The effect was heartbreaking: his head bobbed like that of a horse incurably lame, his gait ugly and slow.

Pat hurried back to the truck to collect a lead rope and returned to fit it to Grey's halter. Even with the rope attached, Grey came slowly. Again, Charl crouched, checking the hoof for any stray stone or piece of brick that might have become lodged in there. Tiny stones like that had been known to cause great trouble before—but there was nothing there.

"It wasn't an accident," Charl said, looking into Grey's sorry, soulful eyes. "He isn't lame because he was attacked. He's lame because . . ." Charl could hardly bring himself to say it. The truth of the matter was Grey had been reduced to this because of lack of water, because of malnutrition, because Charl and Pat had not been on Two Tree to tend to the horses. While the other horses had been able to fend for themselves, with access to grazing and fresh water, Grey's body had started to wither away; his hoof was simply a symptom of his body shutting itself down. Telling Charl that it was not his fault would do nothing to soothe his conscience, nor Pat's; as every good farmer knows, livestock need to be tended to, cared for. Without it, they can wither and die. The same was true of our horses; the once-beautiful Grey had become a living embodiment of what can happen when a horseman abandons his post.

"Come on, Charl. It isn't too late. Not yet . . ."

Slowly, they brought Grey back to Two Tree farmhouse, where Deja Vu, Imprevu, and the rest of the Two Tree horses were waiting. They seemed to snort, sadly, at Grey's appearance. It is telling how sensitive horses can be, whether to one of their own kind or to the humans with whom they have made such a strong bond. Perhaps the horses could see the torment in Charl's eyes too, for they watched him cut a sad figure across the yard.

Grey took little coaxing to limp toward the water trough where the rest of the herd had been drinking. As he took in the water he had been crying out for through his long imprisonment, Pat readied the other horses to get into the truck. His eyes wandered over the fields Charl would never farm again. Already they were going to waste; Mugabe might have claimed that these farms were being handed over to landless war vets, but the reality was they would be left barren, waiting for the bush to reclaim them.

There was movement on the trail below Two Tree, a truck Pat did not know winding its way through the fields with black men—not workers from Two Tree—piled up in its back. For an instant, he froze, his hands resting on the crests in Grey's spine, poking up through his threadbare hide. Then, the truck rolled on, bound no doubt for Crofton or the land beyond.

"Where are we even going to take them, Pat?"

It was a question they had not yet asked themselves. Lady, Duchess, Duke, Marquess, and Fleur were still on Rob Flanagan's farm, but there were no guarantees that they would stay safe for long.

"Do you know Braeside?" asked Pat.

Charl nodded. Braeside was a farm that bordered the land we had been leasing at Palmerston Estates. In a time not so very long ago, Braeside had been an African idyll. It sat near Palmerston, between sheer hills crowned in scrub, where jacaranda trees stood heavy with scent. Its owners, Rory and Lindy Hensman, were farmers like us, but their lives really revolved around the amazing menagerie of orphaned animals who called Braeside their home. Their house was open for all the lost things of the bush. At Braeside, Hoggles, an enormous bristly warthog, dominated the sitting room, taking over settees and armchairs in preference to his basket of woven grass; at Braeside, a scaly anteater, known as a pangolin, wandered along a passage, a kudu calf drank daintily from a china cup, an orphaned owl perched curiously at an attic window, searching for a way in. And, on Braeside, a whole herd of orphaned elephants roamed the tracks or swam in the rivers with Rory and Lindy clinging to their backs.

"The war vets will come there, too," said Charl, gently pushing Grey up the ramp and into the back of the truck, there to be received by Deja Vu and the rest of the mismatched herd.

"Maybe," said Pat. "But better that they're there than . . . here." He turned, surveying the familiar fields through which we would ride no longer. "If there's one place animals can still be safe, it has to be Braeside," said Pat, and he ran his hand tenderly along Grey's sore, patchy muzzle.

Chapter 7

HIGH IN THE HILLS of Braeside Farm, the night was alive with fires, small cauldrons of orange and red stirring in the bush. The same fires could be seen far into the distance; below the Braeside hills, there were rings burning on Palmerston Estates, where ramshackle villages had sprung up in our carefully tended fields. The smell of smoke came on the wind, bringing with it the dull sounds of chanting. Whether it was only the war vets, or the labor force of Braeside forced into a *pungwe*, roaring out slogans in support of Mugabe and ZANU-PF until their throats were raw, Pat and Charl could not say. In silence, their bodies hunched over, they made haste along the track below the shell of the Braeside farmhouse until they reached the stables.

"It's like being in the army again," said Pat.

It was an observation he had made before. Many of Zimbabwe's white farmers had spent their youth fighting in the bush war, and as the farm invasions intensified, all the old instincts seemed to bubble to the surface.

When they reached the stables, Pat and Charl made sure that they had not been followed and then, under cover of darkness, slipped inside. In the first stall, Grey hung, half-suspended, in a great sling made from tarpaulin and suspended from the rafters. His two hind hooves and one of his fore balanced, gently, on the stable floor, while his damaged hoof hung above. His ears turned at Charl's approach, and he let out a muted whinny.

"Hello, old friend," Charl whispered, hurrying over.

"How's it looking?"

Charl crouched at Grey's hoof, the light of his torch sweeping across the stable and picking out different corners: the pile of manure in the corner, Grey's patchy flank where his ribs still showed.

"Better," Charl replied. "But not healed yet . . ."

Ever since moving the horses onto Braeside, Pat and Charl had been coming here to tend to them. At first it had been simple—for, even though Braeside looked down on Palmerston Estates, it had not yet been abandoned to Mugabe's thugs. As war vet activity intensified, though, Rory and Lindy had made a drastic decision—they determined they had to leave while they still could. Rory and Lindy had other concerns as well, for they were not the sort of people who could leave their orphaned elephants behind. After much careful thought, they had set out south, intent on driving their elephant herd across the border into South Africa.

The flight of the Hensmans, however, had left Grey, Deja Vu, Imprevu, and the rest stranded on Braeside. With the farmhouse abandoned, the war vets quickly moved into the farm, settling in its fields and hills. Now their stick huts could be seen along every trail and ridge; their fires burned in the bush, and the night was filled with their songs. What had become of the Braeside workforce, we did not know; terrorized and driven to *pungwes*, perhaps, but some of them limped on, trying to keep whatever portions of the farm they could in working order.

After making certain that Grey was as well as he could be, restrained in his sling, Pat and Charl crept on, into the stables where Deja Vu and the rest were waiting. They seemed to know they were being called upon, and they shifted, excited, at Pat and Charl's presence. Tonight, the men were administering vaccines, and in the dull light of their torches, they prepared the syringes. After palming a fistful of horse cubes into each of the horses' mouths, they administered the injection into the horses' necks. Only Imprevu seemed to object. At the touch of the needle, she bucked, releasing an ill-tempered snort.

Pat and Charl froze, listening out for the sounds of footsteps. So far, they had been fortunate in their midnight trips onto Braeside; if the war vets knew they were here, they did not care or were wary of any confrontation. All the same, until there was another home for Grey, Deja Vu, and the rest to go to, Braeside was all that we had.

Confident that they were not being watched, Charl ran his hands around Imprevu, feeling the horse twitch.

"They're getting restless."

Pat smirked. "You want to take them out on a midnight ride?"

The sounds of the distant *pungwe* were carried high on the wind.

"Maybe not tonight," Charl returned, with a wry smile.

By the time the vaccines were administered, the horses dipped and deticked, and the stables shoveled of muck, the black of night was paling into dawn. Fingers of red sunlight burst over the horizon. From Braeside, Pat could see the contours of the neighboring Palmerston Estates. It was mere weeks since we had left, but it might as well have been a lifetime.

"I think it's about time we weren't here," said Pat.

As they drove back down the track, Braeside Farm was eerily silent. They rolled past the still stick huts of Palmerston, the barren fields where a single rangy cow lowed at them from where it was tethered. Then, out onto the road and past Heroes Acre, a cemetery where heroes of the bush war—those men we had once called terrorists and insurgents—were still being ceremoniously buried. Above the turnoff, a big mural of Mugabe's face peered down.

"Do you ever think about leaving?" Charl asked.

"For where?"

"Anywhere," said Charl. "Anywhere but here."

Late the following night, Pat turned to me in bed and brushed the hair out of my eyes.

"What is it, Pat?" I asked.

"It's Charl," he whispered, careful that his voice not be heard through the safehouse walls. "There was something in his voice last night, on Braeside. I think . . ."

Unsettled, I reeled back. "Think what?"

"He's thinking about leaving, Mandy. I'm sure of it. I could . . . hear it in his voice."

A thought occurred to me, something that had not entered my consciousness until now. "And you, Pat?"

Half of me, I knew, was begging him to say: *Let's go; let's buy our tickets and fly out of here.* But the other half pictured him riding on Frisky, tending to Deja Vu, nursing Grey back to health.

"Never," Pat whispered. "This is *my* country. Those are *my* horses. This is *my*"—his voice faltered—"world," he finally concluded.

I looked at him. It was his country; they were his horses; it was his world. But they were mine, too. My world was Pat himself, and I felt the very same fire in my own chest.

"There was a call today," I said. "I think you should call back."

Pat and I had spent the day compiling data for our agronomy business. Agronomy is the science of agriculture, and ever since Crofton we had run a small business on the side, consulting for farmers across Zimbabwe, analyzing their land and providing suggestions on how they might best improve their yields and profits. Now that we no longer had River Ranch or Palmerston Estates, agronomy was the only way we could make any money. Yet what had once been a straightforward task of taking soil samples from various farms and making recommendations had become more complex since the start of the land invasions. As farms fell, so did our clients, and we had to roam wider and wider for smaller and smaller incomes.

"It'll have to wait," said Pat. "Gaydia will wonder where I've got to."

Gaydia Tiffin was an old friend who worked with Pat on the agronomy business. Gaydia was warmhearted and vivacious, and she and her husband, Roldy, had once farmed in the same area as us. The fact that they were expert polocrosse players, and almost as at home in the saddle as Pat, only cemented the union. Gaydia's daughter, Romaen, had the same passion for horses her mother did. Their home had often reminded me of Crofton, filled with dogs and cats of varying shapes and sizes.

"I think she'll want to hear this one, too."

The call had come early in the morning. Even though we felt secure in the safehouse, a call at that hour of the day had triggered my panic response. Shaking the sudden feeling away, though, I had simply picked up the phone.

"Hello?" I had tentatively begun, half expecting the guttural tone of some CIO official on the other end of the line.

"I'm looking," a soft, female voice said instead, "for Mandy Retzlaff?"

The woman on the other end of the line introduced herself as Katherine Leggott, from a family who farmed on the outskirts of Chinhoyi. I was not familiar with the family, but we soon settled into talking about the land invasions. Even though I knew so little about the Leggotts and their farm, it seemed that, somehow, they knew about ours.

"You'll have to forgive me," Katherine began, "but I'm just going to say it . . . You see, we heard you were the *horse* people."

She gave a strange emphasis to the word *horse*, as if to intimate that we ourselves were some curious mixture of equine and human genes.

"Well," I began, "we do *have* horses—"

"Yes," she interjected, more eager now. "And I heard . . . I heard you were the people who could be counted on to look after them, that you wouldn't let them go the way of . . ."

There had, it transpired, been increasing war vet activity across the Leggotts' farm. Though they had not yet been evicted, the mobs had gathered, the trails had erupted with a plague of stick huts and settlers, and it seemed that the noose was constricting around them.

"We're leaving," Katherine's voice buzzed at me along the line. "My husband, John, has family in Australia. We'd thought about moving before, but . . ." She paused, trying to fill in the blanks of her own story. Just as it felt to so many of us, everything was happening all at once. It would take years for people to look back and put these months into any semblance of order. "We're going there for our kids, Mandy."

She paused. "But it's our horses. Something has got to be done about our horses."

I looked at Pat across the safehouse kitchen.

"Well," I ventured, with a smile, "what else can I say?"

The next day, Pat and I went out to see the Leggotts. Once we had seen their horses, there was nothing else we could do but take them in. The consequences of leaving them behind passed before Pat's eyes, and after that there was never any other option. I was worried, for our horses were already divided—some still out on Rob Flanagan's farm, the rest on the rapidly diminishing Braeside—and there were moments when it seemed an unnecessary strain. It was only as I watched Pat loading them up and taking them to join Grey, Deja Vu, and the rest up on Braeside, smuggled onto the farm under the cloak of night, that my worries relented. While he was concentrating on all these horses, at least my husband did not have time to brood on what was happening to the country he loved. If tending horses was what it would take to keep him from exploding the way he did that day on Palmerston Estates, I wouldn't have minded if he had taken in all the horses in the whole of Zimbabwe.

The day after, I made the trip into Chinhoyi to collect more veterinary supplies. In town, I met with Rob Gordon, a veterinarian we knew well from Crofton and Palmerston. Today, he looked like a shadow of the man who had treated our animals on Crofton. I caught up with him on the main strip that ran through Chinhoyi, the road flanked on either side by busy market stalls and bustling crowds. I tried not to look at the stalls too closely these days, for we were certain that items scavenged from the *jambanja*ed farms lay here. Indeed, we had known farmers whose furniture was piled high for sale here, and across the villages.

Rob looked distinctly harassed as I told him what we needed. His face was etched in hard lines.

"Rob?"

"Sorry, Mandy," he began. "Of course I can help . . ."

I quickly understood why Rob seemed so different. He was, he said, one of only a handful of vets left in the Chinhoyi district. Since the land invasions began, veterinarians had never been more needed—and yet now they were leaving Zimbabwe in droves, just like the farmers themselves. As more farmers were driven from their farms, more and more herds of livestock were being abandoned. If those sheep and cattle were not immediately slaughtered by the war vets, they were left to die slow deaths from sickness and neglect. Dairy cattle were in particular danger, for they need milking several times a day; if just one milking is missed, it is only a matter of time before infection sets in.

"So we're killing them all," said Rob. "If the war vets don't do it, it's down to us."

Rob's words were like dull thunder, sounding on the horizon and growing louder as a storm grows near. The scale of this devastation was vast. Each farm looked after thousands of animals, and each farm's herds were unique to that land, selectively bred over generations to produce a certain strain. Rob and veterinarians like him were moving in where the war vets had been and euthanizing great flocks of animals.

"Rob," I said, "it's madness . . ."

He looked at me as if to say he knew.

"If not us," he said, "who else?"

Faced with this dark new responsibility, many vets had chosen to leave Zimbabwe altogether, finding cleaner work in South Africa; Tanzania; and, like the country's farmers, farther afield as well: Australia, New Zealand, England, and all over the world. In my heart I could not blame them; they had trained to save animals, not to cull them by the thousands.

Yet, as Rob sold me the vaccines we needed up on Braeside, I could not help thinking about the animals left behind, not only the domestic pets stranded on farms from which their owners had fled, but the herds out there in the bush and the fields, waiting in vain for their owners to come back.

"Rob," I said, "are there more horses out there, left behind?"

He looked at me through eyes half-closed, his head cocked to one side as if he was still trying to understand what I had said.

"Mandy," he said, "they're *everywhere*."

I stood for the longest time as he drove off.

I would, I considered, just *have* to tell Pat.

In the days that followed, the safehouse phone rang more and more often. The country was a chaos of rumor and misinformation, and one of the tinier rumors swirling around the streets of Chinhoyi was that Pat and Mandy Retzlaff had opened their arms to horses whose owners were being compelled to leave them behind.

It was Rob Gordon, I knew, who had been disseminating the rumor. As we sneaked more horses—a sleek roan mare, a gorgeous dappled gray gelding—onto Braeside, we could not fault him for it. Rob had put down more animals in the last twelve months than he might have done in a whole lifetime, and the idea that there was even a glimmer of hope for some of these abandoned horses must have been a temptation too difficult to ignore.

The more horses we smuggled up onto Braeside, though, the more danger Pat and Charl put themselves in every time they crept onto the farm under cover of night. With Rory and Lindy gone, the settling of Braeside was intensifying. Villages grew up out of the bush, fields were partitioned, and all through the night the fires burned and the drums were beaten. We could not neglect the horses kept there, for then they might all fall prey to the same withering devastations that Grey had endured—but the longer they were left there, the stronger the danger of going to look after them became. We were living on borrowed time and had been for too long.

With thoughts of the horses being divided circling in our minds, we resolved to make a trip to Rob Flanagan's farm and check on the Two Tree horses being kept there. Before we had even turned off the main highway, we could see the evidence of settlers abounding. On one of the banks there spread a cluster of stick huts. A small boy darted from one to another, and a face I took to be his father's glared at us from the darkness inside. We rolled by barns that stood gutted and empty, a tractor standing, spent and curiously alone, in the middle of a field.

"Was it like this when you brought them here?" I asked.

"There were problems," Pat said, with a withering look. "There wasn't *this*."

We climbed out of the car and came toward the farmhouse where Rob Flanagan still clung on. On the windward side of the house, I saw the looming outlines of the great tunnels and greenhouses where Rob grew his flowers to be exported all over the world.

As my eyes swept around the farm, I caught sight of one of them: Lady, grazing between two of the greenhouses.

"There!" I exclaimed.

The farmhouse seemed dead, and there was no answer when we hammered on the door or squinted through the windows, so we crossed the yard, climbed the fences, and made haste to where Lady stood. She looked in good health, her eyes bright, her ears alert. She had the same sheen to her chestnut coat and did not seem to have lost weight.

I called out to her. For an instant, she spooked, as if she might hurtle off. Then she turned and came toward us. Though there was little ground to cover, the greenhouses rising tall on each side to make a narrow canyon, she broke into a trot. Exuberant, she pushed her nose into my shoulder. She whinnied softly.

"It's good to see you, too," I said. I can hardly describe the feeling of relief that she looked so well; my mind had been filled with images of what had happened to Grey.

We found Duke and Fleur by the foot of the same greenhouse, while Duchess and Marquess emerged, one after another, from the awning at the end of one of Rob's long tunnels. There was little room to draw them together, but Pat and I fussed around each one, inspecting their eyes and teeth, and especially their hooves.

One of Rob's own horses, a beautiful roan, appeared from the same tunnel. We walked on, Lady and the other Two Tree horses falling into line behind us. It must have looked a curious procession, for none of the horses were roped together. We weaved through greenhouses and tunnels, breathing in the scents of cut flowers, the aroma of those only just coming into bud.

Pat nodded, happy but somehow disturbed. "Rob's looking after them, but for how long?"

Lady ambled past me and dropped her head to drink at a trough.

"I was thinking the same thing when we were on Braeside last night. We were with Grey, in his stable. His hoof's almost healed, but just in time." Pat hesitated. "I don't think they can stay up there for long, Mandy."

"No?"

"Now that Rory and Lindy are gone, you can barely call Braeside a farm. It's a dozen farms now, parceled up and cut up and . . . butchered. We've left them up there too long already. Last night, Charl and I were returning from the farm. There were flies swarming over an animal carcass in a ditch. Just slaughter, for no reason, not even for meat. I can't leave Grey and Deja Vu up there for much longer."

"Then what?"

He did not mean to bring them here. Of that I was certain. Rob Flanagan's farm was slowly being eroded by settlers. This was no land for horses. It was time, I sensed, to bring them together. It would be a mismatched herd, made up of horses from a dozen different farms, but they—and we—would be safer together than apart.

"I think it's time we started thinking . . . don't you?" Pat ran his fingers along Fleur's muzzle, his cheek pressed to her, listening to the rhythm of the heart deep in her chest. "About moving on," he said. "It's the way Charl's been talking. He doesn't want Resje living through this. If this is Zimbabwe now, he doesn't want Charl-Emil living it, either."

"Leave for where?" I asked. "Out of the country?"

Pat's face erupted into the most glorious smile.

"No," he said. "This is *my* country." He paused, standing tall at Fleur's side. "Besides, what would we do with this lot?"

"And the rest," I whispered, remembering the calls that kept coming in.

"So," Pat said, "I suppose we'd better find a place. We'd better make a plan."

On our return to Chinhoyi, I put myself to work.

"Pat," I said, trying to control the trill in my voice, "I think I've found it."

It was almost dusk. We had been back in Chinhoyi for several days, and since then I had done nothing but sit in front of the phone, dialing number after number, any old friends and contacts I could dredge up, hoping that something might turn up.

In the safehouse, Pat prowled the edges of the room.

"Found what?" he asked.

"Do you remember," I began, "Fred and Janey Wallis?"

Fred had gone to school with Pat, in a world that now seemed very far away. He and his wife, Janey, lived on a farm about twenty kilometers from Chinhoyi, overseeing the construction of a gargantuan new dam, and Fred had been among the now infamous "Chinhoyi 24," all farmers incarcerated without conviction when they rushed to the aid of a neighbor beset by a baying war vet mob. Though Fred had spent three crippling weeks behind bars, emerging malnourished and ridden with parasites and a bronchial cough that would not go away, he and Janey had refused to give up on Zimbabwe just yet.

"They have a house, Pat, sitting empty."

Pat arched an eyebrow. "And?"

"And it's ours, if we want it. Land enough for all of the horses, too . . ."

Now I knew I really did have Pat's attention.

"War vets?" he said softly, those two words so heavy with meaning, for us, for our future, for the horses. For the country.

"Not yet," I replied. "It would be a home, Pat. It would be *some-where*." I paused. "We could go there tomorrow, if we had to. What do you think?"

I could see the idea blossoming behind Pat's eyes: land enough for the entire herd; somewhere safe for the children; and, shimmering in the distance, the fresh waters of a dam, so that the horses might never again go thirsty like Grey had.

He nodded, sharply and once only. It was all that I needed. Soon, we would be on our way.

That night, the safehouse gathered for dinner. In the downstairs dining room it felt just like one of the dinners we had shared on Crofton and Two Tree. In the middle of the table, a big side of beef billowed with aroma, and, as Pat set to carving it apart, Charl and Tertia gave thanks for the meal we were about to share. Their faith, already strong, seemed to have strengthened since that day on Two Tree. Every time I heard them pray, I could not stop myself from picturing Tertia, holding tightly to Resje and Charl-Emil in the heart of the farmhouse, waiting for the mob to descend.

At the end of the table, Kate played with Charl-Emil. It was time, I decided, to break the news.

"Everybody," I began, "there's something Pat and I have got to say . . ."

A hush descended.

"We've known for a long time that this wasn't forever." I threw Tertia a grin. "Our refugee camp in the middle of town! And with the horses so divided, it's been preying on our minds—how to bring them back together, how to make a life for ourselves in the middle of this chaos. So I've been searching for somewhere we could go." I paused. "All of us. The horses included."

"Mum?" Kate ventured. "Is everything . . ."

I gave her a nod. "Everything's going to be fine, darling. You see, we have somewhere to go to now. There's an empty farmhouse on Biri Farm. A place we could set up a home again. A place we can take Deja Vu, Grey, Lady, and all the rest. There's a dam as big as at Two Tree, and riding trails that run all over the farmland. Janey and Fred Wallis have said we can stay there as long as we want."

"Mandy," Tertia chimed in, "that's such great news . . ."

She reached across the table and took my hand. Yet the way she squeezed told me that something was wrong. I thought I understood.

"Tertia, Charl," I said, trying to mask my smile. "We want you to come with us."

Charl and Tertia shared a strange look. They held the pose for a second. Then Tertia took her hand from mine and reached out to fold it over Resje's. Resje shifted in her seat, and silence settled across the dining room, broken only by a sudden cry from Charl-Emil.

"Mandy," Tertia began, "there's something *we* have to tell *you* as well."

"It won't come as a surprise," added Charl. "We've been thinking of it for some time." He hesitated. I saw Pat's expression change and understood, in that moment, what Charl was about to say. "This isn't home," Charl went on. "Not anymore. We didn't come back to Two Tree just to see it taken away. We'd thought . . ." Words seemed to fail him, as they had been failing so many of us for so long. "We'd thought it would be paradise. Like it was the first time I worked there. A paradise for Resje and Charl-Emil. A part of the country to charm my city girl's heart . . ."

At this, Tertia smiled.

"Not anymore," she said. "Mandy, if it was just us, well, maybe we'd stay. Maybe we'd find a way to make a new life here. But it isn't just us. There's Resje and Charl-Emil, too. I don't want them to have another day like that day on Two Tree. How could we ever feel safe here after that?"

"It *was* paradise for a little while, wasn't it?" I said, my voice barely a whisper.

Charl nodded.

"But a paradise lost," he said. "Pat, Mandy, we've made up our minds. We're going to New Zealand."

Throughout, Pat had not said a word. Slowly, he stretched out his hand and took hold of Charl's.

"Of course," said Charl, "there's the small matter of . . . Lady. Fleur. Grey. Duchess, Duke, Marquess, and the rest."

"No there isn't," said Pat, holding Charl's gaze. "There never was."

"We can't take them with us."

"You don't need to. Two Tree, Crofton . . . It always felt the same thing to us. I've known those horses as long as you. I was there when you pulled Lady out of Lady Richmond. I was there when that Arabian stallion came through. We've watched those horses grow from foals. They're as much family as Deja Vu, Imprevu, and the rest up there. They're as loved as Frisky ever was."

Charl nodded. Nothing else needed to be said.

Except perhaps:

"I think we're going to miss you, Tertia," I said.

Around the table, we all raised our glasses. First Pat, then Charl, then Tertia and me. Resje and Kate lifted theirs too, and, in his high chair, even Charl-Emil seemed to know something was happening. His face broke into an absurd grin, and he seemed to pump his little fist too, eager to join in with the toast.

"To old friends," said Charl.

"Absent friends," I added.

"And to the end of all *this*," Pat interjected.

We drained our glasses, talked of Crofton and Two Tree, of rides by the dam, of the Arabian stallions, of Frisky and Lady Richmond, of all the horses who had lived and died there and not had to know the chaos that was engulfing their country.

We drank long into the night, and, with the children fast asleep around us, we said our good-byes.

Chapter 8

PAT AND I stood at the fences of Biri Farm's new, hastily erected paddocks, the first lights of dawn beginning to spread. We were here to see the horses come to their new home.

It had been a long walk from Braeside, as driving the horses through farms already ceded to war vets and party officials would draw too much attention, but the grooms had reached us at last. They led the horses through the paddock gates. It was a mismatched herd, but with Charl and Tertia gone it seemed strangely fitting that the Crofton and Two Trees horses should have come together. Grooms had walked the horses off the remnants of Rob Flanagan's farm, too. Here were Grey and Deja Vu standing together, Fleur with Lady, Imprevu with Duke. Duchess and Marquess were the last to come through the gate, and as they settled in, we clambered over the fences to run our hands across their flanks and make sure they had reached their new home without any harm. Grey's hoof seemed to have healed perfectly, though we were still uncertain how much weight it could bear.

"It's going to feel strange," Pat called, "living with them again."

It was going to feel strange living *anywhere*, I thought, but perhaps it would feel more like home with the horses nearby. For the first time in what felt like an age, we could try to build some semblance of normality into our lives—and the first step on that road was to take a long ride around Biri Dam.

Once the horses were rested, Pat and I saddled up and set about exploring our new home. Biri Dam, completed only recently, was developed jointly by the farmers (for irrigation) and the government (for water to Chinhoyi). Fred had been employed to manage the finishing touches to the dam and to control the water. All of this seemed so absurd now. The land here had been pioneered long before our own, its contours less jagged and wild than the ones we had hewn out at our own farm. On the slopes above the fields the crowns of bush did not grow as densely, and the air hung heavy with the tang of the citrus groves along the shores of the dam.

We set off around the farm, not knowing exactly which way the paths would lead us. I had chosen to ride Grey, while Pat had chosen Imprevu. The earth did not have the same vibrant redness as at Two Tree and River Ranch, but the land was of a similar quality, hard and unforgiving, laced with the same scree that forbade farming without a careful cultivation of the soil. Here the land had been given to tobacco and, in its fallow years, long grasses for the cattle who still roamed here.

We found a bush trail, steep and punishing for the horses, and followed a switchback to its top. Here, we could look down on the waters of Biri Dam. In the east the great dam wall loomed, while on the farthest side farms much older than our own had been resettled long before. Ten kilometers away, east of the dam wall, stood Avalon, a farm that belonged to Nick Swanepoel, while in the west, along the line of the dam, Biri was bordered by Portland Estates, a cattle ranch belonging to John Crawford. The dam stood, a formidable blue scar in the green land.

We looked down on the houses where the dam's construction workers had once lived, concrete shacks for their foremen and huts of poles and thatching grass for the other staff. In the past few days, those old workers of ours who had been clinging to their homes at Crofton had made the journey down to be with us again. As we rode through, I was glad to see familiar faces: Charles and Albert. For the moment, they would be free from the scourge of Mugabe's ZANU-PF.

The farmhouse in which we lived was next door to the house belonging to Fred and Janey Wallis. As we rode back to our new paddocks, Fred, shaved bald to get rid of the lice from his recent imprisonment, with spectacles perched on his nose, was sitting on the step, as he often did. He called out, and we brought Grey and Imprevu around.

Physically, Fred seemed to have changed little since he and Pat were at school, but the signs of the three weeks he had spent in prison were visible. His eyes did not seem to settle, he moved with the jittery air of a scarecrow, and the cough that had set in during those weeks inside still plagued him.

"Settling in?" he asked.

I threw a look backward. Lady had bounded over to the edge of the paddock and was studying me carefully, greedy as ever and desperate to be doted on.

"Well, Fred, there's a lot to settle in . . ."

Fred rolled his eyes. I think he remembered something about Pat from their schooldays: endless stories of the chicken and cattle he was collecting on his father's farm. It must have been an absurd sight for two people like Fred and Janey, to suddenly have their home invaded not just by Retzlaffs but by a random collection of rescued horses, too.

"I suppose you'll have to talk to John," said Fred.

"John Crawford?"

Fred's eyes lit up, as if he was daring us with a practical joke.

"Didn't you know?" he ventured. "John's finally having to leave. He doesn't have much time left. But he has a Retzlaff kind of a problem . . . fifty horses, stuck out there on his farm. I think you'll be receiving a call."

We knew when we hit the boundaries of the Crawfords' farm, some way west of Biri, for we could see their cattle ranged before us, hundreds of heads watching dolefully from the fields. John's was a good old-fashioned cattle ranch of the kind the first pioneers in this part of the world had kept. We rode in on Grey and Deja Vu. There were horses in the fields, too. A big gray mare, as strong as any stallion, tracked us with her eyes while, around her, two foals tentatively pushed their muzzles at each other. The smaller of the foals held itself much like the gray mare, with the same strong-set shoulders. Most telling of all, both the mare and the foal had two white feet, a mark that they were surely mother and son. These, we would soon learn, were Jade and her foal, later to be named Brutus, two horses I will never forget.

John Crawford was waiting for us at the farmhouse. John was a lovely, soft-spoken man, approaching thirty years old. Pat and I had known his father well, for he also bred cattle and we had often seen him at shows and auctions.

"It's been two years since they appeared," John explained as he helped us water Grey and Deja Vu in front of the low, sprawling farmhouse. "We could ignore it at first. It was only a little thing. A few faces at the gates, a few men at the sides of the roads. It got worse." He paused. "There started being parts of the farm we couldn't touch. Then those sections started growing. They built their huts, brought in their cattle. Brought distemper with them. It killed my dogs. Ticks got into the cattle." He ran his hands along Grey's flank. "A year ago, they told us it wasn't our farm anymore. We stayed. I can't count the number of times we've been told we have to leave."

John led us into the fields where his cattle were grazing. There, we walked among his horses. Some of them, we could see, were strong cattle horses. There were foals as well, six or seven younger than a year old.

Every one of them seemed to spook at our appearance. I watched as a ripple seemed to move through the herd. Mares turned as if to protect their foals, while a dark bay gelding turned tail and kicked into a trot.

"They're *wild*," I said.

"I can't remember how long it's been since we could work these horses. They *know*, Mandy. They get a feeling when something's wrong. It doesn't take many months for wildness to set back in."

My eyes were drawn to the big gray mare we had seen upon approaching the farm. Up close, I could see that she wore a great scar on her left flank. At first I took it for the mark made by some marauding war vet, too stoned or drunk to know what he was doing. I asked John.

"No," he began. "It's from the cattle. There are a few horses with marks like that. Sometimes a horned cow will gouge them when they're feeding at the same troughs." He paused. "She came through it, though. Jade's a strong girl."

John moved as if to run his hands through Jade's mane. It was obvious that he and the horse had once been close, for she did not startle so easily as the others.

"What do you think?" John ventured. "Can you help?"

There must have been fifty horses in the field, and perhaps just as many cattle. Here were the old and the young, the strong and the lame, more horses than we had had on Crofton and Two Tree combined, more even than we had collected up on Biri. When I turned back, the horses blurring in front of my eyes, the last thing I caught sight of was Pat's face. He was wearing an inscrutable expression, as if going through a calculation too complex to comprehend.

Then he simply nodded.

"We'll take as many as we can."

Rounding up the horses was difficult. Perhaps they had seen some terrible things from the invading war vets, but the wildness in them seemed to have made them distrust humans again.

As we were about to set off, Pat's eyes had landed on the big gray mare and her plaintive little foal.

"What about Jade?" Pat asked. "And this foal of hers?"

There was no hesitation. John simply shook his head.

"She isn't just one of the herd, Pat. She's *my* horse."

I knew what that relationship was like. Every horse is an individual, but, just like humans, sometimes those individuals click. That was the way it had been for Pat and Frisky.

"John, you're not thinking straight. See it from Jade's perspective. How long have you got left? Two months? Three?"

"Less," John admitted.

"When it comes, it comes fast. You might not have time. What if you couldn't get Jade off? What if they . . ."

For a young man, John looked suddenly very old.

"If you get the farm back one day, John, I'll ride her back here myself. I'm not trying to steal your horse off you . . . but I don't want to leave her, not when I've seen what's coming." Pat paused. "And I have seen it, John."

Jade seemed to move her head between Pat and John, following the conversation.

"You mean, if it ends, you'll send her back?"

"If it ends, I don't think I could stop her."

In resignation, John passed Jade's lead rope to Pat. Then, he ran his hand along the length of her muzzle. *Good luck*, he mouthed. Jade's ears swiveled and folded forward, her lips turning to nibble at John's hand.

As Pat led Jade off, her foal followed after. In the end we drove twelve horses from John's fields to Biri. That same day we had to work on the foals in a round pen, and by the evening we had them eating out of our hands.

Back at Biri, Pat put his arm around me. I nestled into his shoulder and soaked up his smell: the smell of earth, of home, of our long years of work. We looked out across the land together. On one side of the field, the Two Tree and Crofton horses seemed to be gathering, while on the other, Jade, the little foal whom I had named Brutus—for there was never a less likely looking Brutus in the whole of Zimbabwe—and the rest of the Crawford horses were making a separate herd of their own. In between, the other horses we had taken in looked like dark islands in a sea of green. Then, one of the Crawford mares ventured out and Deja Vu, recognizing her from the day's journey, shifted from her side of the paddock, too. It was, I decided, a sight wonderful enough to make all thoughts of tomorrow, and the day after, simply evaporate away. The horses were getting to know one another.

"I think we've collected enough," I began. My count had reached thirty-five before I started seeing double.

"Mandy," Pat said, grinning, "we haven't even started."

Late that night, Fred came to see us. In the sitting room, he sat down with Pat, opened a cold beer, and looked at him with sad but eager eyes. From the kitchen doorway, I listened to them talking—or, rather, I listened to Fred talk and watched Pat's reaction. Pat, Fred was certain, had to see sense. The more horses we took in, the less able we would be to provide for them; the more horses we took in, the less able we would be to provide for ourselves. Some people, Fred said, had nervous episodes that could manifest themselves in the most curious of ways; the sooner Pat recognized his mania for what it was, the better.

It dawned on me that Fred was probably right. I had seen Pat's mania manifest itself like this before. I had borne the brunt of the hundreds of turkeys he had collected in the early days of our marriage. Farmers around us were constantly losing their heads as their lives unraveled. We had heard of countless heart attacks, divorces, extramarital affairs. Was it really so far-fetched to believe the same thing was happening to Pat, and showing itself in this most incredible of ways?

"There are herds and herds of animals out there," Fred said. "Cattle and sheep. You can't rescue them all."

Pat suddenly looked the way Jay had as a young boy, thrilled to be out hunting with a new bird of prey.

"Do you know, Fred," Pat said, "you might have given me an idea. Cattle and sheep! Somebody has to rescue those cattle and sheep!"

Even though Pat was only joking, Fred looked suddenly downcast, perplexed beyond measure.

In the doorway, my face broke into the widest grin. Pat, I decided, might well have been mad—but in the new Zimbabwe, only the truly insane could ever hope to prosper.

For a while, now, the impact of the land invasions on Zimbabwe's economy had been clear. We watched helplessly as the nation's only real resource—its agricultural land—was systematically destroyed. Most of the farms taken did not go to the local black populace, as was being promised. Instead, they became the country residences of party officials, or else they were simply put to the torch or abandoned. If any farming was happening on River Ranch, Two Tree, or the countless other farms to have fallen, it was simple, subsistence stuff by the settlers. Commercial agriculture was finished and, with it, the Zimbabwean dollar.

In Harare one morning, my mother left home to withdraw her pension. At the bank, she produced her passport and identification. Having withdrawn her money for the month, she set about her regular routine: first to the shops for supplies, and later to a restaurant in town for afternoon tea with an old friend.

It was only upon opening her bag and seeing the money she had withdrawn that she realized: her month's pension, that symbol of the lifetime she had spent nursing, was worth little more than half a loaf of bread and a bottle of Coke.

She looked up when the waitress came to take her order and politely excused herself without ordering.

On the table behind her, her month's pension fluttered on a plate. It was the biggest and yet smallest tip the waitress had ever received.

"Only in Zimbabwe, Amanda."

In Harare, all of my mother's possessions were in cases, carefully being loaded into the back of our car. We had packed as much as possible off to relatives, and it felt strange to see my mother's long lifetime reduced to a few boxes and bags. She was seventy-three years old and now she had nothing.

When I closed the trunk, I saw her slipping into the driver's seat.

"Mum, I'll drive."

"Amanda . . ."

"You don't know the way."

She relented and shuffled to the other side of the car.

"Come on, Mum, let's get out of here . . ."

There had been a great influx of farmers into Harare, those who could not flee the country often finding new homes in the city. Perhaps

Pat and I would have considered it, were it not for the horses out on Biri. Pat was spending his days with John Crawford's foals in his training ring—and the idea of him giving up that life to move to the city felt as objectionable as what Mugabe was doing to the land.

We pulled off into Harare traffic. The roads were ragged at their edges and full of great potholes. Darkness was falling and the street-lights shone only intermittently, so that we had to roll from one halo of light to the next through pools of blackness. In that blackness, I saw that the streets were filled with men in uniform, soldiers out on patrol. I checked the dashboard and saw that our fuel was running low—but every garage we passed had big signs outside declaring that there was no gas, no diesel, nothing in their stores.

"Mum," I began, "how long has it been . . . ?"

"Oh, Amanda," my mother said with a lofty grin, "this is *nothing*."

I wanted to tell her I was glad she was coming to live with us. Biri Farm, at least, was at peace. Then, the thought occurred to me that it might not always be that way, and in silence I drove on.

My mother did not deserve this.

Beryl Sheldon Whitefield was born in Hyde in England in 1929 and did not find herself in African climes until she married my father, John, in 1952. My father was an architect from Galashiels in Scotland and, soon after they were married, answered the clarion call for architects to seek their fortunes in Ghana in West Africa. My grandparents, horrified that their little girl was being dragged off to the Dark Continent, pleaded with my father to reconsider. But my parents had their hearts and minds set on adventure. It was to dictate the shape of their lives.

It was in Ghana that I spent my early years, before my parents finally settled in South Africa to raise me and my two younger brothers. After twenty-one years, my mother and father went their separate ways. Beryl left Africa to live with her mother in Spain, but, on hearing that I had taken up with a Rhodesian and was moving to live in a country at war, she decided to return to the continent that had dominated so much of her life. She found work as a hospital nurse and gave her days and nights to helping old and sick Zimbabweans, both black and white.

Now, that country to which she had given everything for twenty-five years was condemning her to a cruel, impoverished old age.

"Do you know, Amanda, I believe I may even owe the bank. The pension doesn't even cover the account costs now."

When we reached Biri Farm, Albert and Caetano, two of the workers who had come with us from River Ranch, helped Granny Beryl to unload her packs. There was so little, and yet it was the sum of a life.

"Welcome home, Mum."

She looked up at the face of Biri farmhouse.

"Amanda, it's positively a palace."

With a wry grin, I showed Granny Beryl around her new home. In front of the farmhouse sat Pat's training ring, and farther on stood the beginnings of a gymkhana setup he and the laborers were building as part of the training regimen he was instituting for the newest horses. So far, the foals from John Crawford's farm, including the tormented little Brutus, were being handled daily, getting them used to close human contact. Pat would spend long hours settling them, then lifting each of their hooves so that, when the time came to ride and work with them, they would not instinctively kick out. When they were old enough, he would begin a long process of groundwork, fitting them with halters and lead ropes, training them from the ground with long reins, before finally climbing into the saddle. It could take two years to school one of these horses properly; I only hoped Biri lasted that long.

On the hill that backed onto the farm, some of the laborers were working at clearing an eight-kilometer trail for riding. It was to be the last part of Pat's makeshift training program, a twisting track full of surprises—ditches, crests, sudden switchbacks—to help desensitize the horses and teach them not to be spooked. Looking at Brutus, standing forlorn in the field, and Lady, still bounding boisterously about, I wondered if they'd ever get to walk that trail.

We had prepared a room for Granny Beryl and I showed her to it. As she unpacked clothes into drawers, I produced a small bag, no bigger than a school satchel.

"Mum, put this somewhere safe."

"What is it?"

"It's your ditch kit. Don't worry about it—just keep it to hand."

My mother set the bag down, drew back the zipper, and peered inside. One by one, she lifted the items out: first, a clean pair of panties; next, a tube of toothpaste with a new toothbrush; then a bar of soap, some other toiletries, a small roll of U.S. banknotes. Using U.S. currency was still illegal in Zimbabwe, but at least it was worth something in a market spiraling out of control.

"But . . . what's it for?"

"I've been keeping mine ever since Palmerston. Keep your passport with it too, Mum. And if anyone ever comes to the farm, anybody who looks like they're Party or Air Force or CIO . . ." I trailed off. It was not fair to heap this on her after the shell shock of her pension disappearing. "Just keep it safe." I folded my hands over hers.

I was almost out the door, off to find Pat, when my mother stopped me short.

"Amanda, is everything all right?"

"No, Mum," I said, the last few months hitting me with all the power of a train, "things aren't all right at all."

Sometime after dark, a car pulled into Biri Farm, our driver Jonathan at the wheel. From the backseat, Kate tumbled out. The school run was longer than it had been when we lived at Crofton or the safehouse, but for the sake of continuity in her important exam years, we had not wanted Kate to be uprooted. Exhausted, she came into the farmhouse, ditched her bags, and ran straight into her grandmother.

Kate beamed and threw her arms open wide. "What are you doing here?"

"Kate," Granny Beryl announced, "this is where I live."

Momentarily confused, Kate scoured the room until her eyes locked with mine.

I'll explain later, I mouthed.

We drifted into the living room, where a table had been set for dinner. Pat was nowhere to be seen, still no doubt in his training ring with Brutus, and I hurried off to bellow for him. It would not have been the first time he had missed a meal while playing with his horses.

By the time I got back to the dining room, Kate and Granny Beryl were in the midst of catching up.

"And how's school?"

"Mum . . ."

"Amanda, I'm asking the girl a question."

But it was a question Pat and I had been shying away from asking. Ever since Crofton, Kate had come home with rumors she had heard in the schoolyard, her friends' families beset by war vets and driven from their farms. The school ground was a place where stories fermented, but, more than that, it seemed a microcosm of what was happening in the rest of Zimbabwe. It wasn't only in the cities and on the farms that the rivalry between Mugabe's ZANU-PF and the MDC was viciously played out; it was happening in Kate's world as well.

"It's pretty empty," Kate said, turning to Granny Beryl. "Lots of students didn't come back at the start of term."

"Where are they?"

"Australia, mostly. Some of them went to England, I think, like Paul." Kate paused. "Lots of mothers are going, too. They're finding work caring, now they don't have their farms."

"Caring?"

"Old people's homes, Mum," I interjected. "There are agencies for it."

"There was a"—Kate hesitated, searching for the right word—"*thing* after school," she went on. "Some of the older students, they keep wearing their MDC shirts. Some of the others . . . well, they don't like it. They came in with their ZANU-PF shirts. It was like those horses out there, everyone sticking to their own side of the field . . ."

"Politics, is it?"

"It's because of the election," said Kate.

March was not far away. In ballot boxes across Zimbabwe, the battle would be lost or won: four more years of Mugabe and his rape of our country, or a fresh beginning with Morgan Tsvangirai and his Movement for Democratic Change. Knowing how overwhelmingly the nation had refuted Mugabe's referendum two years before, I was convinced that the country felt the same way as we did, desperate for the MDC to take control and stabilize this chaos; what I was not convinced of was that the election would reflect the true will of the people. I had seen how terrorized the workers on Crofton, Two Tree, and Palmerston Estates had been by ZANU-PF demagogues. The same thing was happening nationwide.

At that moment, Pat came into the room, still wearing his chaps. Without stopping to wash up, he wrapped Kate in a big bear hug and dropped into his seat.

"I'm starving," he began, looking at what was left in the bowls. "Oh well, I suppose I'll be the dustbin again . . ."

He proceeded to shovel everything that was left onto his plate. It was a moment before he noticed Kate squinting at him.

"What is it?"

"Dad," Kate ventured, "you *stink*."

Pat lifted his hands to his nose. "I've been dipping the horses," he said. "For ticks."

While Pat rushed off to scrub himself, Kate, Granny Beryl, and I put down our plates and took a walk down to the paddocks. Over the fence, Jade, Brutus, and the other horses from John Crawford's farm lifted their teeth to tear at the low-lying branches of the trees beside them. Having stripped each twig, they proceeded to carefully chew the leaves. It was a habit not even Pat had seen before. Our only thought was that there had been too much competition for grass to graze among the Crawford cattle, and these enterprising horses had found a unique solution.

On seeing us, Lady bounded over. I could see why Pat was having an ordeal trying to properly train her; this little madam was spoiled beyond saving.

"What do you think, Mum?" I asked. "Not bad for a group of desperadoes on the run?"

Granny Beryl nodded sternly.

"Amanda," she said, as if it had only just occurred, "I thought I'd made it clear with that horrible little horse Ticky. Just what are you doing with all these *horses*?"

In the farmhouse, the phone rang. Granny Beryl, sensing an opportunity to help out, strode energetically over.

"Don't worry, Mum. It's probably another call about some horses . . ."

It was with a pleasant surprise, then, that I heard a familiar voice on the other end of the line, vaguely distorted as it made its way halfway across the world.

"Hello, Mandy."

"Hello . . . Charl."

Charl and Tertia had been settled in New Zealand for some weeks, and it occurred to me now how much I missed them.

"How's Biri Farm?" Charl asked.

It was a good feeling to share some positive news. I told him about Brutus and Jade, the other foals who had come from John Crawford. I did not tell him that Pat still believed some of these horses might be restored to their rightful homes.

"How about you, Charl?"

"It's . . . difficult, Mandy. I won't complain. I'm glad we came. It's . . ." He paused. "Work's hard to come by, that's all. But we're not the only ones in this boat."

"Are you working, Charl?"

"I am," he replied. "I'm on a cattle lot."

I had to ask him to repeat it. I thought I had misheard.

"Charl, you've been a farm manager for twenty years! Surely . . ."

"It's for the kids, Mandy. That's all that matters." He meant it, but

I could still hear a hint of defeat in his voice. "But I didn't call to complain. There's something else—and, with all these horses Pat's collecting, maybe I called at just the right time . . . Tell me," he went on, "do you remember a mare called Princess?"

How could I forget? I rode Princess's half brother, Grey, almost every day. I vividly remembered seeing them as foals on Two Tree, a family of noble half-Arabians, and watching them grow. I remembered, too, the day we had been riding across Two Tree, only to see Resje being thrown from Princess's back and, her foot caught in the stirrups, trailing wildly behind.

"Charl, has something happened?"

"Ormeston's gone," Charl replied. "It's where I sent her, after the accident." His voice trailed off. "We sent her there, and now the war vets have it. Isn't it the stupidest thing? I haven't thought about Princess in years, but since I heard . . ."

"It isn't stupid at all."

"I suppose she might be gone already. But . . . it doesn't seem right not to *know*. You and Pat have already done so much . . . but you have Grey and Fleur and the rest. If Princess is still alive, it seems she should be with them."

An image hit me: Pat sneaking onto another occupied farm, but this time without Charl. I was not sure how to feel about that; at least, together, Pat and Charl had been able to cover each other as they moved through the darkness.

"Charl," I said, "let's make a plan."

Ormeston had been *jambanja*ed some weeks previously, and its owners had not been back to the land since. That night, I called the CFU, hoping to hear that Pat and I would be safe going onto the farm in search of Princess. The news I heard was grave: settlers had moved onto Ormeston in droves, the farm was already being partitioned, and under no circumstances could we risk sneaking on.

"Not even under cover of night?"

I looked at Pat, willing him to stop. I shook my head.

The next morning, I telephoned a local member of the SPCA. It seemed a strange contradiction, even in this most contradictory of countries, that the same war vets who had calculatedly slaughtered farmers' dogs just to cultivate fear might let the doughty, often white, women of the SPCA onto the farms in order to rescue domestic pets—but, if there was a way of getting Princess out safely, this was our only hope.

"She's a horse," a flinty voice explained. "Our purview is domestic pets only. We don't have dispensation to take livestock."

Livestock were considered part of a farm, so no longer belonged to the farmers who had raised them for generations. It was part of the reason that countless farmers had taken to slaughtering their herds as soon as they realized they would be evicted. With the market flooded by such wholesale slaughter, the price of beef and lamb had suddenly plummeted; generations of breeding were lost, and all for less than ten cents per kilogram of flesh. In the new Zimbabwe, it was hardly worth the paper it was written on.

"Princess wasn't a working horse," I explained. "How can she be livestock?"

"It's a gray area, I'll—"

"They're not even classed as agricultural livestock, they're domestic animals—"

I realized I was talking over the SPCA member.

"Mandy," she said, "let's see what we can do."

February 2002, and the parliamentary election was only a month away. Coming back into Biri Farm one afternoon, Pat and I saw an unfamiliar truck sitting outside the farmhouse. Instinctively, Pat eased his foot off the accelerator. We crawled along the track, the horse paddock just coming into view over the next ridge of red.

"Who is it?"

At first, I did not venture a reply. Then, I saw a horse trailer decoupled from the wagon and breathed a sigh of relief. "I think it's Princess . . ."

We drew into Biri Farm's yard and climbed out of the car. A man was standing at the edge of the trailer, tall and black, wearing khaki shorts and a simple plain shirt.

"I thought nobody's home!"

"Why didn't you ask the labor and get her in the paddock?" Pat asked, trying not to sound aggrieved. "She'll be burning up in there . . ."

"Boss, they said you should do it."

Pat climbed up into the trailer, disappeared for a minute, and then returned, leading the statuesque Princess by a lead rope. As her head emerged I saw the same Arabian features that her brother, Grey, displayed. It had been more than five years since I last saw her, but she seemed so familiar: her shining bay hide, her dark, flowing mane.

Then she was out of the horse trailer, and what I saw left me without words.

Princess's withers were dressed in gauze that had once been white, now stained a horrible red and yellow, as blood and pus seeped out of some unknown wound at the base of her mane. The dressing was huge, the wound it buried bigger than a clenched fist. Wordlessly, Pat led her around and I saw that the same dressing was applied to her other side.

Pat ran his hands along Princess's flank. His fingers came a foot away from the dressing and she shifted in pain, straining against her lead rope.

Pat whispered, "Let's get her in the stable."

We had turned to lead Princess off when the driver called out.

"Boss, you're forgetting . . ."

Pat passed me Princess's lead rope and turned, as if to bawl at the driver, when he saw another face appearing from the darkness in the trailer. A tiny chestnut mare emerged, blinking into the light. She must have been less than a year old. Except for the wound on Princess's withers, this foal was a perfect replica of her.

"She's called Evita," the driver explained. He began to chatter on, but the words were lost. I approached the tentative foal. She cringed back into darkness.

"Come on, girl," I said. "You're home now."

There had already been stables when we arrived at Biri Farm, but our laborers had built more stalls between them, simple things where the horses might be led for feeding or veterinary care. We settled the dainty Evita in one stall; in the one next door, Pat calmed Princess.

Then, gently, he began to peel back the dressing.

It was a long operation, the dressing matted to Princess's hide. Inside, the wound had been packed tightly with gauze. Pat lifted a corner and teased it out. As far as it came, it seemed there was always more to come. Layer by layer, the wound revealed itself, deeper and deeper. Sinew started to show. Nerves were exposed. I stroked Princess's muzzle as Pat crossed the stall and began to tease at the dressing from the other side.

At last, the wound was open to the air. Pat stooped, stared along the length of the festering wound.

"It's a gunshot wound," he said. "Somebody has shot her."

I watched in growing horror as Pat extended his arm toward the wound. The gaping maw swallowed his whole fist. Were it not for her exposed nerves and raw muscle, he could have put his arm straight through Princess's withers and out the other side.

"The bastards," Pat whispered.

"What are we going to do?"

In the next stall, Evita shifted, as if sensing what we were doing with her mother.

"I'm not going to put her down," said Pat. "I know that. I'm not going to give them the satisfaction."

"Darling, she's—"

Pat's eyes blazed at me. "She's *Charl's* horse. *Resje's* horse." He reached for his medicine bag, fumbled inside for an antiseptic spray and packs of gauze. "I'm going to make her well again. She's going to be so strong I could ride her from here to Victoria Falls and back. And, most of all"—he began to pack the wound with gauze as I steadied Princess's muzzle and looked into her dark, sad eyes—"I'm going to pray this election's lost. Mandy, it *has* to be the MDC."

Grey and I cantered along the line of the dam. I could hear the thunder of his hooves, feel the wind raging in my hair. It was enough to make me forget.

I was urging him to a gallop, and could already sense his excitement at the challenge, when I saw two figures appear on the horizon, back in the direction of Biri farmhouse. Instinctively, I teased the reins, and Grey, acknowledging the gentle request with the barest bowing of his head, slowed back from a canter to a trot. We glided around and headed across the open field.

Pat rode toward the dam, Deja Vu beneath him, and we came together in the middle of the field. It did not seem right to stop, so as the horses acknowledged each other, we turned and followed my trail back along the shore of the dam.

"Mugabe won" was all Pat said. "It's ZANU-PF."

I had, I supposed, been stopping myself from asking the question all day. The champagne we had optimistically earmarked would stay in the storeroom tonight. There would be no popping of corks, no glasses raised in celebration. There would be no midnight dreaming of returning to Crofton.

"How bad?"

"Only just," Pat replied, "but fifty-six percent is still a majority."

It should not have been this way. Instinctively, I squeezed Grey. He gave a burst of speed, but then he dropped back to a slow, languorous walk. Like me, he knew there was nowhere to run to.

"It should have been like the referendum," I said aloud, thinking back to that moment in which the land invasions truly began. "Eighty percent against. The MDC . . ."

"Were robbed," Pat interjected. "Is it any wonder? We've seen what they did to our labor. On Palmerston and Braeside and . . . They knew what they were doing. Driving us off our farms was never about us being white. It was about votes, pure and simple." Pat edged Deja Vu on. "He wasn't going after us. He was going after our labor. What do the votes of a few white people count against all that?"

We came almost as far as the Crawford farm before we lapped around to make the long ride home. Along the way, we barely exchanged a word. Only when we came back toward Biri, saw the rest of the herd in their paddocks, did I break the silence.

"When we took John's horses in," I began, "you said we would send them back . . . when it was over."

Pat nodded.

"Well, it's already over, isn't it? It was over a year ago. We just didn't want to admit it. There isn't any going back home, is there, Pat?"

I did not know if I was saying it in anger or relief, but it was relief that flooded me when Pat nodded. I did not like the idea of his hope being lost, of Patrick Retzlaff having abandoned the wild-eyed optimism that had seen him rampaging into a bar brawl on the very first day we stepped out together, but somehow it was consoling to think he believed it properly, for the very first time. We would not, I knew, stop taking in horses—but at least now we knew what we were letting ourselves in for. The rules of the game had just been forcefully declared. Now all we had to do was play.

"Let's make a plan," said Pat.

Back at the farmhouse, I found my mother asleep over a book. I roused her gently, placing a cup of steaming tea in front of her.

"Mum," I ventured, "did you hear?"

She nodded absently.

"You're not surprised?"

Granny Beryl shrugged. "It happens, dear."

I could not believe she could be quite so sanguine about it, but suddenly all the sourness of our ride home lifted from me in waves.

"What are you thinking, Amanda?"

I was thinking about Paul, our last days on Palmerston, of taking him to the airport and waving good-bye. I was thinking that there were places in the world better than this—and if Pat and I could not go there for fear of leaving our horses behind, perhaps there was yet a way of seeing my mother safe and comfortable in her old age. Mum had been born in England; perhaps there was a home for her there, a place to spend her twilight years without the fear of Mugabe's *panga* hanging over her head.

"I'm thinking," I said, "that it's about time we got you out of here. How would you feel, Mum, about going back *home*?"

Chapter 9

A PLANE BANKED in descent toward Harare International Airport. A familiar city unfolded before me. I had been away for twelve long weeks, and though I had spoken to Pat almost every night, the feeling of coming home was almost overwhelming.

In the seat beside me sat my mother, her closed eyes somehow still betraying her sadness—for, after three hard months of searching, we had not been able to find her a home.

England had seemed such an opportunity, but almost as soon as we touched down, the scale of the challenge felt insurmountable. After spending some time with Paul, now firmly ensconced in London life and living in Wimbledon, south London—a place so filled with exiled Zimbabweans that it had earned itself a new nickname, *Zimbledon*—we had headed off for the country town of Princess Riseborough. There, we had stayed with my cousin Julie while I made some money as a waitress and we tried to steer my mother through the labyrinthine bureaucracy of England's Social Services Department. Though we visited their offices every day, we were repeatedly sent away and told to come back at a later date. Even though my mother had been born in England and worked there for many years, it did not, we were told, guarantee her a state pension or the support of Britain's care homes. We begged and pleaded, but no matter how many times I tried to explain the terrible predicament my mother was in, the officious woman at the office only batted our questions back. I still remember the way she looked at us as she declared, "Political situations in Zimbabwe are not *our* concern . . ." It was as if we were being sent away before we had even presented our case.

After three months of trying, Granny Beryl and I were returning to the country that no longer wanted us. It was only as we began our descent into Harare that the real sense of failure hit me. Granny Beryl still slept, but I wondered what I was taking her back into. As the seat-belt sign flashed on and we prepared to land, I woke her.

"Are we home?" she asked.

It seemed such an absurd question. What did *home* mean anymore?

Coming through Customs in the airport was always tense, but never more so than since the land invasions had started. Slowly, we made our way through. On the other side, our driver Jonathan was waiting. We pulled off into Harare traffic, passing the place where—in that long-ago world—my mother had had a safe, reliable home.

"Where's Pat?" I asked.

Jonathan looked over his shoulder, wearing an inscrutable grin. "He is with his horses . . ."

It was not until we turned from the main road to follow the red dirt track toward Biri Farm that I understood how much I had missed this place. There can be nothing comparable to coming home to Africa, and all homesick Africans, whether white or black, will tell you the same. Africa has a smell. It has a rhythm. The wealth of feeling that bubbled up inside me seemed incredible. Was I really so attached to this place in which Pat and I were holed up? Did I really consider Biri Farm my home? It was August, and the first colors of Zimbabwean spring were beginning to appear in the bush: a soft pink that would harden to mauve, before lines of stark green appeared along the veins of every leaf and spread out to cloak the country.

"Mum?"

Beside me, Granny Beryl, too, was gazing out of the window.

"It looks like Crofton used to look," she whispered.

Jonathan guided the car over a crest of red, banking left, and there, sitting below us, was the glittering blue of Biri Dam. Along the line of the water, a tiny figure galloped on horseback, a shimmer of gray underneath him. We drove alongside, the smell of citrus strong in the air.

"Welcome home," said Jonathan.

At first, it looked like a mirage: the paddock with the glittering water in the background. Somehow, it was unreal. Then, as I stepped out of the car and saw familiar faces crowding at the fence—Lady, Deja Vu, the tiny Brutus with his face still set in permanent concern—I understood why.

"Amanda," Granny Beryl began, climbing out of the car, "what happened here?"

From the paddock, the eyes of fifty, sixty, seventy horses stared back. There were twice as many horses as when I had left. Here were mares and geldings and foals I had never seen before; familiar faces from a farm beyond Braeside and Palmerston Estates; a horse that I somehow recognized from the home of another murdered farmer. I stepped forward. Deja Vu spotted me at once and was weaving her way through the herd, favoring her scarred leg.

I was lost, looking into this sea of horses, when I heard the beat of hooves and turned to see Pat riding up in Grey's saddle.

"Oh, Pat," I said, throwing back my head to laugh. "What have you done?"

"Here she is. Shere Khan . . ."

She was, I had to admit, the most beautiful horse I had seen, regal and lofty and a full hand higher than any of the familiar faces of the herd. She stood, statuesque, a dun mare with glistening black points and big, shining eyes that positively shimmered with intelligence. In the setting sun she looked golden, and as she walked toward us she tossed her dark mane from side to side, seemingly declaring herself the most wonderful horse in Zimbabwe. I reached out so that she could draw in the scent from my fingertips and nibble at my hand, but she simply dropped

A much older Frisky at Crofton in the mid-1990s. By this time she no longer lived up to her name and had become much more gentle and quiet in her advanced years. We will miss her always.

Author collection

Frisky, my husband Pat's beloved horse and childhood companion, was with us when we came to Crofton, but by that time she was more than thirty years old. This picture was taken earlier, in the late 1970s.

Author collection

Pat riding through the surf in Vilanculos on Jade, whom we rescued in Zimbabwe from our friend John Crawford's herd.

Courtesy of Wrenne Hiscott
www.wrennehiscott.com

Here I'm riding Bridle, Pat's father's horse, and Pat's cousin Roy is on Frisky. This picture was taken in Enkeldoorn, where Pat grew up, at the paper chase in 1979; it's one of the few photos we have from that time.

Courtesy of Anita Brukjackson

My two boys with their sister in the middle in 1988. Pictured from left: Jay, Kate, Paul.

Author collection

As a young boy, Jay hated leaving the farm. Here he is with Pat on his way to boarding school. As you can see, he doesn't look too happy at the prospect.

Author collection

Jay and Kate dressed in their school uniforms at Crofton with our dog Opal, a harlequin Great Dane.

Author collection

A view of Crofton during happier days in the mid-1990s. Our mango tree is visible, the round-topped tree to the left of the house.

Courtesy of Ben Young

My middle child, Jay, looking at what remained of Crofton farm on a return trip we took there in 2012. Everything we loved was now gone, burned by the war vets who took it over. You can see Jay's despair as he stares in disbelief; he had loved roaming the wild African bush as a boy.

Courtesy of Madeleine Pacheco

My two high-spirited boys in the early 1990s. Paul is driving with Jay on the back. They loved to ride Dad's motorbike around the farm.

Author collection

Deja Vu, who was born on Crofton, waiting patiently for her food bucket on Zimofa farm, 2005. A most loving and gentle horse, she came to a tragic end in Mozambique.

Courtesy of Heather Trezona

Our faithful Fanta. She has blessed the lives of so many children, in both Zimbabwe and Mozambique, who learned to ride on her. Here she is in the Chimoio riding school, 2007.

Courtesy of Stefaan Dondeyne

My husband, Pat, the avid horseman, riding Duke while competing in the gymkhana we held for our riding school children in Chimoio, 2006.

Courtesy of Stefaan Dondeyne

Here I am with Squib and little Sebastian, 2006, at the Chimoio riding school. We are indebted to the parents, both NGO workers and ex-Zimbabwean farmers, who supported our school there.

Courtesy of Stefaan Dondeyne

Ramazotti, Pink Daiquiri's beautiful foal, in 2005. Both horses were taken by a corrupt farmer who claimed they had destroyed his wife's soybean crop. These sorts of false claims were part of the nightmare we had to endure on our journey.

Courtesy of Heather Trezona

Pat with Fleur, the day after arriving in Vilanculos. He was worried that the horses would be terrified of the sand and sea, but with the temperature a scorching 113 degrees Fahrenheit, the horses immediately took to the water.

Author collection

The beautiful Lady, named after her mother, Lady Richmond, by our friend and neighbor Charl. Here she is sticking out her tongue, waiting for a treat after a riding lesson in Vilanculos, 2011.

Author collection

My beautiful daughter, Kate, with Tequila on Benguerra Island, off the coast of Vilanculos. Tequila, a determined but lovable horse, stays on the small island because of his expensive escapades; he is forever trying to return to his home in Zimbabwe. On the island he has tried on three occasions to do the same, but found no way off.

Courtesy of Benguerra Lodge
www.benguerra.co.za

Pat and Tequila enjoying a swim on Benguerra Island the day after we arrived in January 2008.

Courtesy of Benguerra Lodge
www.benguerra.co.za

Our longtime worker and loyal friend Jonathan Mazulu, who helped us on our journey and remains with us to this day.

Courtesy of Wrenne Hiscott
www.wrennehiscott.com

Martini, from Umboe Estates, Chinhoyi. Here he is up to his hocks in lush green grass and looking a little chubby on Benguerra Island, 2012.

Courtesy of Robyn Dunne

Tequila (left) attempting to remove Slash's halter. He is an expert at this, and Slash is always a willing partner. They both remain on Benguerra Island.

Courtesy of Robyn Dunne

Charl and Tertia Geldenhuys, our neighbors on Two Tree Hill farm. Many of their horses became a part of our growing herd after they were forcibly removed from their home.

Courtesy of Hester de Jager

Pat and I love the view from the Red Dunes. Together we have traversed countless miles and suffered incredible loss, all while doing what we could to save the horses we love. Now, in Vilanculos, we are thankful for each new day and the promise it brings.

Courtesy of Katharine Easteal

her head to snatch a clump of grass and flicked her tail disdainfully. Only when Pat called to her did she come to the fence. Regally, she dropped her head to nuzzle him, but she was promptly bustled out of the way. Lady, it seemed, could not stand to share.

"Where did all these horses come from, Pat?"

"All over. It's been getting worse, more and more farmers leaving . . ."

"Is that Tieg Howsen's horse?"

I had spied a small, dark Arabian stallion standing among the herd, a horse much older than the Crawford foals who milled around him, and recognized him as Uzuk, who had once lived on a farm neighboring Pat's brother's.

"There's a story to that horse," Pat began. "You see that foal?" He pointed, but it was difficult to make out where he was pointing; the field was full of foals. "Uzuk's daughter, I think. Tieg had named her Horrid . . ."

"Horrid?"

"I couldn't call her that. She's Holly now."

"Isn't it terrible luck to change a horse's name?"

"It didn't do Frisky any harm. She had another name when I met her." Pat paused. "Tieg called me up. She'd left the farm and found a place in Harare, but there were too many horses for her to take with her. So I helped her by taking Holly, Uzuk, and an old mare. She'd wondered if I could put the old girl out of her misery . . ."

It would not have been the first time. Back before I had left Biri, we had had calls from distraught farmers who thought the kindest thing would be to destroy their beloved horses, rather than leave them to the war vets.

"She loved that horse," I said.

"I promised I'd look after her, if we could take Holly, too. I just couldn't stand the thought of leaving her up there, Mandy. So here she is."

"What's she like?"

"Deranged. I wanted to get her in the training ring as soon as I could, get her joined-up, get her used to being handled . . . She panicked. I think it was because she couldn't see through the walls. She just dropped her head and *charged*. But the walls wouldn't give. She flopped down. Just collapsed. I thought she was dead . . . but, when I crept over, one eye opened up and, groggily, she got back to her feet. She just stood there, staring at me like she's staring now . . ."

In the paddock, Holly was considering us both with a calculating gaze. "How's their training going?"

Pat gave a crumpled grin. "I thought I knew about training horses. Turns out, I don't know a thing. I don't think you can know about training horses until you've trained a hundred of them."

I arched an eyebrow. "Well, how many have we got?"

"Seventy-one." Pat smiled. "But there's time yet. Come on, I'll introduce you to the rest."

Shere Khan looked imperious, the queen of the herd, but her subjects were many and varied. Among them was an ear-less mare Pat had taken in from the same farm, who had foaled down almost as soon as she arrived on Biri. The foal, silvery gray, had been named Nzeve ("ear" in Shona) in honor of his mother's missing ears and seemed already to have struck up a friendship with a bay foal named Slash.

I watched Nzeve and Slash running at each other. Soon they were joined by a collection of other foals. Brutus hung at Jade's side at first, but finally wandered over to join them, nosing tentatively forward. They seemed to be lining up, as if to race.

"They're at it again," muttered Pat.

The foals nearest, Pat explained, had come from Gary Hensman, who farmed close to where his brother Rory had farmed on Braeside. Gary still managed to cling to his farm, but sections of it were constantly being taken by settlers and he was worried how long he might last. On the farm he had bred polo horses, and two of the foals who now pushed among the others had been too small. They were Slash, a bay with a white slash on his brow, and Mouse, a timid, inquisitive chestnut gelding.

Above them stood Stardust, a chestnut mare who had belonged to one of Tieg Howsen's friends. I watched them for the longest time. It was, I supposed, good to be back.

I searched the herd for signs of Princess, but she was nowhere to be seen.

"How is she?" I finally asked, fearing the worst.

"Let's take a look."

Pat and I walked the circumference of the paddock, followed by the boisterous Lady on the other side of the fence. As we made our way to the stable where I had last seen Princess, a Thoroughbred eyed me dolefully from the paddock.

"That's Terry's horse, isn't it?"

Pat nodded. "He's called Fordson." We lingered for a moment, the horse's eyes tracking us. "I was at Terry's funeral. I couldn't not take them in, not after what happened."

Terry Ford was the tenth farmer to have been murdered during the land invasions. Terry had been a good friend, and we had spent many years showing sheep together at the Harare shows. Like countless other farmers, Terry had given up living on his farm many months ago. His farm was under particular scrutiny, for Sabina Mugabe, the president's elder sister, had declared her interest in taking it over—but, on hearing that his son was coming to visit from where he now lived in New Zealand, Terry had made the trip back to tidy, clean, and prepare for the homecoming.

It was the last trip he ever made. That night, the farmstead was besieged. Terry made frantic phone calls to his friends and neighbors, but they would never see him again. When his body was found, his beloved Jack Russell, Squeak, was standing guard, refusing to let anybody near.

"I took two others as well as Fordson," Pat explained. "I couldn't stand the thought of them being destroyed."

In the stable, Princess was waiting. If she recognized me at all, she did not react. Pat and I walked along her side, where one end of her wound was open. In the dark cavity I could see that the passage carved by the bullet had narrowed. Even so, a sour, steamy smell rose from her, and the edges of the wound glistened with pus.

"Fistulous withers," Pat began. "There isn't enough blood supply to a horse's withers, so she won't heal."

"Won't heal at all?"

"It closed up once, but as soon as it does, infection sets in, and the new tissue starts dying away . . ."

I reached out to stroke Princess's muzzle. "What will you do?"

"She's come this far. We just have to believe she'll get all the way."

"It's been a long time."

Pat's hand ran along Princess's flank, stopping only when he began to feel her tremor at his touch.

"I'm sorry, Princess," he said, "it might take a lot longer . . ."

Pat turned to lead me back to the farmhouse, recounting endless stories of the first time he had taken the foals into the ring, the way Lady refused to be trained and demanded to be pampered, the panic that set in whenever Brutus was led away on his own. I knew he was trying to make me laugh, but I barely heard a word. As we crossed the farm, I found that I could barely look at the horses. Every last one of them was a symbol of what was happening to the country we loved.

I had been away for only three months, but it seemed the evil would never end.

In the weeks to come, family reunion was more and more on my mind. And so, it was with pleasant surprise that I put down the phone one morning and turned to Pat with the wonderful news: Paul was coming home.

It was the first time Pat had seen Paul since he left for England, and no sooner had he arrived on Biri Farm than father and son took out along the training trail with Imprevu and Grey. At the farmhouse, Granny Beryl and I supervised the preparation of a family feast to welcome Paul back, and we eagerly awaited Jonathan's arrival with Kate from school. Jay, meanwhile, had managed to get a week off from his apprenticeship and was, even now, making his way across Zimbabwe to be with us.

It felt good to be together again. Shortly after Kate arrived, Pat and Paul returned from their ride. I looked out of the farmhouse window to see Paul surrounded by the Crawford foals, tempting the ever-reticent Brutus to eat horse cubes from his hand while Lady tried to get in the way and Shere Khan looked disdainfully down, and watched Kate rush out to meet him. Even in the months he had been gone, she seemed to have grown. Surrounded by foals, he hugged her, putting her down only when Lady pushed her head between them.

As Granny Beryl was making the final preparations for dinner, I went out to join them.

"So, Paul," I began, "is it anything like you imagined?"

Across the paddock, Pat was running his hands over Deja Vu, his fingers softly stroking the scars on the leg she had trapped in the wire fence on Crofton, all that time ago.

"No," Paul replied, "it's even crazier than that . . ."

We were a long time waiting for dinner, for Jay was nowhere to be found. As plates went back into the oven to be heated and the bowls of potatoes and meat were covered in tinfoil, I returned time and again to the veranda. Dusk was settling on Biri Farm, the horses settling down for the night, and still there was no sign of our returning son. I was beginning to get worried.

"What do you think, Pat?"

"It's Jay. He'll be okay."

I was not so certain. I could not forget the feeling of realizing how much Zimbabwe had worsened in the time I had been away.

In the farmhouse, Kate sat, held rapt by Paul's stories of England. On the couch she had her knees tucked up under her chin, hanging on to his every word. I listened to the ebb and flow of their conversation. England must have seemed so exotic to Kate. I wondered if she might ever follow her brother there. Perhaps she would have to.

The darkness was already absolute when I heard the rumbling of an engine. Two tiny orbs of light appeared in the distance, their beams growing. I called for Kate and Paul, who rushed out to join me on the veranda. At last, a Land Rover hove into view, grinding to a halt in front of the paddocks. The eyes of more than seventy suspicious horses watched from the gloom.

Out stepped Jay.

As he ambled over to say hello, he had the same cocksure swagger of old. His hair, blond and wild as ever, had grown longer. It hung in curls below his ears. He ambled to a stop in front of the veranda and squinted into the light.

"We were worried sick," I said.

"So was I," Jay replied. "I was held up."

"Held up?"

"It was because of my gun."

"What gun?"

"The police stopped me at a roadblock, wanted to search the car. I told them to go right ahead." Jay stopped, shaking his head. "I'd forgotten all about the hunting rifle I'd stored behind the seat back at camp."

I remembered the police on Palmerston, who had flagrantly helped themselves to our crops. I remembered the farmers summoned to stations and imprisoned without charges or trial. Even though I knew Jay was safe, I was not sure I could hear the rest of this story.

Silent as ever, Jay tramped on into the house, his nose leading him straight to the table where dinner was slowly getting cold.

"Well?" Kate asked, as we all followed after.

"Well, they wanted to arrest me."

Jay slumped into a chair and started piling his food up.

"Arrest you?"

"It was okay, though. I knew the member in charge from the hunting camp. I had to call him to straighten it out."

"And they just let you go?"

"Not quite." Jay's mouth was now full. "They told me to bring my gun license in on the way back through." He paused. "Hey, you don't know where it is, do you?"

I dreaded to think. Probably it had been lost on Crofton, along with everything else—but, before I could answer, Jay threw me a look, his dark eyes glowing.

"Mum," he said, "is there any beer?"

The next morning we rode together across the length of Biri Farm. For a few scant hours we were a family again. It felt as if we had never left Crofton. Even Jay, so rare a rider, cantered along the line of the dam, sitting in Lady's saddle. In the afternoon, Kate and Paul helped Pat in the training ring, leading in each of the Crawford foals, and I tried to coax Brutus out of his shell.

When it came time for the boys to depart, Jay back to his hunting camp via an unwelcome trip to the Harare police and Paul off to stay with friends in Harare, Kate and I stood in the doorway to wave them off. Jay and Paul hugged their little sister and playfully punched her on the arm. Never one to take a beating, Kate punched back, repelling them down the steps. She was sixteen now, but she would always be their little sister. Those few days we had together felt more golden, even, than the long years of Crofton.

"When will they be back?" Kate asked.

"Let's not worry about that now," I said. "Look over there . . ."

In the paddock, Pat was besieged by a dozen foals.

"We'd better go and help," said Kate.

I put out a hand and stopped her. "This is your father's madness." I grinned, watching Lady butting him in the behind. "He brought this on his own head. Let's just watch for a while first . . ."

Chapter 10

GRANNY BERYL AND I had made it to the top of the training trail, following in the prints Pat and Imprevu had left behind. We looked down on the dam for a long time before turning to make the trek back, weaving our way downhill. We were halfway there, overlooking the farmhouse and the horses in their paddock, when I saw the plumes of dust. In the distance, a Land Rover cut along the farm road.

"Where's Pat?" Granny Beryl asked.

"Out riding," I said. "It isn't him."

"Then who?"

The Land Rover quickly grew nearer. At last, I could pick out the outlines of figures behind the windshield. The vehicle was laden down with passengers.

"Come on, Mum," I said. "Before they reach the house . . ."

We made haste along the trail, picking our way as quickly as we could around all the obstacles Pat and our workers had built in to desensitize the horses and prepare them to be ridden. Along the way, I scrambled for the phone in my handbag. The signal was weak, but I lifted it high and tried to raise Pat. The phone just rang and rang.

Hoping he was in the farmhouse, we tumbled down the end of the bank and rushed along the paddock's edge. In front of Biri farmhouse, everything was still. We paused. There was no sign of the Land Rover.

"Get inside, Mum," I said. "Come on!"

We crashed from room to room, but Pat was nowhere to be found. Again, I tried him on the phone. Again, it rang and rang.

"Mum, maybe you should go and . . ."

I was about to tell her to go and make some tea, take a rest, anything so that she didn't have to see me panic, when one of our drivers, Albert, appeared in the doorway. For a second he stood, framed there, before I beckoned him in. He was holding his hands in front of him, and in them was a crumpled piece of paper.

"What is it, Albert?"

His eyes were downcast, as if he did not want to say.

"There was a Land Rover."

I threw a look at my mother. Thankfully, she was retreating farther into the house.

"We saw it, Albert. Where is it?"

"It came to the workshop. There was a . . . police officer." He stressed the last two words, as if to imply that the man had only dressed up in a policeman's clothes. It did not matter. There were no true police officers in Zimbabwe any longer; it was just another way of saying Mugabe's thugs. "Please," Albert went on, "you must read."

His fingers were trembling as I took the note. My eyes scanned the words. Then, they shot back up to meet Albert's own.

"You know what this says?"

Albert nodded.

"Chanetsa," I breathed.

Again, Albert could only nod. Peter Chanetsa was the governor of Mashonaland West. He was also a member of Mugabe's inner circle. I vividly remembered him as one of the men who had gone out to Two Tree on the day of Charl and Tertia's eviction to oversee the kangaroo court outside the farmhouse.

The letter in my hand declared that Biri Farm was now the property of Peter Chanetsa. We had only four hours to vacate the property.

I could hear my mother shifting upstairs. I left Albert in the door-way and, the note screwed up in my hand, tried again to call Pat. When there was no answer, I dialed for Janey at the neighboring farm store instead. The phone just rang on.

Hanging up, I bustled past Albert.

He coughed politely, as if to get my attention. "This is serious," he said, pleading in his tone. "You must start packing."

"We will, Albert. I have to tell Janey . . ."

I hurried past the paddock, ignoring Lady's demands for attention, and up the steps to Janey's house. I found her in the farm store, sorting out boxes.

"Janey . . ." I realized I was brandishing the piece of paper as if it was some sort of weapon. "Janey, listen!"

Janey stopped. "What is it?"

I couldn't bring myself to read the note, so I passed it to her instead. Her eyes glazed over. Then they drifted up, as if to look into the house.

"Mandy," she breathed, "my parents are staying. And Fred—Fred isn't here . . ."

Like me, Fred had decamped to England in an attempt to make some money. The last I had heard, he was slaving in a supermarket warehouse while Janey remained here, struggling to make the farm shop work.

"The police drove into the workshop. They cornered Albert, made him deliver the note . . ."

"The *police* are issuing evictions now?"

"What does it matter? We've only got a few hours . . . Janey, we have to pack."

She took a step backward, slumping into a chair, her dark eyes enor-mous. "Why now? With Fred away and . . ."

"It doesn't matter *why*. This is real, Janey."

There was a moment of pure silence, and then Janey nodded. "Thank you, Mandy," she said and, mysteriously, turned back to her boxes.

As I hurried back to our farmhouse, a thousand thoughts turned in my head: What should we pack first? How would Granny Beryl cope? Where could we possibly go in such a short space of time? It was Thursday, and I thought suddenly of Kate, coming back tomorrow from her week at school. I looked up. The sun was almost directly above. The clock was ticking.

Rushing past the paddock, I saw that Imprevu was back from her ride, standing alongside her daughter, Deja Vu. Pat must have been somewhere near. I reached for my phone and was about to dial him again when I saw movement down by Princess's stable. I cut through the paddock, ignoring Lady's pleas, and crashed in.

Pat was standing with Caetano, one of our drivers, re-dressing Princess's wound. He looked at me. We said no words. I simply handed him the note.

Pat studied it for a long minute, seemingly reading and rereading every word. Then, he crushed it in his fist and cast it down where it belonged, mired in Princess's muck.

"Start packing now," he said and, bustling past me, hurried to the paddock.

I came into the farmhouse and felt as if I was about to start scaling an unconquerable mountain. The sides were too steep, the cliffs too sheer to climb. We had lost everything at Crofton, but, somehow, we had accumulated so much at Biri. Furniture donated from friends who had fled, horse gear we had inherited from abandoned farms and rescue centers, pots and pans, household utensils, all the clothes we had been able to spirit off Palmerston Estates. Caetano appeared behind me, and I soon realized that our other workers were assembling. Chanetsa was robbing them of a home as well. Jonathan and Albert and Denzia and all the rest. Perhaps, if we all worked together, we might yet get off Biri Farm.

Then I looked around. Pat stood in the paddock, surrounded by our seventy-one mares, geldings, and foals. He threw his head back, ran his hands through his hair.

Four hours might have been enough to get ourselves off Biri Farm, but there was no hope of leading the horses off in time.

My heart sank.

Three hours to go.

At Biri farmhouse, the packing had begun in earnest when another vehicle appeared on the horizon. This time, my heart did not sink. It soared. The car pulled into the yard outside the farmhouse and Carol Johnson stepped out.

"Carol," I said, rushing to her. "Thanks so much for coming . . ."

"When could I ever resist the urge to be your knight in shining armor?"

We walked up the steps into the farmhouse. Boxes were scattered around, as Jonathan, Albert, Caetano, and the other workers helped to pile our belongings inside.

Ruefully, Carol looked me in the eye. "We're getting rather good at this, aren't we?"

Caetano looked up from his box. "Not good enough! Madams, we are not going fast enough! This Chanetsa, he is a dangerous man . . ."

Carol launched into the kitchen, where Denzia was packing up the kitchenware, while I ventured upstairs in search of my mother. Granny Beryl had been dispatched to pack up her own belongings, and, as I climbed the stair, I was struck with that same terrible sense of failure I had had on returning to Zimbabwe: I could not provide a home for my children, nor for my mother in her old age.

I pushed open the bedroom door. In front of her wardrobe mirror, my mother was looking at her reflection longingly. I froze—this was absurd. I closed my eyes, but when I opened them again, the vision was just the same.

Granny Beryl was wearing a blue nurse's uniform, one she had not worn in more years than I could remember. She considered herself carefully and then moved, struggling to fasten her epaulets.

"Mum!" I cried. "What are you doing!?"

It took a second for Granny Beryl to snap out of her reverie. When she turned around, she seemed to be looking at me, not only from the other side of the room, but from some distant past: a normal Zimbabwe, when we had all led normal, everyday lives.

"Amanda," she began, "can you believe it? I found this old thing in a suitcase, and it still fits!"

I could scarcely believe my ears. I stepped farther into the room, closing the door behind me.

"Mum, we barely have three hours . . ."

"Three hours?"

"If we're still on the farm when Chanetsa comes . . ."

Granny Beryl waved her hand, as if to dismiss the commotion. "You don't need to bother yourself with that, Amanda."

I rushed over to her, picked up a suitcase from where it lay on the floor, and heaved it onto the bed.

"Please," I said. "Just get everything together . . ."

I could hear another commotion downstairs, Carol calling my name. I turned, opened the door, took a step out.

"Mum, promise me . . ."

Granny Beryl looked at me with that same perplexed look.

"Mum, be ready in an hour. I need to get you off the farm . . ."

Leaving Granny Beryl dressed up like the nurse she used to be, I rushed down the stairs, half expecting to see Chanetsa already here. In the front room, surrounded by piles of boxes still unfilled, stood Pat.

"We're going to Avalon," he began. "Nick Swanepoel's going to put us up for the night."

Avalon was the farm to the east of Biri, ten kilometers away, beyond the defiant dam wall. Nick Swanepoel had been a good friend, but the thought that he would help us now was overwhelming; it lifted whatever stone had been sitting on my chest. Gaydia, who still worked with Pat on what was left of our agronomy business, had herself been living in a cottage on Avalon's grounds, along with her two children. The thought of her cheery face welcoming us as refugees was enough to temper my anxiety, if only for a second. Gaydia was an expert horsewoman too, and instinctively my thoughts turned to the herd sitting out in the paddocks, Shere Khan looking loftily over them.

"All of us?"

"All of us," Pat said, turning over his shoulder, "and all seventy-one of them. We just have to figure a way of getting them off . . ." He stopped, scanned the room. "Why isn't everything packed?"

I thought I might explode. "Packed!?" I thundered. "What do you think we're doing!?"

Pat considered the room methodically. "Put white sticky labels on everything you need to take. Only the important things. The rest we'll leave." He paused. "Mandy, do it now."

Two hours to go.

I hurried to the office and rifled through drawers of stationery until I produced a box of the white sticky labels Pat used for marking agronomy files. Back in the house, Carol and Granny Beryl, still dolled up in her old nurse's uniform, were kneeling together, packing box after box. The room buzzed around them, and, for the first time, I could see the fear etched into my mother's face. Perhaps at last she understood.

I passed the box of labels to Albert, and together we rushed around the house, planting labels on everything we had to take: boxes of books and the agronomy files first; everything Kate had accumulated in her new bedroom; the countless saddles and bridles and girths we had collected along with the horses.

I was in the kitchen, pasting white labels left and right, when I heard the rumbling. Instinct drove me to the window, but my fears were unwarranted; it was not Chanetsa arriving early, but only the first of the tractors coming to haul our goods the ten kilometers to Avalon farm. Sitting in the driver's seat, Jonathan leaped off and joined the stream of workers ferrying boxes aboard.

When I looked back, I saw that the kitchen was full of boxes with white labels. Albert stood in the doorway. With a flourish, he peeled off one of the remaining labels and planted it firmly on the breast pocket of his overall.

"Don't leave me behind," he said. "I'm important, too!"

I opened my mouth to laugh, but a strange feeling was welling up inside of me, and I had to turn my head so that he could not see the tears that now flowed, unchecked, down my cheeks.

One hour to go.

The tractors were making their way in convoy off Biri Farm, following the red dirt roads to Avalon in the east. Down at the paddocks, Pat, Jonathan, and Albert were readying the horses with halters. I looked, again, at the sun in the sky. I imagined Chanetsa on his drive out to Biri Farm, even now.

A plume of dust worked its way along the farm roads. At the paddock, we all froze, watching as the vehicle arrived. When it pulled into the yard, the relief in the air was palpable. Paul stepped out. I rushed to him. He had been visiting friends in Harare before flying back to England, and half of me wished he was already gone.

"I'm sorry, Paul," I said, remembering Palmerston. "I didn't want you to be here when . . ."

He silenced me with a hug.

"What's the plan?" he asked, striding toward the paddock.

"We're coming back for them as soon as it's dark," Pat replied from the other side of the fence. Paul reached over and let Imprevu nibble at his hand. "Nick Swanepoel promised us paddocks at Avalon."

"And then?"

Pat smiled, wryly. "We'll have to make a plan."

As he began to explain the route he and the grooms had charted off Biri, I hurried to find Janey. Although packed boxes were spread around her house, she still lingered in the farm store. She seemed to be tallying up prices, taking inventory.

"Janey," I ventured, coming tentatively through the door, "it's time to go . . ."

Janey looked up. "Not now, Mandy. I just need a little more—"

In that instant, I heard the gunning of engines. Rushing back to the veranda, I looked down the farm road. Trucks had appeared from the fields and I could see people pouring out. As I looked at them in their shabby clothes, with their axes and *pangas* hanging at their sides, the old fear ran through me.

"Janey, please, it's starting. The war vets are here . . ."

"Not yet, Mandy. We're not *ready* yet . . ."

I turned, rushed back to the paddocks. There was nothing to be done—we had to leave. Already, I could hear the settlers shouting as the trucks unloaded around the farmhouses. Somewhere, a chant was going up. I saw a group of men tumble from a truck and begin to yell at Albert and Caetano. Damn them, but they were beaming, taking glee in the chaos they were about to create. In the corner of my eye, I saw three men take to one of the giant fig trees with their axes. They were getting ready to block the roads.

"Pat," I called. "We have to go . . ."

In the middle of the herd, he looked up. One of his hands lay on Shere Khan's flank, as if both Pat and the queen of the herd were preparing to repel these invaders together. He was wearing the same face I had seen that day on Palmerston. I willed him to stay calm with my eyes.

"Get in the car, Mandy," he said, taking his hand softly from Shere Khan's side. "We're right behind you . . ."

Darkness fell suddenly across Avalon Farm.

Avalon was one of the prettiest farms I had known. In addition to its main farmhouse, there were other cottages and buildings stretched around. Workshops and barns sat in a great semicircle, and in their cradle land had been roped off for a makeshift paddock. The lights were on in the main farmhouse, where Nick Swanepoel and his family lived, and beyond its wide verandas lay the grasslands where Nick had promised our horses pasture. Beyond that were the fields where he grew soybeans, wheat, tobacco, and maize. That night, Avalon seemed to me to be some kind of oasis, a farm somehow managing to march on while all around it others tumbled.

Nick was a big man, a few years older than Pat, and Avalon was his pride and joy. Across the empty paddock, I could see his silhouette in his farmhouse window. Pat and I made preparations to move in with Gaydia, whose cottage was next door to the main homestead. On the other side of the Avalon farmhouses sat Nick's private game park. Here he kept all kinds of African antelope, giraffes, and zebra. I could sense their presence, and for a moment it was like stepping out of Crofton in the dead of night to breathe in the bush.

We had been here scant hours. In the little cottage behind me, mattresses had been spread out, and the kettle was constantly on the boil. If I was grateful for anything, it was only that Kate was still at school and did not have to live through this again.

Some of the trucks were being unloaded, but our car still sat, heaped high with boxes, outside the cottage. In front, Pat gathered with Albert, Caetano, and Jonathan. They had collected clusters of lead ropes and halters, and as the stars revealed themselves, plastered across our African sky, they knew that the time was nigh.

The moon rose high above Avalon.

Paul emerged from the house behind me. As he dropped down the steps to join Pat, I took hold of his arm.

"Make sure your father stays out of their way."

Paul nodded. I was not only asking him so that Pat might not see red and find himself locked into an altercation with the war vets; my hope was that if I burdened Paul with looking out for his father, he too might avoid a confrontation.

"We'll be back soon, Mum." Paul paused. "I promise."

If only the promise had been within his power to keep, I might have believed him.

Pat and Paul climbed into the cab of one of the farm trucks, while Albert, Caetano, Jonathan, and some other workers climbed in the back.

Then the engines fired and they wheeled away into darkness. The only sounds were the rumbling of the truck and the whisper of wind in the long grass.

I drifted back inside, where Gaydia sat with Granny Beryl, nursing a cup of tea.

I could not sit. I prowled the house, walking up and down the hallway, lingering on the veranda for long moments, squinting into the blackest night. An hour after they had gone, clouds drifted over, beaching the moon in a silvery reef before obscuring it altogether. Now the stars were gone. Somewhere out there, my husband and son stole through impenetrable night.

I clung to my mobile phone as if it were some totem, a symbol that Pat and Paul were still alive. The green display screen flickered, but there was no signal tonight.

Long hours seemed to pass, but the dawn did not come; the night only grew thicker.

I heard movement behind me. It was Granny Beryl, coming to check on me. "Have you heard from them?"

I shook my head. "Soon," I said, willing it to be true.

Fleetingly, the moon broke through the clouds, shedding silver light onto the fields. And, at last, I saw shapes in the darkness. At first, they were mere shadows, different parts of the night—but soon those shapes began to have texture, definition. I saw *eyes* glimmering at me.

It seemed to be the charge of a ghostly cavalry. On either side of each groom two horses were roped, so that they came out of the mist four abreast, with a tiny man huddled in the middle. I saw no sign of Pat and Paul, but here was Grey, here was Fleur, here were Jade and Duke and Duchess and Marquess. Behind them came the foals, Brutus and Evita and all the forgotten foals who had come to us from the Crawford farm. I tumbled from the veranda and rushed to meet them.

Albert was the first groom to reach the boundary fence. As I hurtled to meet him, I saw that the white sticky label was still stuck to his chest. In his right hand he held the ropes to Grey and Fleur; in his left, he held ropes to Imprevu and Jade. I ran my hands through Grey's silvery mane and took his rope, leading him along the bank, in front of the Avalon farmhouse, and toward the new paddock we had set aside. Behind me, Gaydia helped Albert and the grooms steer the first of the herd through. In the paddock, they stood looking around curiously, seemingly wondering if their journey was at an end.

"Albert," I began, as he guided Fleur in to meet me, "where's Pat?"

"He is coming . . ."

I turned. The herd had appeared en masse now, dozens of horses' heads pushing forward, as if through a curtain of mist. The darkness swirled and, out of the vortex, there cantered Lady, Caetano struggling to keep hold of the boisterous mare.

At the opening of the paddock, I took her rope, then crouched and fussed over her until she had calmed down. Even then, she would not leave my side. As I stood and guided the other horses in—Brutus clinging meekly to Jade's flank, Nzeve straining away from his earless mother—Lady pushed her head into my armpit, still eager for attention.

"Mum, where is he?"

Granny Beryl simply turned and pointed.

The night was filled with horses. There must have been a dozen in the paddock, but fifty more now crowded the yards, nosing out of the outer dark. There, among them, Shere Khan standing regally at his side as if to personally oversee the exodus of her people, stood Pat.

Damn him, but he was beaming. Positively *beaming*.

With some struggle I left Lady behind and weaved between several horses recently rescued from various locations—Tequila, Martini, Kahlua, and the sunken-backed Pink Daiquiri—until I could reach him.

"What happened?"

They had taken the long back road onto Biri Farm, parking the truck some distance from where the war vets were camped and venturing forward on foot.

"Paul and I couldn't get close," Pat explained as, behind him, the truck reappeared, Paul hunkered over the wheel. "They're everywhere. But the grooms went on and roped them up. We met them out on the trail, north of the dam wall. They just walked out of the mist like ghosts."

I breathed out. Beyond Pat, Paul had brought the truck around and gently eased Princess down the ramp, the wound in her withers still bandaged up. There would be no stable for her tonight, but the grooms would tend to her in the paddock with her daughter, Evita, and the rest of the herd.

"Pat," I said, "I think you deserve a drink."

I tried to take Pat's hand and lead him up to the farmhouse, but his feet were planted squarely in the earth and he would not be moved. When I looked at him, he shook his head and led me toward the truck. Above us, the night clouds shifted and came apart, revealing another sliver of moon.

"Pat," I whispered, "what is it?"

"It's Janey." He paused, helping me swing up into the cab. "Something has got to be done about Janey."

An hour later we were back on the road skirting Biri Farm, keeping our distance from the house.

"You see?" said Pat.

The war vets were everywhere. Makeshift camps had sprung up around the trucks from which they had poured onto the farm. In places along the main road, trees had been felled. The night was alive with drums. Occasional chants flurried up, only to die away. The sounds whirled together, an unholy chorus designed to inspire fear.

We pushed on until I could see the empty shell of Biri Farm squatting in the lights of the fires. Beside it sat Janey's home. The war vets were ranged around the back of her house, dominating the fields where the workers' huts and paddock used to be.

"Why wouldn't she leave?" I whispered, cursing her for being so stubborn.

"What matters," said Pat, "is how we get her out."

We approached Janey's house from the dam itself. With the waters fading in our rearview mirror, we came to the front of the house. There were no war vets camped here, for they were all out back, stoking their fires and sending up their chants. As Pat ground the truck to a halt we could still hear their drums and revelry from the far side of the house. I stepped out onto cold hard ground and was thankful, for the first time, that the clouds obscured the stars.

Pat climbed from the cab and Paul appeared from the back of the truck. The only thing separating us from the front of Janey's house was a tall brick wall. Beyond, Janey was trapped with her parents, sitting among all their packed boxes and suitcases: on one side, a wall too tall to scramble over alone; on the other, the horde of war vets and their insidious din.

Pat stepped forward. There was no point trying to dissuade him. I squeezed his hand and told him to be careful.

"You know me," he said—and, with Paul's help, hauled himself up until he could see over the top of the wall.

He hung there for a second, peering into the darkness beyond, before scrambling his way up. Then, he turned to extend his hand. Paul took it, and as Pat dropped down the other side, my son found himself hauled up. In an instant he was at the top of the wall, and then they were gone.

I was alone, and suddenly the sounds of the war vets seemed so much stronger in my ears. I fancied I could make out words in the chanting, but they were singing in languages I did not understand. Perhaps if Jay were here, he would have translated for me, but listening to the terrible sounds invading my ears, I decided that I was happier not knowing. Beneath the chanting, drums played a demonic percussion. These, I realized, were nothing other than war drums. Their incessant punctuation forced the songs to greater and greater heights. The chanting reached a climax, ebbed away with the drums, and then flurried up again, as if led by a malevolent conductor.

For some reason, I could not climb back into the cab of the truck. It felt like a prison cell, as if I were trapped. Perhaps that had to do with the song of the war vets. I dreaded to think how Janey and her parents felt, surrounded by those sounds.

I propped myself against the cab and tried not to feel the cold of night. I seemed to wait an interminable time. After some minutes, the chanting of the war vets seemed to fade. It wasn't that it had disappeared, only that I was so used to it that my mind seemed to be processing it out. I snapped myself from my reverie, listened to the terrible chanting come flooding back. The relentless, deafening pounding of the drums. I went to the wall, wanted to cry out for Pat—but, fearful of giving him away, I held my voice. Every shift in the darkness startled me. I found myself counting down each second that he was gone: ten, nine, eight . . . Yet, every time I reached zero, I remained alone.

Waiting is the most terrible thing. There was nothing I could do, and time seemed to stretch on. I pictured Pat and Paul creeping into the front of the house. I pictured them confronting Janey and her parents, coaxing them away. I pictured them sneaking across the garden, approaching the wall—but every time I conjured up the images, another one broke through: war vets tumbling into the house, realizing what was going on, and dragging Pat and Paul out to face one of their dramatic kangaroo courts.

Then, at last, I heard the hissing of my husband's voice.

"Pat?"

"Mandy, get over here!"

There was desperation in that voice, and I rushed to the wall, just in time to see Pat's face cresting the top. With help from the other side, he heaved himself up, perching precariously there while he reached back down and hauled Janey up. As he steered her over the other side, I took hold of her hands and helped her down. For a second she was shaken. Then, she seemed to whisper to herself and she straightened, forcing all the tension out of her body.

"Mandy, start the truck . . ."

As Pat and Paul helped Janey's elderly parents scramble over the wall, I rushed back to the truck and started the engine. As the rumbling kicked in, I froze, wondering whether they might hear it on the other side of the house. It was too late to care. Janey's parents dropped down the wall, shaken but still holding themselves defiantly, and Pat and Paul tumbled after.

We took the same road back along the dam, going east toward Avalon with the chanting of war vets fading behind us. By the time we reached the farm, the first lights of dawn were breaking. We rounded the Avalon workshops and came to a juddering halt outside the paddock. As we climbed down, the herd seemed to turn to us. Grey was contentedly grazing the long grass. Princess stood in the corner of the field, with Albert still re-dressing her wound.

The sun burst, suddenly golden, over Avalon Farm, spreading fingers of color across the land, setting the msasa trees alight with rich green and burnished red. At the side of the truck, we watched as the sunlight reached the paddock, dappling the horses one by one. They, too, seemed to sense it, turning in unison to soak up the sudden warmth.

"Where now, Pat?"

He didn't answer. For the moment, waiting for those fingers of sunlight to reach us, it just didn't matter. We had escaped again, and without a second to spare.

Chapter 11

THE PEAKS OF the Bvumba and Penhalonga were lost in low clouds. No wonder they were called the Mountains of the Mist. Beneath me, Grey shivered, silvery as the mist through which we rode. On each side, the steep escarpments were covered in thick woodland, with leaves of rich gold and red. Clouds billowed in low gullies, swirling in the grasslands where the forest thinned. We wound between walls of dense pine forest, at last reaching the highlands where the trees grew more sparsely and the crags were covered in smaller scrub, succulent aloes, and the gentle mauve sugarbushes with their feathery faces and razor-edged leaves. The valleys around us were home to small coffee plantations, and when the wind blew in the right direction, their scent filled the air. We rode on until at last we broke out of the tendrils of cloud and we could look down through the shifting reefs: the ravaged farmlands of Zimbabwe on one side, the lush green bush of Mozambique on the other.

It had been two years since we had fled Biri Farm; now we rode through these mountains plotting yet another move. This one was to be bigger than the many we had made before; this time, we were not merely going to another farm but plotting our way out of the country itself. Beside me, Pat was riding Shere Khan, her regal eyes looking first at one country and then at the next; behind me, Kate and Deja Vu brought up the rear. The Bvumba had been a good home, a place of peace in which we could regroup and consolidate our herd as well as take in many new horses—but we had known from the very first that, like all good things, it wouldn't last. In the east lay the wild, virgin bushlands of Mozambique, a nation just recovering from a bitter twenty-year civil war. We had come into the mountains searching for a way to herd the horses through without facing the tyranny of the official border crossing; that we were even contemplating such a move was proof, if ever it was needed, of the madness consuming our own country.

The Bvumba was the eastern highlands, running down the border between Zimbabwe and Mozambique like a jagged serpent's spine. We had been living among the mountain peaks at a cottage called Partridge Hill, clinging to a steep escarpment with rich green forest on every side. Partridge Hill hung above the beautiful border town of Mutare, where the wide streets were lined with trees heavy with blossom and the people were so peaceful it was easy to forget the ravages Mugabe was wreaking on the rest of our country. Our new home was small, just big enough for Pat, Kate, and me, with some workers in the grounds. Granny Beryl had stayed with us for a time, until we were at last lucky enough to find her a home back in England, but there had been absolutely no space for the horses. It felt strange not to have them near, but we had found grazing land for them on several smallholdings and farms dotted around Mutare itself, as well as the fields of a game park where they could roam with antelope and giraffe. They'd had to be separated into smaller groups, but though it was sad to see them divided, we knew it was a good thing. If one of those farms was to fall, we would always have a backup onto which we could take its horses.

For a time, we had found peace. For a time, we had been able to forget. Then, the reality of the new Zimbabwe caught up with us. One by one, the farms at which the horses were kept began to fall. One by one, we had to find new homes for the horses. Now, every last smallholding or farm around Mutare was gone, taken by some crony from Mugabe's inner circle. The herd, vast and unwieldy, had been brought together again. They were all holed up on the grounds of Kate's school, but they could not stay there long. We were running out of food, we were running out of space, and we had been living on borrowed time for too long.

I turned in the saddle and looked over my shoulder, realizing that I had pushed some way ahead. Through the mist, Shere Khan's muzzle appeared, her head held high as if she considered herself queen of the mountains. For a moment she hung there, as if suspended in the swirling gray mist, before Pat appeared, sitting tall in the saddle.

"Which way?" I began.

Pat shook his head. "Back the way we came. There isn't a pass this high."

We coaxed the horses to turn and dropped back down a gully, entering a clearing between tall gum trees.

"Nothing?" Kate asked, bringing Deja Vu around.

I shook my head. "Not yet."

At once, Pat hauled Shere Khan to a halt and lifted a hand to wave us down. Behind him, I squeezed Grey with my thighs and guided him to a stop. Kate and Deja Vu drew alongside.

"What is it?" I asked.

"There's been army here," said Pat. "Look . . ."

In the roots of one of the tall gum trees lay a ragged backpack. There had been a camp here; I could see the circle of stones and charred earth where somebody had lit and then quickly doused a wood fire. It was not the first time we had seen such a thing. We were not the only ones who had dreamed of jumping the border, and army patrols on either side of the frontier knew how tempting it was to try. Whoever had been here had been waiting for the most opportune moment to pass, unseen, over the invisible line between nations. A patrol must have stumbled upon him, and, ditching his worldly possessions, he had fled.

A terrible shiver ran down my spine. I wondered how close we were, even now, to watchful eyes.

"Dad . . ." Kate began, as if about to voice the same fear we all had. "What if there are border patrols when you try to take the horses through here?"

I tried to imagine what it might be like: more than a hundred horses herded through these mountains, only to come face-to-face with some opportunistic border patrol.

"The border patrols are the least of it," Pat responded. "A border guard you can buy off, if you've got the right mind and money." He looked back, as if he might see some wily Zimbabwean border guard watching us from the mountain range. "It's the Mozambican authorities I'm worried about. Once the horses are in Mozambique, how will we be able to account for them?" He stopped Shere Khan. A strange look ghosted over his face. "Damn it, Mandy, we just can't take them through here . . ."

"Pat," I said, coaxing Grey closer to Shere Khan, "we *have* to. You said it yourself. We can't stay in Zimbabwe any longer."

It was the reason we had come to the Bvumba in the first place. Those first nights after fleeing Biri Farm had been terrible, but we had known we had to make a decision. It had seemed like a prophecy: one day, we would be fleeing Zimbabwe and taking our horses with us. In anticipation of that, we knew we had to head for a border, find a place to stay, and organize ourselves. Wherever we went, our new home had to be a place from which we could very quickly escape. The nearest border to Biri Farm had been the Bvumba, the nearest nation the poor Mozambique, still reeling from its bitter civil war. That was why we had headed into the east.

"We can't risk marching them through the mountains." Pat's hands tightened on Shere Khan's reins, as if he did not mean to let her go. "We didn't save them from those farms just to lose them here."

I looked up. Perhaps we had been fooling ourselves, thinking we could lead the herd through the mountains unnoticed.

"What now?" I asked, my hands tangled in Grey's mane.

"Now," said Pat, "we round up the herd. We take them to the border crossing." He reined Shere Khan around and pointed her to a sloping mountain road, back to Mutare. "And we pray, Mandy. We pray the fates are with us."

· · · ·

Two years ago, the idea of abandoning Zimbabwe forever had been a distant dread. Now that it was real, I got to thinking about how the past two years had changed us and the herd, the exact circumstances that had brought us to this. I could hardly believe how wildly our lives had transformed since the day we brought our young children to River Ranch and Crofton. That we were about to lead the horses into the unknown again scarcely seemed credible.

After being driven off Biri, we had found a home at another friend's farm while he marshaled his resources to find a new home in Australia. The farm was in Headlands and called Bushwazee, but we had been there a scant four months when Mugabe's war vets descended again. Once again, we were left rustling our own horses off the farm. Headlands had been east of Biri, and then we traveled even farther east, until the dark spine of the Bvumba Mountains promised us sanctuary. We set up house high in the hills at Partridge Hill, found Kate a new school in the town of Mutare—where she could live with us through the weeks and stop boarding—and began to make alliances with all the local farmers so that we could bring our horses with us, too. In the end, the herd was divided and taken to a dozen farms around Mutare. Pat threw himself into working with the horses, establishing training grounds as we had done at Biri Farm, and approached schooling all the foals in the herd as if it was not only his profession but his very calling. I had never seen my husband so energized since the earliest days of Crofton, when we were trying to found the farm. Pat was no longer a farmer; he was a horseman through and through, rising at dawn each day to go out training with Brutus, Lady, and all the other foals we had gathered.

And, meanwhile, the phone just kept on ringing as people called to tell us about their horses.

Rob Lucas was a farmer who had first contacted us while we had the horses at Headlands. He was not the only one. The rumors of what we were doing seemed to have gone before us, and the calls began to come from farther afield. Fanta, a fifteen-year-old chestnut, came from a prominent farming family in the Marondera area, along with a group of older horses, some of them lame, whose owner insisted they had to accompany the beautiful mare. Fanta was one of the most delightful horses I have ever come across, and her friendly nature and wonderful personality instilled confidence in the many children who learned to ride on her. There were others too—but by far the most intriguing plea we heard came from Rob Lucas. For Rob, like us, had turned his home into a refuge for abandoned horses.

Here was a man we simply had to go and see.

We drove back along the winding Bvumba roads, through the wide, floral streets of Mutare and past the site of Kate's school, Hillcrest. Mutare did not seem as barren and run-down as the rest of Zimbabwe, for its shops were lined with goods smuggled over the mountains from Mozambique. Here, people did not have to go hungry while watching their hard-earned wages evaporate in a mist of hyperinflation. We stopped, briefly, to look in at the farm where Grey, Fleur, Duchess, and the other Two Tree horses were grazing in their paddock, before taking the road deeper inland.

We reached Rob Lucas's farm, leaving the highway to follow a dirt road up to the farmhouse. Just like in Zimbabwe's towns and roadways, there was a sense of decay about the place. The fields sat empty, devoid of all crops, and in places the trees had been felled and carted away.

We saw the horses in the field before we reached the farmhouse. There must have been fifty of them, including ten foals. From the look of them, some of them must have been stranded on *jambanja*ed farms for long weeks or months before being spirited away. A strawberry roan appeared to have a sunken back, much like Pink Daiquiri, and his withers were thin and ragged. The silvery mare at his side looked weak and rangy, and when a dark gelding turned to shuffle away from our oncoming car, I saw that he was trailing behind him a lame leg.

Pat climbed out of the car and hung over the fence for a moment, gazing at the herd.

"They're huddling together," Pat observed.

He was right. The herd seemed skittish, moving as one to shuffle away from us. The only one who did not move was a tiny blue roan foal, its eyes wide with bewilderment.

"There's something wrong here."

"What do you mean?"

Pat moved to swing back into the car. "Not even Princess is as spooked as those horses, and think about what she went through."

We rolled on up to the farmhouse, where Rob Lucas was waiting to meet us. Rob was a big man, in his fifties, with the same harassed look we had seen on countless others from whom we had taken horses. He shook Pat's hand vigorously.

"That's a big herd out there," I said, wondering just how many Pat thought we might take.

"It's been a nightmare," Rob admitted, tramping around the corner of the farmhouse as I hurried to catch up. Curiously, we were walking away from the horses. "The war vets came a year ago. We fought them off. We even managed a court order . . . but what does that matter in Zimbabwe?"

"What changed?" I asked as we rounded the corner.

"Oh, *everything.*"

At the back of the farmhouse, tall fences marked the edge of a small game park, just like the one Nick Swanepoel had kept on Avalon Farm. In front of the gates, Rob's Land Rover was parked. He slipped behind the wheel and gestured for Pat and me to climb up front.

"Just make sure you keep the windows wound up," he said.

"Why aren't we going toward your horses?" I asked.

"You'll see."

One of Rob's workers pulled back the gates and we rolled within. The game park was wild and fairly wooded—though, in truth, it did not look so very different from the rest of the farm, now that so many of the fields had been ceded. Once we had driven through, I looked back. There was something ominous about the blank expression of the man on the other side as the gates came together and sealed us within.

We drove along a meandering, dusty road, potted with deep holes, and ground to a halt in the shadows cast by a stand of msasa trees. In the front seat, Pat moved as if to step out of the car, but Rob reached out and held him back.

"Just look," he said, lifting a hand to point. "Over there."

I squinted through the trees. On a great mound of red ringed with small bushes lounged a lioness. The sunlight spilled around her, but she was not asleep. I could very clearly see one eye open, methodically considering her surroundings.

I saw a flash of yellow in the corner of my eye and turned suddenly.

"There!"

The lioness on the mound was not alone. Now I could see a huge lion, perhaps the leader of this pride, coming up out of dense scrub. My eyes must have become attuned, as suddenly I could see other patches of scrubland moving; long grass and thornbushes resolved themselves into the forms of other lions. We were, I decided, quite surrounded.

"They're rescue lions," Rob explained, "from the droughts in the 1990s. You remember?"

"Oh," I said, remembering Crofton withering under that interminable sun, "we remember."

"I've kept them here for so long, done everything I could for them . . . They're happy. Strong. Free of disease. You see how well they look? But it's coming," Rob said, his eyes still trained on the king of the pride. "I'm getting out."

Rob looked suddenly downcast, and my heart went out to him. I know only too well what it was like to feel trapped, that you couldn't just pack your bags and flee, no matter how difficult the circumstance. Rob had the same look in his eyes as Pat sometimes had, as I sometimes saw staring back at me out of the mirror. Just as we could not abandon our horses, Rob could not abandon his lions.

"We had friends," I began. "Neighbors of ours where we used to farm—Rory and Lindy Hensman. They took their elephants south, tried to get them into South Africa."

"I have it in mind to do the same. Botswana, Tanzania, South Africa . . . It's all the same."

"Mozambique?"

Rob weighed it up. "They don't have lions there. They don't have anything. They massacred it all during their war. No, I think I'm heading south as well."

"Rob," Pat suddenly interjected, "where do all those horses come from?"

"Well, Pat, during normal times farmers used to send carcasses of animals that had died on farms to the lions. This included old and sick horses. Since the land invasions, desperate farmers who have to leave in a hurry have been loading up their horses and dumping them here." I heard the exasperation in Rob's voice. "We've had ten mares foal down in one of the pens." He looked at Pat in despair. "I can't just shoot them all.

"I can't just leave them to the war vets, either," Rob went on, "and I don't want to have to put them all down. I was hoping you might . . ."

Rob brought the engine back to life and we trundled on. In the long grasses at the edge of the mound, a giant, broken rib cage sat, stripped of all meat and slowly being bleached by the sun. No farmer, no horse trainer, no man who had studied animal sciences could mistake that rib cage for anything other than what it really was.

"You release the horses into this game park?" Pat's voice was cool, but I wondered what was happening inside.

"No!" Rob gasped. "I shoot them, Pat. When the lions need to feed, I go out into that field and I shoot one of them." He paused, shaking his head in disbelief. "I mean, I'm not a monster!"

The horror of it struck me hard in the face. That was why the horses had seemed so skittish. Yet, when I looked at Rob, the way his face was creased, the horror seemed to evaporate. There was horror of a different kind in the modern Zimbabwe—the war vets, the government-sponsored violence, the murders on the doorsteps of once happy farms; that Rob had been reduced to this was not something to hate him for.

We drove back up, circling the wary lions and leaving the game park by the same gates. In the paddock, the horses were waiting. When we climbed over the fence, they seemed to turn in nervous circles against one another.

"They can smell it," I said. "They're petrified."

I noticed a beautiful gray horse with a silvery mane staring at me from the middle of the herd. I felt close to tears. I did not want to imagine what these horses might have been through, only to wind up here, their grisly end delayed but not forever. If things had been different, any one of our herd might have landed here. I pictured Deja Vu, Princess, Brutus, and regal Shere Khan—all of them, lining up to be shot and served up.

Pat and I drifted into the herd. A string of blue roan foals scattered at our approach. Behind us, Rob Lucas lingered at the fence.

"Pat," I tentatively began, "I know what you're thinking, but . . ."

Pat was not looking at me. He had his eyes fixed on the smallest foal, pushed up against the flank of a big gray mare whose eyes flashed back at us.

"How can we not look after them?" he asked.

"Because we have more than we can cope with already. Because we don't have a farm. Because our horses are scattered on smallholdings that might be taken away any minute. Because, the more horses we have, the harder it's going to be to get over those mountains and escape, if the time really comes. That's why, Pat."

"You said it yourself—they're petrified. What would you do if it was Grey here? Deja Vu? Shere Khan?"

He had me tied up in knots, spinning a web with the very same fears to which I dared not give voice.

"How much money do we even have, Pat?"

Pat would not answer.

"How are we going to keep them?" I stopped. I could see that the gears were grinding in his head; he knew that I was right. "What if we can't look after them properly? You're going to have to shoot them, Pat. When that day comes, you're going to have to line up the horses we love so much and put bullets into each of their heads."

Pat stopped dead. "Better a bullet then or a bullet now?"

I looked at him, hopeless.

"Let's get a truck." He paused. "Load them all up, Mandy. Every last one . . ."

On a smallholding outside Mutare, we stood among ten terrified blue roan foals and a mother mare who would not let us near. Getting a halter onto her had been an ordeal, heaving her onto a truck even worse, but now she stood here, among the foals who might easily have ended up as lion food. They milled hopelessly in a makeshift corral. At the rope, Pat and I considered them closely. Kate, who had the week off from Hillcrest school, was trying to coax the tiniest foal, a feeble little thing we had named Texas, to the rope, but Texas only huddled by the mother mare, Montana.

The land belonged to Sally Dilton-Hill, and most of the Crawford horses were already grazing here. In fact, every time I came here, there seemed to be more: Viper, a purebred Arabian whose owner had been forced to find him a new home when he had somehow managed to nip off a groom's nipple; a big gray mare named Megan; and Spicegirl, a young bay mare with a Thoroughbred-type gait and a sweet, gentle face. We had brought the Lucas foals here, from the jaws of the lions, because Sally was renowned as an expert trainer, and we wondered if she might help us get them over their instinctive terror.

The arenas that had grown up here dwarfed what we had built at Biri Farm. Here was a great training ring of gum poles where horses could be isolated from the outside world and have their join-up performed; here was a field where dressage routines could be practiced and drilled in; here was a gymkhana arena where a horse ready for riding could be put through its paces. Many of the Crawford foals and the youngest horses we had taken from Two Tree were being saddled and schooled—and, with the herd having swollen to many more than a hundred, training them was a full-time occupation. Indeed, we had taken to treating it like a business. Along with Sally Dilton-Hill, we employed many people to help with the training; perhaps Pat's favorite was the eighty-year-old veteran who had been a significant figure in the Rhodesian military, back in the days before Mugabe and Zimbabwe had ever begun.

Sally climbed tentatively into the corral. The horses, sensing danger, moved as if to scatter—but there was nowhere to go.

"What do you think? He must have just been shooting them in front of each other," Pat said.

"A horse is never lost," said Sally. "Certainly not a foal."

We had first learned about Sally's skill in training animals when we met her donkeys. By some strange enchantment, Sally had taught her donkeys how to count. I could see them, even now, in a paddock on the other side of the corral. All Sally had to do was lift up her fingers to illustrate a simple sum, and Arabella the donkey, with her wonderful black eyes and long lashes, would scratch out the appropriate answer in the dirt with her hoof. A woman like that, we thought, could do wonders with our most unruly horses.

In the roped-off corral, Sally tried to get close to the mother mare, Montana. Around her, the foals—Texas, Arizona, California, Indiana, and Colorado—scattered, but Montana stood firm. She rolled her head angrily, eyes shaking. Then she released a vicious snort, rising slightly from her forelegs as she did so, as if to box Sally back. Sally lifted her open palms, as if to convince Montana she was no threat, but the big mare was not convinced. My heart sank. What had this horse been through on her *jambanja*ed farm? How many of her old herd had she seen shot down and carted off to the lions?

One eye on Montana and one eye on us, Sally backed away.

"I think we have our work cut out for us here, Pat."

Among the foals, Montana threw her head back and glared.

The peaks surrounding Partridge Hill were home to other families as well, many of whom had abandoned their farms and come for sanctuary here, just the same as we runaway Retzlaffs. One morning, as Pat prepared to take Kate into Mutare for school and run a circuit of the surrounding farms, checking on all our horses, one of those neighbors appeared on the doorstep with a plaintive look in her eyes.

The visitor introduced herself as Colleen Taylor. She lived just down the mountainside, her little smallholding—a tiny flower farm, replete with greenhouses and tunnels—besieged on all sides by the dense Bvumba woodland. Colleen was tall and dark, and almost as regal-looking as Shere Khan.

"It's Pat Retzlaff, isn't it?" she began.

Pat nodded stoutly.

"Pat, I wondered if I could beg your help. You see, I'd heard you were the *horse* people . . ."

Colleen Taylor's smallholding sat lower in the Bvumba than Partridge Hill, a wide basin of open land between fringes of forest, from which several gullies climbed and others dropped away. Though it was not very far, the way between the two homes was treacherous, so Pat and Colleen traveled there by road. As they turned from the sheer mountain pass along which Kate and I were hurtling, already late for school, they were flanked by Colleen's greenhouses and tunnels. Aloes grew in great banks along the sides of the track, mingling with wafts of coffee from a plantation deeper in the mountains to make a curious scent.

In a paddock outside the small farmhouse stood three horses: a beautiful dark bay mare, a similar gelding who could easily have been the mare's brother, and a smaller, lean foal, a bay who seemed to be forcing his head between the sparring adults.

Pat stood with his foot propped against the car.

"You see my problem?" Colleen asked.

"I'm not sure I . . ."

"You soon will. Come on, Pat, let's take a closer look."

Pat climbed into the paddock and tentatively approached the dark bay mare. The mare seemed to lock her eyes on Pat, shifting to face him head-on. At her side, the foal cantered away, but the black gelding stood firm, eyeing Pat with a look that could only be described as gleeful malevolence.

Pat went to lay a hand softly on the mare's muzzle, but before he could touch her, the gelding sprang into action. Thrusting himself between them, he rolled back his lips and whipped his head from side to side, teeth bared, preparing to nip. Quickly, Pat whipped his hand away, took a step back. He was just craning a look over his shoulder when suddenly Colleen cried out.

"Pat, quick!"

Too late, Pat realized what she was saying. In the corner of his eye, he saw the dark bay mare lift her foreleg and kick it out with the precision and ferocity of a bare-knuckle boxer. Turning against the blow, he stepped to his left. The mare's leg whipped past him and back again. Once it was planted firmly on the ground, the mare lifted her eyes to pierce him, while the gelding at her side still rolled his head, lips parted to show razor teeth.

"They're devil horses," Colleen began, on the other side of the fence.

This time, Pat did not take his eyes off the mare.

"She's Magie Noire, or Black Magic in English. The gelding's Philippe."

"Brother and sister?"

"I never had that bond with my brother . . ."

"These aren't your horses, are they?"

"What gave it away?" Colleen paused. "I'm not a horse person, Pat. Not like you and Mandy. I know a skewbald from a piebald, a stirrup from a halter, but . . . There used to be a family, lived high up in the Bvumba. The Nielsens. They had a holiday plot here, so they came to stay when they were thrown off their farm. In the end, they could only stay a year. It got to them. They had to get out. They're back in Belgium, but they had to leave their horses behind. I said I'd do what I could, but . . ." For the first time, the beautiful Colleen betrayed her worry; her face creased and she breathed out slowly. "I can't deal with them anymore, Pat. I can't get near them, can't feed them, can't dip them. I certainly can't ride them . . ."

Pat's focus was still trained on the mare Colleen had called Black Magic. She was a small, statuesque mare, perhaps fourteen hands high, and her coat shimmered like a black tar road under heavy rain. Her brother, Philippe, had calmed down, but he stood so tightly to his sister that Pat did not doubt what would happen if he tried to get close. These two horses were inseparable.

"What did you say the farmer's name was?"

"Nielsen. He farmed in the Mvuma area."

Pat arched an eyebrow. A thousand warm childhood memories came to him.

"I knew Nielsen," Pat breathed. "From when I was a boy." A smile blossomed on Pat's face, quickly dominating his every feature. "He was the most wonderful rider. I used to go to those gymkhanas. I used to go to those paper chases. I watched him playing polo. Those horses of his . . . I'd never seen anything like them."

His eyes returned to Black Magic and Philippe, the foal hidden behind them.

"Nielsen's horses?" he wondered, aloud. "What about the foal?"

"He's Rebel. He was with Nielsen, too. He was one of the wild horses."

"The wild horses?"

"You know, the herd they had, down near Mvuma . . ."

In the land around Mvuma, south of Harare, there lived almost three hundred wild horses, a herd made up from the descendants of farm runaways and old Rhodesian cavalry horses, unaccounted for at the end of the war. A trust of farmers in the area had collectively taken over stewardship of the herd, letting them roam free but taking care of their veterinary needs and rescuing injured animals whenever the need arose. Nielsen, it seemed, had been one of those men.

"Rebel's all that's left . . ." said Pat, as the terrible story seemed to tell itself.

Colleen nodded. "When they started being driven off their farms, the farmers got together. They couldn't leave the herd to be butchered by the war vets. They didn't deserve that."

The image was a dark and bloody one and brought to mind the vet Rob Gordon's heartbreaking recollections of putting down countless herds of livestock.

"They shot them," breathed Pat.

"But Rebel was just a tiny foal. Nielsen took him in, brought him up here with Black Magic and Philippe. And now . . ."

Pat stepped out of the paddock. "I don't know how I'm going to get them out of these mountains," he admitted.

Colleen's face seemed to light up. "Then you'll help?"

"I'll be back tomorrow morning, with halters and ropes," Pat said. Then, with a final look at the tempestuous, snorting Black Magic, he rolled his eyes at Colleen. "And help," he said. "I think I'm going to need it."

The next day, Pat and I went back to Colleen's plot and, distracting Philippe from Black Magic with handfuls of horse cubes and hay, managed to fit halters and ropes to each. With Rebel trailing behind, we wound our way down the mountain road and around Mutare's border, at last reaching the land where Duchess, Marquess, and twenty of our other mares were grazing. Black Magic had been tempestuous beneath Pat, twisting her head against his every command, but Pat was growing to be an expert horse trainer now, and he had an idea. Sometimes, if a human cannot convince a horse to behave, other horses might be able to do a much better job.

We released Black Magic into the herd of mares. As one, they watched the new intruder. Pat reached his hand out, and I followed it to see Shere Khan, gazing imperiously at the devilish horse who had just joined the herd.

"You just watch," he said. "In a month's time, they'll have sorted her out."

It was true. Every time Black Magic kicked out or butted one of the other mares, the herd turned against her, driving her out to stand on its edges, refusing to allow her back in. Every time she was readmitted and kicked out again, they would drive her out again, and again after that—until, at last, she would stand among them and graze contentedly, betraying her devilish spirit only in the gleam of her eyes, the fleeting flick of her mane. It was a psychological tactic that Pat and his trainers were employing in breaking and training all of the new foals and rescued horses who had come to the herd: a horse wants nothing more than to belong to its herd, and there is no better way of convincing it to behave than by making it confront the very real fear of being ostracized completely.

Fearing his malign influence on his sister, we took Philippe, along with Rebel, to join some of our horses on another patch of land, a small-holding owned by a wonderful woman, Sue Elton, where Brutus and Duke were roaming. And, in the days to come, it was a joy to see Black Magic slowly learn manners, shed her wicked ways, become a real part of the herd. The magic worked on her so quickly, so perfectly, that I was left agonized that I hadn't known this sort of psychology back on Crofton, when our children were small. Perhaps it might have worked on Jay and some of his wilder, more unruly ways . . .

In the morning, Pat bounced out of bed, flexed his muscles, and—for a reason that will always evade me—did a little John Travolta side-shuffle dance routine. I rolled over in the covers, burying my head in the pillow.

"Really?"

"Really, Mandy. You know what today is, don't you?"

"It's not your birthday."

"No," said Pat. "It's better. Today is *Brutus day.*"

The training had been in full swing for several months, and its most recent graduate was Brutus. Though he hadn't yet shed his permanently worried expression, or the furrowing around his eyes that made me want to throw my arms around him and console him every time we met, Brutus was growing into a strong horse. Pat had been looking forward to this day for some time—a chance to finally get in the saddle. Brutus had been trained and schooled in how to behave with a rider on his back, and—or so his trainers swore—he was as ready as he was ever going to be.

"You're coming, aren't you, Mandy?"

He was, I decided, as excited as a little boy at Christmastime. I rolled over for another five minutes' sleep.

"Wouldn't miss it for the world, darling."

A couple of hours later, high up in the Penhalonga Mountains, at the training grounds, a small crowd had gathered: Gaydia; Sally Dilton-Hill; Sally's daughter, who had been working on Brutus; and a few onlookers.

In a paddock beside the fields where other horses were grazing, Brutus was waiting. As I chatted with Gaydia and Sally, Pat strode heroically from the crowd and swung himself over the fence. Sally waited eagerly at Brutus's side.

"How's he been doing?"

"Wonderfully," Sally insisted. "He's taken to it like a natural."

Brutus, now fifteen hands high and wearing a smart saddle, flicked a look at him as he approached, but dropped his head sadly, as if what was coming was the most horrendous thing in the world.

"Come on, boy," a beaming Pat said, "we're in this together . . ."

Stopping only to make sure that there were no rocks or small stones left in the grass around Brutus, Pat swung himself into the saddle. He sat there for a moment before lifting his leg to adjust his left stirrup. When he was certain both he and Brutus were comfortable, he turned and flashed a grin at me through the crowd. Taking the reins in his right hand in classic African fashion, he coaxed Brutus gently around.

Suddenly, Brutus lifted his head. His permanently worried expression transformed itself into one of abject horror. In the saddle, Pat froze. He knew what was coming.

Brutus lifted his forelegs, stamped them back down, and performed a buck. In the middle of the field, he lifted himself, smashed back down, lifted himself again, shaking his head fiercely. In that first buck, he shook off Pat's grip on his reins—but, still, Pat held on. His hands grappled out for Brutus's mane, his legs clenched tight.

Then, he was in the air—and then, he was lying spread-eagled on the ground at Brutus's side. He did not move.

Sally was the first out of the crowd and over the fence to reach him. I hurried behind, catching hold of Brutus's rein to stop him bolting. By the time I was there, Pat was stirring, turning over, and looking up with bleary eyes.

"Pat, are you . . ."

Pat seemed to be trying to stand, but then he winced and took another deep breath. His eyes drifted sideways, and mine followed. Lying at his side was a single piece of brick, the only one left in the whole field. His chest had crashed down upon it.

"How does it feel?"

"Broken," uttered Pat, as I helped him to his feet.

"Let's get you out of here . . ."

Pat's face twisted. From the corner of his eyes, he took in the bank of watching faces. "Not a chance!" he rasped. "I can't let them see me like that, Mandy."

"Pat, if you've really broken your ribs . . ."

"A couple of broken ribs?" Pat agonized. "I've been waiting to ride Brutus ever since John Crawford's farm . . ."

There was no use arguing further; I had seen the steel in Pat's eyes. Either that or the vain foolishness. I handed him the rein and helped him get his first foot in the stirrup.

"You're being . . ."

"Heroic?" interjected Pat, wincing as he swung his leg back over the saddle.

As Pat sat uncomfortably in Brutus's saddle, Gaydia led the other horses out and made sure they were tacked up properly. I had not ridden in several weeks now, and I was longing to be back in the saddle, but now also a bit apprehensive. Behind me, Gaydia fastened a girth and swung into her saddle to adjust her stirrups, while Sally readied another horse. We pulled onto the trail and began the gentle walk off the smallholding. At the head of the procession, I pulled my horse level with Brutus.

"Are you sure you're okay?" I asked.

Pat whispered to me out of the side of his mouth, "Brutus hasn't been trained at all. He just hasn't taken to it."

"How does he feel?"

"Like he wants to be back in a paddock with Jade, grazing on some grass."

"Unresponsive?"

"*Dejected . . .*"

That *did* sound like our poor little Brutus.

The sun was almost at its highest point above Penhalonga, but in gullies and crags, the morning mist still lingered. We nosed Brutus and the rest through a cold reef of gray, emerging in brilliant sunshine at the head of the gully beyond. For a while, the trail cut circles around the foothills, before following a ridge with the scrubby escarpments dropping away on each side. Then we were up, high among the pine trees, climbing to what seemed the top of the world.

At the head of the procession, Pat rode Brutus. Though I could not see his face, I could tell from the way he was sitting in the saddle that he was tense. The disgruntled little horse did not want a rider on his back, nor to be high up in these mountains. He wanted, I knew, nothing more than a paddock of long grass, a trough for water, and the rest of the herd all around him.

I looked back to wave to Gaydia, coming up in the rear on one of Sally's horses. When I looked back, Brutus was gone.

A streak of brown was hurtling up the road ahead, my broken husband clinging to his back.

Brutus had taken off. I urged my horse to follow, but it was already too late. Brutus was careening wildly around a bend in the road, and Pat was gone.

In the saddle, Pat clung on for dear life. He squeezed with his thighs, rocked backward—but if Brutus had ever learned his commands at all, he no longer wanted to take them. As I came around the next bend, I saw Pat craning to his left, peering through the trees. Still, Brutus plowed on. I cried out, my voice lost on the wind, and saw Pat crane left again, as if he could see something through the trees. My eyes darted the same way.

It was then that I realized what was coming.

Up ahead, our road came together with another, running almost parallel, to meet the final stretch of road winding to the very top of the mountain pass. Brutus and Pat were rapidly reaching the apex where two roads became one.

Through the trees, motoring blindly along the other road, came a gargantuan semi truck, piled high with tree trunks felled from the forests. Approaching the junction, the truck and Brutus were almost neck and neck, each straining for the lead as they charged toward an inevitable, very messy meeting.

I closed my eyes, drew my horse to a sudden stop, and muttered a prayer. The sound of the semi exploded in my ears, a horn blasting out as it sailed through the trees, cruised through the junction, and took off up the mountain road.

All was silent. All was still.

At last, unable to keep them closed any longer, I opened my eyes. At the top of the road, only yards from the junction, Brutus had stopped dead. Pat was still in the saddle, gazing back at me as if shell-shocked.

I very carefully made my way up the road to Brutus's side. "That was close, Pat."

"This horse," Pat wheezed, dragging his arm across his brow to wipe away the fear, "hasn't been trained at all."

I looked down. Brutus's gaze met my own. His brows seemed to be pinched and his eyes loomed large, protesting his innocence.

"Time to go home?" I asked. Behind me, Gaydia and the rest of the procession were only just arriving.

"Home," Pat said, "and bed." Then, he gripped his chest. "Oh, and a doctor. I probably need a doctor . . ."

That night, back at Partridge Hill, I stripped back Pat's shirt and saw a dark square of black bruising where he had fallen on the brick. I tried to run my fingers around the marks, but instinctively he recoiled, as sensitive as Princess had been around her open withers.

"Broken," I said.

Pat fingered his wound. "But not completely."

It was, I decided, exactly how I had come to think of Zimbabwe.

We had been in the Bvumba two peaceful years, and around us the herd had swollen. Kate neared the end of school, Paul called to tell us that he had met the girl he meant to marry in London, and Jay left to complete his final exams and began to look for work, not only in Zimbabwe's hunting areas but all across southern Africa. Never since the earliest days of Crofton had I seen Pat so industrious, riding out each morning to train another horse. Partridge Hill had proven the oasis in Zimbabwe's storm that we had craved ever since Crofton.

Yet, if I ever allowed myself to believe we were safe, it was a feeling that quickly passed. There was always the whisper in the back of my mind, a little voice telling us we had delayed the inevitable but that, one day, it would come for us, too.

When the ax fell, it fell swiftly and viciously, just as it had always done in Mugabe's Zimbabwe.

I was returning from England, having finally found Granny Beryl a home and a small state pension, when the first news came in. With so many of the nation's farms already fallen to Mugabe's war vets, it was only a matter of time before his relentless gaze fell on Mutare and the borderland between this country and the next. Immediately on my return from England, we heard the news that one of the farms at which we were keeping our horses was about to be seized. We marshaled our resources to ferry the twenty horses, including our precious Grey and Deja Vu, to one of the other farms we were using. Only days later, that farm too was taken, and we had to ferry the horses again. Now, the land grab gathered pace. The calls came at midnight, in the smallest watches of night, in broad daylight as we drove through Mutare's wide, flowery avenues. One after another, the farms where we were keeping the horses fell to Mugabe's war vets.

We had reached the end of the line.

A small part of the herd had been kept on the grounds of an old game park, where most of the animals were aged or already dead. As the farms fell, we ferried the horses here, so that soon the herd was roaming wild where once antelope, giraffes, and elephants had been kept. Our days became an endless zigzagging across the countryside as we tried desperately to bring the whole herd back together on safe country: foals splitting from their mothers in the confusion; a gelding going astray only to be discovered grazing, oblivious, at the edge of the road; Black Magic momentarily finding Philippe again and rediscovering the sheer

joy of being a truculent, aggressive prima donna. You could see the confusion in the faces of the herd, mares disgruntled at having to leave good
grazing behind to be driven to some farm where the fields were already
shorn flat. Among them, Brutus wore his old expression of permanent
alarm. Perhaps he, alone of all the horses, understood the true severity
of what was going on.

If the farms kept falling, there would soon be no place for them to go.

We arrived at Partridge Hill, late at night, to a meal of leftovers from
the night before, Pat and I both longing to fall into a deep sleep and not
wake up for days. Kate was waiting in the living room, her schoolbooks
splayed out around her. Her eyes looked heavy, ink stained her fingers,
and I doubted very much that she had eaten properly tonight.

I hated this country then. If none of this had happened, if we still
lived on Crofton, if we hadn't had to take Kate away from Lomagundi
School . . . how different her studies might have been.

"How's it going, Kate?"

Kate nodded. "It's okay."

"Are you sure?"

"Actually, Dad . . ." Kate stood. "Tell me if I'm going crazy, but I was
in the library today, and I swore I could see . . . *Brutus*, out on the playing
fields. I thought I was seeing things, but when I looked again, there were
Duke and Duchess, too. Black Magic. Deja Vu . . ."

"Kate," said Pat, "there's something we have to tell you."

Kate slumped in the sofa. "I think I get the picture . . ."

"They announced they were taking the game park," Pat went on.
"We couldn't risk them being there when the park falls. But"—he
paused, sensing Kate's amazement—"the school has land. All the land
beyond those playing fields and tennis courts."

Kate nodded, sadly. "But they can't take the school, right?"

"Not even Mugabe can steal a school," I explained. "It's a last resort,
Kate. Hillcrest School might have the final piece of grassland in the
whole of the district that Mugabe can't take for himself. There's enough

grazing there to buy us some time. That's all it is. We're moving them all there over the next few days."

Kate breathed the information in, seemed to weigh it up, and nodded sharply.

"I don't know how I'm going to live *this* one down." She grinned.

"Just pretend we're not your parents?" I said.

"Mum, I've been doing that for years . . ."

I pulled up at the gates of Hillcrest School, and all I could see were horses.

The fields were not much larger than ten tennis courts—and there, more than a hundred horses were packed, the grass around their hooves already bitten down to scrubby stubs. Along one side of the fences keeping them in, three farmers' trucks were parked. They were not only from the farms on which we had kept the horses, but from farms and smallholdings farther afield as well. Figures were unloading bales of hay from the backs of the trucks, carrying them over to where the horses might feed. These were acts of selflessness and generosity to make me certain there was still so much good in the world, even in the madness of Zimbabwe.

It took me a moment to pick out Pat in the throng. He was standing with Shere Khan and Jonathan, who was wearing his backpack for spraying the horses with a dip solution. When Pat saw me, he weaved through the herd to meet me at the fence.

"They're bringing the last ones up from the game park."

"How are we going to fit any more in?"

Pat gazed around. Lady's head had appeared to root in his armpit, and he fought her down. Even after long months of training, there were some habits that would not be broken.

"Mandy, we're not."

I was not surprised. A piece of me had known he would say this, ever since I returned.

"Where, then?"

Pat's eyes drifted east, to the peaks of the Bvumba and beyond. "It's time."

I nodded. We had rallied against it too long: Crofton and Palmerston, Biri and Headlands . . . and now here. Pat looked at the bales of hay lined up at the fence. We could not rely on it forever. Mutare's farmers would soon be disappearing. Some of them might even flow over the mountains into Mozambique. It was where we would have to go too, we wild-eyed Retzlaffs and our horses. Even in spite of the two years' peace we'd had in the Bvumba, that, I reminded myself, had always been the plan.

"How long have we got?" I asked.

"Days, Mandy. Maybe a couple of weeks." Pat pushed Lady's head away; she was getting far too impatient—but then, so were we. "It's time to make a plan."

I made my way back to the car and sat behind the wheel. Across the herd, I could see the front facade of Hillcrest School. A shrill bell rang, and moments later the girls began to stream out. Among them, I saw Kate emerge. She looked smart and proud in her school blazer, but at the top of the steps, she stalled. She gazed out across the fields filled with her father's horses and I saw her visibly squirm. In the middle of all this, Pat and I had become Zimbabwe's most embarrassing parents.

Yes, I thought, it really was time to leave. My eyes drifted to the mountains, and thoughts of the lush country of Mozambique sitting beyond. Tomorrow we would go up into the mountains, Pat with Shere Khan, Kate with Deja Vu, me in Grey's saddle, and search for a way through. We would look down on the valleys of Mozambique, those untouched lands, and it would suddenly be very real: after years of struggle, we were fleeing Zimbabwe, and taking one hundred and four horses with us.

MOZAMBIQUE

Chapter 12

THE TOWN OF CHIMOIO, where we had found a small house, sat one hundred kilometers east of the Bvumba, in the heartland of Mozambique. Pat and I sat at traffic lights in town, sweating in the blistering heat, dry dirt caked across the windshield of our Land Rover. In the back, Jay lay with his head rolled back and his mouth gaping open. How he could sleep in this heat, I had no idea.

Taking the horses through the Mountains of the Mist had proven a bigger ordeal than I might have imagined. As I looked at Pat in the driver's seat beside me, I could distinctly see the toll it had taken on him: his hair seemed to have turned gray overnight. I could tell how the lines had deepened in his once-youthful face, but I knew he wouldn't have taken it back for a second. We had made it out of Zimbabwe alive, and we had brought one hundred and four of our precious rescued horses with us.

It had not been easy. In the end, we had decided not to risk driving them through some secluded mountain pass, for fear of meeting soldiers and bandits along the way. Instead, we had faced the tyranny of the official checkpoints. There were enough obstacles to getting ourselves over the border, what with Mugabe's border guards keen to clamp down on any little irregularity and bleed some kind of bribe money out of it, and for the horses the challenge had been almost insurmountable. It had taken weeks. Each day we had loaded our precious horses into the backs of trucks and taken them to the border crossing, nestled deep in the heart of the Bvumba—but every time, we had been turned away, told that our paperwork was not correct, that we did not have authorization to take grass across the border, that the horses needed passports, that the passports were incorrectly bound, that we had to pay fees and charges— and yet more bribes. Time and again our horses were sent back. Time and again we tried. Then, just as the lines deepened in Pat's face, as we began to talk at night about the very real possibility of abandoning half of our herd, we tried one last time. We loaded up the whole of the herd and approached the border. By some strange mercy, that day the border guards smiled kindly on us. We sailed into Mozambique unharmed, and with us came Grey, Deja Vu, Shere Khan, Black Magic, Lady, and every other horse to whom we had devoted our lives.

In the column of cars behind us a chorus of horns started to sound, but they were not making the lights change any quicker.

We had been in Chimoio three months, but I had not yet gotten used to the heat. It seemed a world away from the other side of the Bvumba. Lower and less temperate than the Zimbabwean side, Mozambique's very air had a different flavor. Chimoio was the fifth-largest town in Mozambique, the capital of Manica Province, which bordered the Bvumba. The town seemed to have lived a multitude of lives. In some areas, the evidence of its old colonial days was clear, with Portuguese architecture still standing and the language plastered across billboards and street signs; in others, the old town was derelict and slowly being reclaimed by new businesses and homes. The streets, wide and dusty, put me in mind of some frontier town of old, and as we navigated and got used to the town's backstreets, I began to understand that though we were only a hundred kilometers from Zimbabwe, this was an Africa like no other: a Portuguese Africa, a Communist Africa, a postrevolution Africa in which the rule of law still felt like only a guideline to most.

"Jay," Pat barked, "wake up. We're here."

We had come to the very outskirts of town. There, beyond the shell of an old Portuguese building that was slowly being rebuilt and patched up with new fences, walls, and wire, I could see the heads of Grey, Shere Khan, and Black Magic grazing on their bales of dried grass. Lady's head lifted from behind a bale to greet us.

"Thanks, Dad," Jay muttered, "I was having a bad dream. I dreamed that we lived . . ." Jay stopped and stepped out of the car. "Oh, wait . . ." He grinned. "That wasn't a dream."

We had timed coming over the mountains into Mozambique well; perhaps, I reflected, it was one of the only things we had done properly in the whole of our journey. Having just graduated from Hillcrest School, Kate was accepted to study chemistry at university and had gone down to South Africa to earn her degree. Jay, meanwhile, had graduated from his hunting apprenticeship and accepted a post in Mozambique's premier national park, Gorongosa, where he was training guides and introducing the first tourists to the wonderful park. Mozambique did not have much big game left, most of it having been slaughtered to feed soldiers in the war that had finished a decade ago, but season by season it was returning, and a private philanthropist named Greg Carr was financing the return of elephants, lions, and all kinds of antelope to Gorongosa.

We left the Land Rover and crossed the dusty street, eyeballed by a billy goat chewing on a small bush at the edge of the road. On the other side of the fence, we met the horses.

"Dad," Jay began, "they look . . . terrible."

Of the one hundred and four horses we had brought with us, forty lived in the paddock here, while the remainder were out on Zimofa, a farm thirty-five kilometers beyond the town limit. We had found the property soon after coming over the mountains, and it was here that we had founded our riding school. As more and more Zimbabweans poured into town, bringing businesses and agricultural ambitions with them, so too had foreign NGOs begun to populate the town. Chimoio had become a melting pot of southern African, Portuguese, English, Dutch, American, Canadian, and even Chinese and Indian immigrants. Many of them brought families with them, and our fervent hope was that, at last, the horses could start working together with us, helping to pay their way. Now, whenever we could, we gave riding lessons and led rides out into the wild, untamed bush of Mozambique.

Yet what Jay had said was true. All was not well in the herd. I walked over to Philippe and put a hand on his muzzle to stop him grazing. At first he seemed to be in good health, but when he turned his head to look at me, I saw the dark, ugly cavity where his right eye used to be. The grooms had led the herd out grazing one morning, and come the evening, Philippe had wandered back to his paddock at the riding school blind on one side.

He was not the only one who had suffered. In the corner of the paddock, Grey stood with dark pink lesions coloring his withers and the underside of his neck, while Black Magic wore the dark boil of ringworm around both her eyes, along her muzzle, and creeping around her hairless lips. Others wore the marks of the fungal infection deeply scored into their hides. With so little veterinary support in Mozambique, we were struggling to keep on top of all these ailments.

"Ringworm's the least of it," said Pat. "Come this way."

Jay trudged after his father into the stables at the center of the riding school. In the first stall, Princess was contentedly being dipped for ticks by two of our grooms. Against all the odds, the wound in her withers had finally sealed—and, though she would forever be sensitive when anybody touched her, it had not festered and opened up again as it had done so many times before. In the next stall, however, stood a different story.

Little Fanta looked bereft. She hardly looked like a horse any longer. In the stall, a creature of skin and bone looked up, not a single hair left anywhere on her body. Her rib cage showed, stark and grisly, through her skin; her teeth were ugly yellow protuberances from the tip of her muzzle.

"It's like an allergic reaction to the heat," Pat explained. "She started losing her hair and then lost the ability to sweat. Everything just shed away." He paused, putting a tentative hand out so that Fanta could nibble at it. "By rights, she should be dead."

I stroked Princess's muzzle. By rights, she should have been dead, too.

"She just won't give up the ghost," said Pat.

"Dad, you should get a vet."

Pat gave Jay a withering look. "Nice idea, genius. You tell me—where are we going to find a vet for these horses?"

We explained that there were local vets, that much was true, but not one of them had any experience in treating horses. We had found that out as we came across the border. When, at last, we made it through to the Mozambican side, huge crowds gathered to see the horses led from the trucks and watered and fed. Hundreds of people had flocked out of the border buildings and houses to catch a glimpse of the herd. Horses, we were told, had not been seen in Mozambique since the dawn of the civil war—and that was more than thirty years before, in 1974.

"They thought they were big dogs," I said, as Jay and I left Fanta wheezing and returned to the open air.

"Big dogs?"

"You know, big dogs you could ride. Dogs who eat grass . . ."

Across the riding school, Lady bounded up to the edge of the paddock. "That one *is* like a big dog," Jay muttered.

In the paddock, Lady was standing with a collection of tiny foals.

"Someone's been busy," Jay said with a smirk.

"They're . . . accidents," I said.

One after another, I introduced Jay to the illegitimate foals who had started to appear in the herd. One of the problems with maintaining such a big and disparate herd, especially in Mozambique—where the veterinary aid was almost nonexistent—was managing unexpected births. Because our horses came from such checkered backgrounds, and because we could not often determine their real ages, we had not always performed the necessary geldings in time. The horses we had taken from Rob Lucas and his lions had, it turned out, been a little older and friskier than we had imagined. It only took one boisterous young stallion to come of age more swiftly than expected, and suddenly the younger mares across the herd had come into foal.

Pink Daiquiri was one of those mares. She had given birth to a beautiful colt we had named Ramazotti. They stood together now on Lady's left side, Pink Daiquiri with her sunken back and soft, beautiful features, Ramazotti with dark markings on each of his flanks, with pronounced facial bones and shimmering eyes.

"She's better-looking than *that* one," said Jay, indicating another colt.

Some of the other illegitimates were not as blessed with good looks as Ramazotti. On the farms outside Mutare we had been keeping the foals together in a kind of equine nursery where they could learn to play, get to know the social structures of their herd, and go through the first stages of their training together. One of the downsides of this arrangement was that young stallions, just reaching maturity, could mate with their sisters. The foal that Jay had pointed out was named Vaquero, and he was the result of just such a union. As far as inbred accidents go, he was very healthy—but he had a disjointed, gangly look about him, and his eyes seemed to wander.

"Any horse would look ugly next to Ramazotti," I began, following Vaquero's roaming eye.

"That *isn't* a horse, Mum."

Vaquero must not have sensed the insult, for he pushed his muzzle over, eager to inspect these two gawking figures on the other side of the fence.

"One day, Jay, you might know what it feels like to have an ugly little brute of a son and still love him."

I was halfway across the riding school, hurrying to join Pat at the car, when Jay figured out what I meant. Jay and Vaquero, I thought, were going to get on just fine.

In the afternoon, Pat and I rode out to Zimofa Farm. Though the rest of the herd was grazing contentedly in the pastures, we were not there to inspect them or medicate their ringworm for the hundredth time. Zimofa Farm was one of the many farms in the area we were hoping would help us get back on our feet, provide us and the horses with a permanent home once again. We were here to look at paprika.

Chimoio was in the middle of a gold rush. There were no mines in the hills, no gold panners in the riverbeds, nor any great stamp mills scoring the land. There were gold mines in the border country between Mozambique and Zimbabwe, but there was another kind of gold in Chimoio as well: the land itself.

For farmers like Pat and me, Mozambique was untouched, virgin land. There was agriculture in the country, but not on anywhere near the same scale as we had known it in Zimbabwe. Here, farmers kept smallholdings or grew crops simply for subsistence—but there was land aplenty here, waiting to be opened up, irrigated, and transformed into healthy, functional farmland. As Mugabe drove commercial farming out of Africa's breadbasket, it was inevitable that some of those farmers would turn their eyes toward the open country to the east and dream of what the land might look like if people with ancestral knowledge of farming poured their lives into it. High up in the Bvumba, the same thoughts had occurred to Pat and me.

It began, as these things often do, with paprika. We had been consulting with Zimbabwean paprika growers with our agronomy business since before we were forced out of River Ranch and Palmerston Estates. We had worked closely with a large company known as Highveld Paprika.

Highveld Paprika had financed the growing of paprika across Zimbabwe, but, like us, the company's leaders had been drawn to the east, to the fresh world of Mozambique, ten years out of its civil war and desperate for development. There was so much virgin bush here, and so little organized agriculture, that to the exiled farmers of Zimbabwe it must have seemed a promised land. It certainly seemed that way to the directors of Highveld Paprika. Their plan was to open up countless hectares of bush, investing in both local farmers and people like us who were streaming over the border, and watch the bush roll back, bountiful fields of paprika crops growing in its wake.

Overnight, Chimoio had become a boomtown, and we were at its epicenter. Investment in the land encouraged investment on a much wider scale. Across town, new houses were being built, and new traders were opening their stores. Engineers were setting up bases to help in building works and irrigation schemes, while money was being poured into the town's utilities, a new medical practice had sprung up, and foreign NGOs cascaded in.

Pat and I had been tasked by the two directors of the company with being their intermediaries on the ground. Though we would not farm ourselves, we were to oversee the farmers in whom Highveld Paprika was investing. The plan involved Highveld Paprika lending a vast amount of money that we would manage and dispense among the Chimoio farmers involved in the program, by way of buying them tractors, harvesters, and irrigation equipment—and, of course, advising them on how best to treat and manage the crop. We did not plan on doing it forever, but the opportunity, we knew, was far too good to miss. For the first time since being driven from our home, we had the tools to claw our way back to the top, earn enough money to found a new home and build a permanent life for ourselves and our horses. It would never be Crofton, but deep inside I still dreamed of a place our children could come back to, a house to which they might bring our future grandchildren.

Pat strode along the trail, tracked by Tequila and Marquess in the paddock beyond, and walked between two banks of paprika plants. I followed. The paprika plants were shin high, wearing rich green leaves and budding fruits. I trailed my hand across their feathery tops, feeling the cold rustle of leaves across my fingertips.

For a second, we were fifteen years in the past, back at River Ranch in our earliest days. I was standing in the middle of one of our tomato fields, inspecting the leaves for signs of infestation or disease and calling out to Pat whenever I found something suspicious. *Opening up the land,* I constantly reminded him, *is not only about driving back the bush. There are smaller, more insidious enemies to beat back as well.*

"It's really going to work here, isn't it, Pat?" I called out.

Too lost in his dreams of the land, Pat did not turn back.

"Isn't it, Pat?"

He looked back and nodded. "This is good land, Mandy," he said, grinning.

"Better than home?"

He crouched, fingering one of the unripe fruits.

"It'll do."

I supposed that it would.

At first, I thought the voice was a dream. Half-awake and eager for the comfort of sleep, I rolled over, wrapping myself around Pat. He had kicked the sheets off in the night—the air beneath our mosquito net was so hot and clammy as to be almost unbearable—but a deep sigh told me he was still asleep. I was glad that one of us, at least, could get some rest.

"Wake up!"

This time, the voice jolted me from my tormented slumber. I sat bolt upright, happening to elbow Pat in the face as I did so. With a single giant snort, not unlike the disparaging sound Black Magic might have made, Pat awoke.

"What is it?"

"There's somebody at the door . . ."

I moved to push out of the mosquito net, but, muttering some incomprehensible complaint, Pat pushed me back to the mattress and climbed out himself. Too nervous now, I followed him to the bedroom door and listened down the hall.

"There has been a terrible accident."

It was the voice of our night guard, a local man we had employed to keep the horses in their paddock safe at night.

"What kind of accident?"

"The fencing wire has been stolen . . ."

Pat growled in discontent. "That doesn't sound like much of an accident to me . . ."

It was only when the night guard next spoke that the true purpose of his moonlit visit became clear. "There are horses on the road. You must come quick."

Pat pulled on a shirt, I quickly heaved boots on over my nightclothes, and we set out into the hot Chimoio night.

Our first stop, the night guard in tow, was down at the riding school. As we climbed out of the Land Rover, Jonathan and Albert were down at the end of the paddock, shoring up a hole where the fencing wire had been stolen. Among the horses gathered at the other side of the paddock, I could see Lady, Black Magic, and Deja Vu eyeing us curiously. As Pat and I came to the fence, Lady began to amble over, but she quickly realized something was wrong and came no farther. Above us, the sky was streaked with thousands of stars.

"How many got out?"

"We counted three missing."

"Who?" I asked, gazing into the dark silhouettes of the herd.

"Grey is gone," Jonathan began. "Treacle, Romans . . ."

Pat stepped through the hole in the wire. "Which way?"

Jonathan pointed into the darkness. Grey and the other two run-aways seemed to have turned their backs on the town and headed into the wild, open scrub. Yet out there lay as many dangers as there were here in Chimoio.

"The main road, Pat. What if they were . . ."

Pat cut me off. "Get back in the car, Mandy."

We left Jonathan and Albert looking over the herd and screeched the car around to follow. Our headlights arced across the road, illuminating the potholes, and then we took off, out of Chimoio. The night rushed past around us. Streams of burning sand kicked up by the wheels twisted across the windshield, finding their way through the open windows to whip and sting us.

We hit the main road and turned west. My eyes roamed the verges, but in the darkness I could see no sign of where the horses might have gone. If there was grazing nearby, perhaps they had remembered it from their rides and were bound that way—yet all around, there was only the dry, thorny scrub.

A full moon was on the rise. Fleetingly, in its ethereal light, I saw a spattering of horse dung in the middle of the road. I breathed out a sigh of relief—we were headed in the right direction. Then something twisted in my chest.

"Pat," I said, "they're walking on the main road." I paused. "In the dead of night . . ."

He looked at me, expressionless. The thought had occurred to him, too.

It felt cooler outside of town. The shadowy silhouettes of a stand of msasa trees, with their familiar fingerlike leaves, blocked out the silver of the moon and stars for a second—and, when we emerged on the other side, we saw a vast shape looming ahead.

Uncertain at first, Pat pressed his foot on the brake, and the Land Rover ground to a halt.

Our headlights picked out the shape of a truck at the side of the road, its back wheels up on the bank.

I moved to get out of the car.

"Stay there," said Pat.

But something compelled me to stand, and I joined him on the side of the road.

We walked in the path of our own headlights, up toward the truck. The driver was already climbing back into the cab, gunning the engine back to life. With a crunch of gears, he hauled the truck around, crashed down from the bank, and took off up the road. Exhaust choked out of the back of the truck, enveloping us in an acrid cloud.

As the cloud parted and we emerged on the other side, I stopped dead. The shapes lying in the middle of the road were not great boulders of earth, nor cargo dropped from the truck. In pieces before us lay the bodies of the three horses.

I rushed forward, stalled, rushed forward again. I froze. By the time I came to my senses, Pat was on his knees at the side of the first horse. He gestured wildly for me to go back to the car, but I was drawn on, like a moth to a naked flame. I guessed that this had been the first of the horses into which the truck had plowed, for his haunch was torn half away from his body, and a mess of meat was open to the stars and insects of night.

My eyes panned up the ruined carcass, and I saw Grey's head, stiff and lifeless. His tongue lolled out, caked already in hot dry dust.

In a daze, I stepped past. Farther on, up the road, hanging half in the ditch between the stone and a scrubby field in which subsistence maize was being grown, lay Treacle. At first, my heart soared, for her body was not pulverized like Grey's. I dropped down to touch her flank, and my hand sank into her hide. Underneath, her ribs were shattered. Her body was a mere mask, for inside she was shredded. I ran my hand up her spine, into her mane. She had died with her eyes open and they stared at me now, pleading.

Between Grey and Treacle, Romans lay. Pat sank to her side, pressed his head to her chest as if to listen for her death rattle. There was only silence.

The truck was long gone, its exhaust trails clearing. We sat in the middle of the road, surrounded by the devastation.

I was too numb to cry, but images rained down on me: Grey, a lovable foal on Two Tree; then, older now, taking me high up into the forests in Penhalonga as we searched for a way to drive the horses over the border.

"What do we do?" I breathed, still stunned.

Pat was beyond speech. He wheeled around, as if to climb back into the Land Rover, but then stopped dead.

"We need a truck," he uttered. "You'll have to go . . ."

"Pat . . ."

"Well, I'm not leaving you here, am I?" he roared. Then, suddenly, he calmed. "Tell Jonathan to get a truck out here quickly."

I could still see Grey's tongue lolling in the corner of my eye. I tried to shake the image away and found that, for the first time, my vision was blurred by tears. Perhaps it was a good thing; at least now I did not have to see their faces staring up at me. Grey had survived war vets, come back from being stranded out on Two Tree, been rustled off farms, and somehow made it through the rush of disease and parasites that had feasted on the herd when we first came to Chimoio. The thought that he was dead on account of us was awful.

I climbed back into the car. There I saw the cadavers, trapped in the headlights as if I were the one about to run them down. I tried not to look as I swung the car around and drove the long road back into Chimoio.

Half an hour later, I made it back into the riding school. Jonathan and Albert were just cutting off the last strands of wire in the new stretch of fence. I asked Jonathan to bring a truck round.

"Will you drive, madam?"

I looked down. I had not realized it, but my hands were shaking. "No," I said. "You . . ."

It took an interminable time to get back. In the passenger seat I could not sit still. I wound down the window, wound it up again, played with the phone in my hands and toyed with calling Pat, each time fighting down the urge. In the back of the truck, Albert and another one of our grooms bounced around, waiting to help with the grisly task.

"I remember a time on Crofton," I began. The memory had not occurred to me in such a long time, but for some reason it had resurfaced now, as vivid as if it were yesterday. "I was riding with Charl, who was on Grey, with Kate and Jay riding up behind us. Suddenly, Grey was so agitated. He stopped dead, refused to go on. It took me a while to see what he had seen." I looked at Jonathan, my eyes glassy. "In the bush, there was a python, just gorged itself on a sable calf. Her mother must have been off grazing and came back to see her calf in the belly of this snake, straining at its skin from inside. She was hammering her hooves up and down, pulverizing that snake . . . but she could never set the calf free. It was already gone." I paused, kneading my hands. "How did Grey know? Why did he care?" My voice broke. "I loved that horse."

By the time we came back to the spot in the road, I realized we were not the only ones. The truck headlights picked out Pat, standing between Grey and Romans, with Treacle on his other side, but around him I saw groups of local villagers. Three figures, two women and a man, stood in the maize, while another crouched at Grey's ruptured back. As I stepped out of the cab to hurry over, Jonathan maneuvering the truck so that we might heave the carcasses inside, I noticed others as well. One of them cried out in his local language. Though I knew he could not understand, Pat shot him a look like daggers. Turning, he saw the man bent low at Grey's side and, with a great stride, drove him back to the edge of the road.

"What's going on?" I asked.

"They want the meat," Pat said.

I stared, as if asking him to say it again.

"We need to get them out of here, before more come . . . Jonathan!" Pat barked. "Help me here!"

There were more faces on the banks of the road now. I felt a hand tugging on my elbow and turned to see the questioning faces of two local women, shrouded in the blackness. Whether they were speaking Portuguese or their local language, I could not tell; the words were blurred, indistinct, as I watched Grey being loaded onto the truck.

When, at last, all three horses were aboard, Jonathan edged the truck around so that Pat and I could squeeze up front. When the headlights swept round, they illuminated not only the mass of local men and women, whose confusion quickly turned to anger at the thought of us hauling their meat away, but also the stains of gore where Grey, Treacle, and Romans had fallen.

I shut my eyes to it, but I could not block out the baying of the horde.

As the pink lights of dawn rose that morning, illuminating the snaking dust along Chimoio's back streets and the blinking horses in the riding school yards, Pat and I stood with Jonathan, Albert, and some other workers in a small stand of gum trees on the very outskirts of town. There, in the holes we had excavated, lay the cold remains of Grey, Treacle, and Romans.

I could not bring myself to shovel the dirt in on top of them. I simply stood and watched, and knew, with a terrifying finality, that one of the last connections we had to the old world of Two Tree and Crofton was gone.

In the morning, I stirred late, my eyes heavy with sleep. Pat was already awake, hauling on his jeans on the other side of the mosquito net. When he saw that I had woken, he looked down.

"Go back to sleep."

"Where are you going?"

He stopped in the doorway. "There's something I've got to . . . Mandy," he said, "you need to rest."

Sensing that something else was wrong, I scrambled out of the mosquito net and followed him into the hall. By the time I reached him he was already out the door and climbing into the Land Rover.

"Where are you going?"

"I'll deal with it, Mandy."

Still barefoot and in my nightgown, I flung myself into the passenger seat. "*Tell* me," I insisted.

At last, Pat relented. "Better put some clothes on, Mandy. We need to take a drive."

Half an hour later, my eyes still heavy with sleep, Pat and I stood in the same stand of gum trees in which we had lain Grey, Treacle, and Romans. The ground in front of us was open, the graves empty, the only sign that our horses had ever lain here the dark earth where Grey's blood had pooled in the ground.

"They took the meat," I breathed.

"Followed us here and dug them up," Pat said, too stone-faced to betray any emotion.

"We have to get them back . . ."

Even as I said it, I knew it was too late. That meat was already gone, out into the villages or off to market.

"What good would it do Grey, anyway?" Pat said as he led me back to the car. "We failed him."

Morning's light was spilling over the riding school when we arrived. In the office, staring through the dusty window at the horses in their paddock, it struck me that I would never see Grey among them again. It seemed such a foolish thing; I had seen him sprawled on the road, I had watched them lower him into the earth, I had seen his grave spoiled and his body carried away—but it was only when looking at Lady, Deja Vu, Shere Khan, Black Magic, and the rest that his absence really sank in. I buried my head in my hands and wept, long and hard.

At that moment, one of the grooms appeared in the office doorway to beckon Pat. He was holding out a mobile phone.

"It is ringing," he said.

Silently, Pat went to take the phone.

"Is the madam all right?"

"It was the horses last night," Pat said, the phone still chiming in his hand.

"And you are upset?"

I looked up. I couldn't reply. The grooms we had hired locally could never understand what these horses meant to me. They had not seen Grey limping off Two Tree, his hoof almost hanging off; they had not been there to see the gunshot wound through Princess's withers, nor had they watched foals like Brutus escape the *jambanja*ed farms.

"I better answer this," said Pat. "It's Highveld Paprika."

He walked away, bustling the groom before him. In the office, I was left alone. Then, after drawing in my tears, I decided there was only one way to face this new day.

I went out to find Lady and lose myself in the herd.

"It's happening with tobacco," Pat said over dinner that night. "It could happen with us, too."

Nervously I poked the food around my plate. Then, deciding to get a grip on myself, I began to eat properly. I might as well eat while I had the chance.

The call had come from a very concerned director at Highveld Paprika. Rumors had reached them concerning various tobacco farmers in the Chimoio district—some of whom were the very same farmers in whom we had invested to grow paprika. According to Highveld, some of the farmers were refusing to harvest their tobacco crops, claiming that the prices they had been offered were far below market value. Rather than harvest, they planned on holding the crops as ransom to force the price up; every day they did not reap in the fields, the crops were another day closer to simply rotting in the ground.

"You know how much money we put into those farms," I began. "What if Highveld just walked away? We'd be left . . ."

It was Pat and I who had sourced the farmers, found the farms, employed agronomists and laborers, purchased tractors and harvesters and countless kilometers of irrigation pipes. Out on those farms the results of our work were clear: the bush was being driven back and beautiful, bountiful fields were appearing in its wake. Another few seasons, another few years, and Chimoio could be the heart of a new agricultural wonderland. The country was untouched; the farms could grow and spread. But, for all that to happen, it demanded good, honest, hardworking people—and an insidious thought had taken root in my gut. Perhaps, in our haste to forge a new life beyond Mugabe's control, we had been too naive.

"So what now?" I asked.

Pat shoveled in his food. At least one of us still had an appetite. "I'll go out to the farms," he said, "and see if I can get wind of what's going on. In the meantime, there's still the riding school to be thinking of . . ."

I nodded. Where had all my old Zimbabwean resolve gone? We had come through war vets and worse; whatever was happening on these paprika farms had to be a piece of cake compared to that.

That night, my thoughts were filled not only with Grey, Treacle, and Romans. If our farming investments disappeared, it would touch every single horse in the herd.

I woke in the dead of night, my heart thundering like hoofbeats, and lay awake until dawn.

Mozambique was putting us through hardships, but in return it promised us a great future. Yet all it took was one phone call from Highveld Paprika and that promise turned sour.

It wasn't long before Highveld's fears became a reality. Only a week later, Pat received a phone call from one of the farmers we had backed. He was demanding a greater price on the paprika in his fields and threatening to let it rot if we did not agree. Soon, other farmers joined the chorus, demanding prices for their paprika that we could not promise. Giving in to this blackmail was not an option we could even consider; the prices were set in stone by Highveld Paprika, and contracts had long ago been signed. Of the dozen farmers in whom we had invested, only three had subscribed to the plot—but three was enough to cripple our operation and ruin the scheme for the rest. Such were the fine lines on which farms succeeded or failed. This was a line we were all too familiar with from our earliest days on River Ranch. As our new world, once filled with such promise, began to crumble around us, Pat spent his days driving out to the traitorous paprika farms, reclaiming as much of the crop as he could. We would still be able to sell it, and every little bit would help. Meanwhile, I remained with the herd, committed more than ever to taking out rides and giving lessons, finding any way possible to eke a living out of these horses that meant so much to us. If we were to claw our way out of this chaos, the horses were our only hope—and yet, as the farming boom collapsed so spectacularly, I feared that the people too would begin to leave Chimoio. It seemed that we had rescued our horses from Mugabe's war vets only to lead them into another disaster.

At the riding school, I cupped Lady's head in my hands and prayed for better times.

A few days later, Jay appeared on the doorstep, bedraggled but rugged, with hair falling in curls around his shoulders.

"You look like you might need a wash."

"It's nice to see you too, Mum."

I welcomed him in and set about fussing as only a mother can. Once a huge breakfast was heaped on the plate, Jay set about demolishing it. If Kate and Paul had been there, the room would have been filled with banter, but Jay was as silent as ever. I propped myself against the counter and drank my tea, waiting for him to finish.

"I have something for you," Jay began. With a flourish, he produced an envelope from the backpack at his feet. He twirled it over the table.

I wandered over, opened the envelope, and lifted out a stack of Mozambican meticais.

"If this is payment, that was one expensive breakfast . . ."

"It's not for breakfast," Jay replied. "It's my pay from Gorongosa. It's for"—he shrugged, noncommittally—"you know, for the horses, for helping with the farm debts. For . . . food, water, *life*. That kind of stuff."

"Jay, we can't take . . ."

I tried to push the money back across the table, but Jay was already standing to slouch away. "You already did," he replied. "Just don't spend it all at once."

I stood in the kitchen after Jay left the room, counting the money he had given me and feeling a terrible welling in the bottom of my stomach. It should not have come to this. The money Jay had given me was all he had saved from his work in the national park. It would tide us over for a little while, but it would not make such a significant dent in our debts that we could flee Chimoio and start again somewhere else. My mind was reeling, wondering how on earth I was going to convince Jay to take his money back, when the telephone rang. Preparing myself for yet another disaster, I picked it up and cheerily said hello.

"Mandy," said Pat. "I'm at the riding school. You'd better come."

Half an hour later, Jay and I stood with Pat at a shredded fence at the riding school. In the early hours of the morning, somebody had evaded the night guard and taken off with a roll of wire.

"I don't have time for this." Pat cursed. "What's the head count?"

Jonathan stood on the edge of the paddock, with Lady on one side and Shere Khan on the other.

"We're one down."

Pat kicked a stone out through the hole in the fence. On the dirt road, it shattered.

"Who is it?" I asked.

"Tequila," Jonathan replied.

Pat opened his mouth as if to bark out another oath, but in frustration he swallowed it down. "Well," he said, "let's go find him."

Jay, Pat, and I took a truck and drove out along the same road on which Grey, Treacle, and Romans had met their fate, but there was no sign that Tequila had come this way. When, at last, we reached the spot of the accident, we pulled to the shoulder of the road and stepped out.

"Lightning doesn't strike twice," I muttered, as if trying to convince myself.

A truck appeared and rumbled past us, blaring its horn.

"It's not lightning I'm worried about," answered Pat.

My phone rang, and I answered it. On the other end of the line was Jonathan. We spoke for a moment, and then I hung up.

"He's been seen," I said, hurrying back into the truck.

"Where?"

"The other side of Chimoio. He's going west." I slid into the seat and Jay jumped in back just as Pat coaxed the engine back to life. "Pat, he's fifty kilometers out. He thinks he's going back home."

We cut around Chimoio on the back roads and joined the highway back to the border on its farthest side. On the horizon, the heights of the Bvumba sat, their crowns almost merging into the blueness of the sky. Slowly, the mountains grew bigger. Their peaks became more defined, their forested escarpments burst forth in rich color. The day's light waned.

At last, we saw Tequila. The highway was long and gun-barrel straight, and we could pick him out, a tiny dot trotting toward the mountains, long before we reached him. When we finally drew near, we could see that he was walking, head down, at the side of the road, refusing to be distracted. Afraid that we might spook him, we pulled the truck onto the verge a hundred yards behind and hurried to join him.

"Tequila," I said, approaching on his flank with enough room between us that he would not be frightened off, "where do you think you're going?"

By increments, Pat crept near. Tequila gave a shallow snort of recognition, and Pat laid a hand on his flank.

"You dumb old boy . . ."

Pat lifted a halter and rope from his shoulder. Even then, Tequila walked sedately along. If he was listening to my commands at all, he did not seem to care. Either that, or he cared about Zimbabwe—about the idea of *home*—so much more.

Pat put himself in Tequila's path and told him to stop. Tequila tried to weave one way, then another, but in the end it was a simple thing to slip the halter over him and attach a lead rope.

"Did you really think you could get over the mountains?"

His eyes lifted, locking with my own. He gave a sudden shake of the head, his mane falling down.

"Back to all that?" I went on. "Nowhere to live for more than a few months, no money, no food, never knowing if they might come knocking in the dead of night?" My voice seemed to trail off. Tequila's eyes were fixed again on the Bvumba, but mine had drifted up. Over Tequila's back, I was staring straight at Pat, and he was staring back. "You don't really want to go back *home*, do you, my boy?"

Upon hearing those words, Tequila kicked into a trot, as if he did not want to listen. Cursing, Pat hurtled after him. For a moment his trot quickened; in response, Pat slowed his gait again, until Tequila slowed down.

"Mandy!" he called back, in half a whisper. "Get Jay to fire up the truck, in case he bolts."

I turned and ran back to the truck, where Jay was resting in the baking sun. Back in the cab, he fired up the engine and we began to trundle forward. Up ahead of us, Tequila had slowed to a walk. Pat was keeping pace with him, though I could see my husband had developed a stitch in his side.

We stopped the truck again, for up ahead Pat had his arms draped around Tequila. Speaking to him softly all the while, he fitted the lead rope and gently teased the horse around. As I watched, a shiver seemed to run down the length of my spine, even despite the searing heat.

"What is it, Mum?" Jay asked.

"I was thinking . . . I don't know how I'm going to manage the herd. Not when he's gone . . ."

"What do you mean, *gone*?"

Pat and Tequila were drawing near now. For the first time, Tequila was facing away from the Bvumba, retracing the prints of his own hooves.

"I wasn't going to tell you like this," I began, "but . . . your father's leaving."

"Leaving?"

At exactly the same moment, and in exactly the same tone of voice, Tequila let out a whinny of surprise. Through the windshield, I cocked a look at him. He needn't have been so shocked; we had told the herd three days before. Obviously, he hadn't been listening. Or perhaps that was why he had turned tail and fled.

"It's no good here, Jay. We've lost too much." It was difficult to make sense of it, but I struggled to find the right words, eager that Jay should understand. According to our friends at Highveld Paprika, the farmers in whom we had invested were being advised by a shadowy business-woman who never showed her face in Mozambique and operated from a house in Harare. It was this woman who had advised the farmers to leave their tobacco in the ground and ransom a better price out of their buy-ers, and it was this woman who was advising them to do the same thing with the paprika in which we had invested.

"Highveld cut its losses. Just walked away," I explained. "As soon as the directors understood, they were gone." I saw the way Jay was look-ing. "You can't blame them, Jay. They made a bad investment. It's big business. They took it on the chin and got out."

"But you can't do the same . . ."

"We owe too much to too many people. All the equipment, all the irrigation, all the seedlings, all the agronomists and laborers we employed . . . It's all on our heads. It would have worked. The paprika would have paid for it. There could have been farms here for genera-tions. But they butchered it, looking for a quick buck . . ."

It was worse than that, but I didn't know how to find the words. When we discovered that three of the farmers were refusing to harvest, we were devastated. We hurried onto their farms, confronted them, tried to persuade them to do the honorable, honest thing. That they were holding us and our goodwill to ransom was terrible enough—but then we received a telephone call, instructing us that our paprika had been harvested in secret and was, even now, being shunted across the border at the capital city of Maputo, far to the south, for sale outside the coun-try. Somehow, the same farmers who had accepted our investment and reneged on their promises had gotten ahold of signed export licenses and other government documentation. We were being stolen from wholesale—and all with the signature of a government official.

"So Dad's leaving . . ."

"He's going to Vilanculos with some of the horses to drum up work. I'm staying to salvage what we can from this mess. I'll go after him as soon as this is over."

Vilanculos was the closest coastal town, 450 kilometers from Chimoio. It was small compared to the northerly port of Beira, tiny compared even to Chimoio, but it was the gateway to the beautiful Bazaruto archipelago, a ribbon of unspoiled islands in the glittering Indian Ocean, with golden beaches and a vast, serene bay in which people came to snorkel, dive, and sail on the local dhows. Perhaps some of the tourists those places attracted could be tempted to take a ride.

"Mum, I'll send you more money," Jay said, his face as stony as his father's.

"I know, darling . . ."

"For Kate's university fees, if nothing else."

I don't know if my heart had ever felt warmer. Jay and Kate had always been close, ever since those days in which she trotted off after him into the bush to foil his attacks on the local birdlife, but the idea that he should send his pay home to keep her in school was too beautiful for words.

"Jay, it's for the best. He's taking seven from the herd. Lady, Fleur, Jade, Black Magic, Squib . . ." I paused. "Spicegirl and Megan, too. He'll put them to work there. There has to be more trade there. More tourists." I hesitated to say it, but I added, "More hope. Chimoio's going bust. We have to get out."

"Who are you kidding, Mum? You haven't been apart all your lives . . ."

I smirked. "There was a time before your father, Jay."

"You were younger than me. *Much* younger." He stopped. "Are you going to be okay?"

"Well," I said, "it's not like I'll be *completely* alone. Jonathan will go with your father, but there'll still be Denzia, Albert, Never, and the other workers . . . And there'll still be the herd. We'll always have them."

"The *herd* . . ."

I thought I sensed vitriol in Jay's voice, as if it was the herd's fault we were in this mess.

At that moment, Pat and Tequila drew level with the truck. Tequila seemed to have given up straining back for the Bvumba now. I slipped out of the cab to greet him.

Tequila dropped his head. I took hold of the lead rope and, conceding defeat, he ambled up the ramp.

Back in the cab, Pat pulled the truck around.

"It almost seems unfair," he said, "to take him away from home like that . . ."

I thought of Mugabe, that day on Palmerston Estates, rustling the herd off Biri Farm, my mother in England, Paul still in London, Kate in South Africa, our family scattered to the four corners of the earth while, here, the new world we were trying to forge came apart at the seams.

"No," I said, "it hardly seems fair at all."

From the back of the truck came a mournful snort. I had always understood that we were here to care for the horses—but now the thought struck me that they did not understand, that to Tequila and the rest it might have seemed that we had dragged them here, that we were the ones keeping them from home. I longed for a way to tell them: we love you; we'd take you back, if only we could. But there was a gulf of language and understanding between us, and I could never tell them exactly how I felt.

At the riding school, Pat was fitting halters to Black Magic, Lady, and Jade, while Jonathan and Albert shepherded Spicegirl, Fleur, and Megan into the back of a truck. At the edge of the paddock, I stood with a reluctant-looking Squib. He was to be the only male horse accompanying Pat to the coast, but he didn't look particularly pleased about it.

"Come on, Squib, Pat's going to need another man about the place . . ."

Once Spicegirl, Megan, and Fleur were safely inside, Pat led Lady out. We stood together, in front of the truck, and I put my arms around the dainty, precious little mare.

"You look after each other," I said.

Lady flicked her mane. Whether she was telling me no, yes, or simply not to be so melodramatic, I couldn't tell. I watched her disappear up the ramp, into the darkness beyond. Jonathan slipped in afterward to help tether her and make sure she was secure.

The last to board the truck was Black Magic. Once she was safely within, Pat and Jonathan lifted and secured the ramp. The last thing I saw was Black Magic's darkly glimmering eyes looking back.

Pat heaved a backpack into the cab of the truck. After the numerous times we had packed up our houses and fled, it seemed surreal to think it had boiled down to this: seven horses and a single pack, like some pioneer of old.

"Hard to think she was one of the nastiest little horses when we found her . . ." I said, still looking at Black Magic peering out of the back of the truck.

"What are you talking about?" Pat grinned. "It's the nastiest horses that are the best. She's got *fire*, that old girl . . ."

Jonathan had already climbed into the passenger seat of the truck, and now Pat swung up beside him, taking the wheel.

"So," he said, cocking his head.

"So," I replied, looking up.

The engine fired, and the horses shifted up back, as if readying themselves for the trip. They must have been used to riding in trucks by now.

"You'll call me when you get there?"

Pat shook his head. "I'll be calling you on the way, every half an hour," he said. "You'll be sick of the sound of my voice." He paused. The door closed between us and, for a second, it was as if Pat was already gone. "You'll let me know how it goes here. If I have to, Mandy, I'll be back on the road . . ."

"It's four hundred and fifty kilometers from Chimoio . . ."

Pat shrugged. "It's a straight highway."

I stood watching until the truck had disappeared. Then, breathing in sand and stinging dust, I turned back to the riding school. In the paddock, Shere Khan stood out from the herd, a full hand taller than the horses crowding her on either side. She seemed to have craned her neck to watch Pat leave.

"You'll have to put up with me now, Shere Khan . . ."

I wandered across the yard and propped myself at the fence. In the field, Brutus and Tequila stopped grazing to wander over. From between them, Princess approached. As I ran my hand along her neck, she suddenly cringed away, her withers still tingling with sensitivity where her wound had healed. I was reminded, starkly, of the ringworm eating its way through the herd; Fanta standing bald in her stable stall, rasping desperately in the heat; Philippe with his rotted eye; and all the other ticks and parasites, so alien to Zimbabwe, that had taken to our horses.

Somehow, I was going to have to get them through it, while at the same time juggling our debts and navigating a route to the other side. A route, I was determined, that would one day take us all along the same road on which I had just watched Pat depart: to Vilanculos, and the Indian Ocean.

There was much to do, but for now it would have to wait. I would have my hour of peace before I walked willingly into the chaos. I called for Albert to help with a saddle and girth and stepped into the paddock to rope Benji, one of my favorite horses and one of the stars of the riding school, who always cheered me up when I felt down.

I hoisted myself into the saddle and Benji carried me out of the paddock, across the riding school, and onto the road along which Pat had traveled. We would follow him, if only for a little while, out to the town limits and the bush beyond. And one day, we would all follow this road—every last one of us—and never look back.

I was sick of new starts. We had had too many.

"This time," I said, hand entangled in Benji's mane, "this time will be our last."

Chapter 13

THE HEAT OF CHIMOIO was vicious. Dust clouded the road. A stray dog stopped to consider me from a mound of grass on the far side of the street. I was on my way back to the stables, and my heart was heavier than it had been since the moment Pat left. In my hands, I held a contract I had just signed with one of the town's moneylenders. With nowhere left to turn, I had drawn on him to repay some of the outstanding farming debts. Now that there was a figure to put to our desperation, I felt both depressed and elated: depressed because I could guess how long it might take me to claw back enough money through the horses to repay the debts and go to join Pat; elated because, in Africa, elation in the face of utter madness is sometimes the only way of getting out of bed in the morning.

By the time I had reached the riding school, the dust caked the side of my face. In the ring, Aruba was tacked up and ready for riding. Beyond him, Vaquero was having his feet inspected by one of the grooms. He seemed to be looking around mischievously, waiting for the moment to kick out or slink away. I made a mental note; we would have to watch out for that tricky brute.

Albert appeared at my side. "Is everything okay, madam?"

I nodded. "I hope so."

"And Mr. Pat?"

"Good, I hope."

It had been only a week since Pat left for Vilanculos, but it might as well have been an age. Those kilometers were the whole world. His voice sounded tinny in my ear whenever he called, and I could not stop myself dwelling on how long it would be before I could follow. By my best guess, it would take me almost a year.

On the first day Pat had arrived in Vilanculos, he had staked the horses in a roped-off ring of grassland by one of the lodges overlooking the coast and woken up the next morning, not knowing where to go or whether any work would come his way. He felt a strange mix of relief and trepidation, then, to learn that a group of three travelers staying at the lodge had seen the horses and wondered whether they might go for a ride. In Black Magic's saddle, with Jade, Squib, and Lady following behind, Pat had taken the travelers along the beach. Not knowing any trails, he had followed his nose, rising up sheer sandstone escarpments, blazing a trail where it seemed men had not gone since the coming of the first Arab traders so many centuries before. What he found sounded more beautiful than I could imagine, stuck here in dry, dusty Chimoio: the azure waters of the sweeping bay, the islands of the Bazaruto archipelago hanging on the horizon, everything between them just sea and golden sand. When he called me that night, he was buoyant; perhaps there was a future in Vilanculos after all. Yet I went to sleep alone in Chimoio at night and woke alone in Chimoio in the morning.

"What have we got today, Albert?"

"Lessons this afternoon."

I nodded sharply. I would have to get the horses ready; selling rides and lessons was the only way I could raise enough money to make it to Vilanculos myself. Shaking those dark thoughts away, I stepped into the ring and approached Shere Khan. She considered me with mild reproach, perhaps even blaming me for sending Pat away, before she dropped her head and deigned to nibble at my hands.

"We're in this together, Shere Khan. The sooner we can pay this off,

the quicker we can get to Vilanculos. The quicker we can get to Pat . . ."
Shere Khan looked up, her eyes alive with dark knowing.

In the morning I woke early, long before break of day. My bedsheets were tangled around me, and somehow I had even kicked my mosquito net free. I lay there, thinking of Pat, so far away.

The next thing I knew, slivers of daylight had worked their way into my room. It was time to get up, but I buried my head in the pillow, silently pleading for some kind of sedation. What snapped me from my wallowing was the ringing of my mobile phone. Thinking it might be Pat, I scrambled out of the strangling sheets and snatched up the phone.

"Miss Mandy?"

Not Pat, then.

"Denzia?" I asked. "What's wrong?"

"Miss Mandy, you must come quick. It is horrible."

"What's happened?"

"It is better if you just come. Meet me at the paddocks?"

Remembering how the crowd had bayed for Grey's meat, I scrambled into some clothes and hurried off into the still Chimoio dawn. At the riding school paddocks, Albert and Jonathan were already up, mucking out the stalls and inspecting the horses. Denzia was waiting at the gates, her arms wheeling like a mad old buzzard.

"It is the Veterinary Department," she exclaimed. "Miss Mandy, they have found horse meat at market."

"Horse meat?"

"They are quite sure. They called me themselves."

An image of Grey and Treacle lying in the road while the locals swarmed around them like flies hit me. Mozambique was not a hungry country like so many others in Africa, but sometimes a free steak was still a free steak.

"Come on, Denzia, let's find out who . . ."

We hurried around the paddock, saying hello to Nzeve's young brother Echo, along with Brutus, Vaquero, Pink Daiquiri, and the others, but a quick head count convinced me that nobody had rustled a horse away from the riding school in the dead of night.

"What about Zimofa?"

Even as I said it, it barely seemed credible. Zimofa Farm was thirty-five kilometers away. It seemed madness to think of a man rustling a horse and riding her all that way to market.

"Denzia," I said, "I can't deal with this . . ."

"They have the woman in custody."

"The woman?"

"From the market."

"They arrested her . . ."

"Miss Mandy, we have to identify her."

The sun was climbing, spilling golden light over the riding school. There would be lessons today. Rides. A way to keep limping on until I could get back to Pat.

"You go, Denzia," I said. "Do whatever they ask, and get back here fast."

When I got home to ready myself for the day ahead, the bed seemed too inviting, and I crawled back under the covers. Fastening my mosquito net tight, I promised myself I would just lie down for a few minutes. Half an hour later, I still wasn't asleep, but there was something comforting in burying my head in the pillow and pretending that the day didn't exist.

Then, as was its wont, the phone rang again, and I had to face reality.

"Miss Mandy, it was Timot."

I barely acknowledged the name. "Timot?"

"It was his wife in the market," said Denzia. "She has confessed. It was Timot who took the horse."

I sat bolt upright. "Wait a minute . . . *Timot*?"

There had been a local man named Timot who had worked for us until just before Pat left for Vilanculos. Against all the odds, we had found in Timot a man with substantial knowledge of horses, and we had been sad to see him go. I still saw him around Chimoio sometimes, in the company of an Indian man named Aslam who was now his employer.

"But *why?*" I asked.

"He went out to Zimofa, cut the fence, and led a horse back to Chimoio. It was his wife chopped her up for market."

Perhaps I was only just waking up, for suddenly the horror sank in. I pictured this horse, whoever it was, blindly following a man she knew out of her paddock, only to make a long ride through pitch darkness to meet her slaughterer's blade.

"Do we know who?" I whispered.

"Miss Mandy, the commandant here at the station, he wants to see the meat."

I kicked out of the mosquito net, abandoning all my hopes of snatching another hour's sleep. "The *meat?*"

"He must *inspect* it."

Denzia had put so much emphasis on the word that implicitly I understood what she meant. The commandant wanted nothing other than to take the meat for himself.

"Where's the meat right now?"

"In market. We must get it to the commandant . . ."

On the wall, the clock began to chime. The hours seemed to be whirling by. In only an hour, I would have to be back at the riding school to take out a group, young tourists who were staying at one of the lodges on the edge of town.

"Phone for the abattoir, Denzia. They'll have a truck. They can take it from the market to the commandant . . ."

"Miss Mandy, there is one more thing . . ."

In spite of myself, I snapped back, "What is it, Denzia?"

"The commandant, he is hopelessly drunk."

"Of course he is. It's Mozambique." I stopped. "Denzia, do what you have to do and get out of there."

After I had put the phone down, I took a few moments to splash some water over my face. I looked at myself in the mirror. It was, I decided, not a very pretty picture. Then, on the way out of the door, I dialed Pat's number.

"Mandy?"

"Pat . . ."

"Is something wrong?"

"Oh, you know," I said, nonchalantly, "just *everything*. How about you?"

"I'm going on a ride."

"Me too." I hurried down the Chimoio thoroughfare, in the direction of the riding school. "Pat, something happened out on Zimofa. Timot came back and cut the wire and . . ." My voice trailed off and I noticed that there was only static coming from the other end of the line. "Pat, are you there?"

"Mandy," came Pat's broken voice, "I'll have to call you back. The guests are here . . ."

When I got to the riding school, Albert and Never had brought out the horses for our ride. Brutus and Mushy were already saddled, while Viper, Texas, Gambler, and Philippe were being prepared. Philippe glared at me accusingly with his one remaining eye, as if insulted that he should still have to work to pay his way. There was still a half hour until the riders would arrive, so I took the opportunity to look in on Princess.

I was there, stroking Princess's muzzle and telling her how I longed to one day get in her saddle, when my phone rang again. For a second I just let it ring. Only when Princess rolled her eyes at me did I pick it up.

"Yes?" I snapped.

"Miss Mandy, they've impounded the truck . . ."

I swirled around, passing the phone from hand to hand. "Denzia, what do you—"

"It is the commandant. As soon as the truck came with the meat, he decided he had to impound it, because it holds the evidence. They are *accusing* us . . ."

"Accusing you of what?"

"Aiding the slaughter . . ."

"But it's *my* horse!"

"Miss Mandy, the commandant, he is *very* drunk . . ."

"Get out of there, Denzia. Just get back here fast." I was about to go on when Albert appeared at my shoulder. Whirling around, I could see our riders for the day lingering at the edge of the paddock, cooing over Brutus, their hands full of horse cubes to palm into his mouth. He looked so startled to see them that their hearts must have gone out to him. If only they knew what a mischievous sort he was under the saddle. I nodded firmly at Albert and turned back to my phone call. "Denzia, the riders are here. Just tell them no. Drive out of there if you have to. Drive through them . . ."

I hung up, straightened myself, and looked Princess square in the eyes. "Sometimes," I said, "I think a bullet through the neck might be preferable to all this." Princess gave me a withering gaze, as if she did not appreciate the joke. "Just a few more months, a few more rides, and we can get out of here for good. How does that sound?" She blew through her nostrils disparagingly, and I turned on my heel to leave.

I met the riders at Brutus's side. There were four of them, two married couples, and they seemed raring to go.

"So sorry to keep you waiting. Beautiful morning for a ride, isn't it?"

Well, it *was* a beautiful morning, if what you wanted was searing heat and choking dust, and horses who would much rather be dipping their heads into a trough in some cool stable. I put my hand on Brutus's flank, begging him to be good.

"Can everyone ride?"

There are people who can really ride, and then there are people who *say* they can ride, and then there are those honest enough to admit that having gone on a few pleasure rides in some seaside resort does not really constitute *riding*. To my relief, the four tourists I would be riding with today belonged firmly in the last camp. I decided I would introduce them to the horses one by one and share a little of their history.

"This young troublemaker's name is Brutus. I'll be riding him today." I looked over the tourists, my eyes settling on the biggest one, a six-foot-tall Englishman with short-cropped red hair and skin that clearly did not like our African sun. "You'll be on Gambler. Treat her properly—she's very sensitive . . ."

I was about to show Philippe to one of the girls, relating the story of his mysteriously missing eye, when I heard the roar of an engine and, in a ball of churning smoke and dust, a van came spluttering into the riding school.

I turned to face it and saw the markings of the local abattoir up and down the van's sides. Denzia was hanging out of the window, gesticulating wildly. I took tight hold of Philippe's reins and watched as the van slewed first left, then right, skidding around just on the other side of a fence.

As the van stopped dead, the back doors flew open. Three big black bags exploded out of the doors and landed in a heap in the sand, spilling their contents.

With horror, I looked down to see meat piled high.

Denzia leaped out to snatch up the bags, but she was too slow. The first toppled to its side and, out of its black opening, something rolled.

Handing Philippe's reins to Albert, I crossed the dusty expanse and looked at where the bags lay. Among them, her glassy eyes staring up as if in petition, was the head of a mare I had known for so long.

What was left of Deja Vu stared back at me.

I bent down and took her head by the strands of mane that still cascaded down. As I brought it level with my own face to gaze into her black, lifeless eyes, I could see the four riders ranged around me. Their faces were masks of terror, but they were nothing compared to the expression I could see, stained forever across Deja Vu's death mask. Shreds of her spinal column dangled from her neck. I found it difficult to imagine that this had been the very same foal born on Crofton, the very same foal whose leg had been entangled in wire outside our home, who Pat refused to put down, who Kate loved and nursed until, scarred but not defeated, she could run and ride once again.

"I'm sorry," I whispered.

In that moment, I hated Mozambique. I hated the sun and sweltering heat, the disease, the laws in which we had become entangled, the farmers who had robbed us blind. We had come so far, brought so many with us, but one by one they were falling by the wayside. First Grey—and now Deja Vu.

Albert was at my side. Softly, I handed him Deja Vu's head.

"I think you must come to Zimofa. It really won't wait."

I was, I thought as I looked into the mirror with a toothbrush dangling out of the side of my mouth, getting far too used to this kind of phone call. This time the summons was coming from one of the local grooms we had employed to look over the half of the herd out on Zimofa Farm.

"Is it really so urgent? There are riders coming this afternoon . . ."

"I think you must come straightaway."

I checked the time. Forfeiting any business at the riding school was out of the question; it was only the money that came from taking tourists on rides that kept the moneylender from my door. If I was going to go out to Zimofa, it would have to be now.

I hung up and called for Denzia.

"Saddle up," I said.

"Miss Mandy?"

"The Land Rover," I said, scurrying across the front room. "I meant the Land Rover . . ."

We made the thirty-five-kilometer trip to Zimofa at speed, as the roads were empty and had been ever since the farmers abandoned this corner of the world. In the fields outside the farm, the horses milled. Wild little Rebel weaved his way to the fence to greet me as I stepped out of the Land Rover, but I could not stay and fuss over him for long. Our groom was standing at the end of the track, beckoning me with a wild whirl of arms.

Denzia and I hurried over.

"I don't have time for this."

"You must make time. It is urgent. The horses, they have . . ."

I threw a look back in the field. Forty faces contentedly turned grass in their lips. "Have what?"

"It is one of the neighbors. You must meet him."

The groom turned and scuttled in the direction of Zimofa farm-house. Once a palatial building with white colonnades, it now lay in ruins, but there was a mango tree still standing proudly in front, spilling shade across the garden. The tree's boughs were heavy with fruit, and, for an instant, I was drawn back to Crofton. I pictured Kate dangling like a monkey from the uppermost branches, spying on Jay as he set out into the bush to hunt some helpless bird.

There were two figures standing underneath the mango tree, a white man and his local Mozambican wife. The groom hurried over, still beckoning me with his hand. Denzia and I stepped into the shade, and I saw the deep scowl set into the white man's face.

When the white man opened his mouth to speak, Portuguese flew out. I could understand only one word in ten, and he spoke so quickly that even those seemed to blur into the rest. I threw a pained expression at our groom.

"He is very angry," the groom explained.

"I can see he is angry—but what's he angry about?"

"The horses."

Around me, the Portuguese grew louder and seemingly more fierce. Spittle showered down.

"I rather gathered that as well. Do you care to explain?"

At that precise moment, the Mozambican lady at the Portuguese man's side cut in. Her accent was thick, but her English was evidently better than her husband's. As soon as she opened her lips, her husband's voice faded away. I wondered who really ran that household.

"Your *animals* have eaten our field."

"Eaten your . . ."

"Twenty hectares of soybeans I have planted, and now all gone! All because of your big dogs . . ."

Twenty hectares of land was a vast area to graze unnoticed. I threw a look back and could still see the diminutive outlines of the herd in their field.

"I'm sorry," I said, "you'll have to explain . . ."

"It is very simple. Your 'horses' broke through their fence and onto our land. They ate our soybeans, and now you must pay."

I shared a sidelong look with Denzia.

"I think," I said, "I'd better see these soybeans first."

The lady and her Portuguese husband shared a sudden look. A conversation erupted in a language I did not understand, then quickly trailed off. The lady looked back to me with fiery eyes.

"There is nothing to see. The soybeans are gone."

"Presumably," I began, "the field is still there?"

There was another explosion of vitriolic conversation. For a second the man seemed to be losing his temper, but the glare of his wife quickly cowed him.

"The field is still there."

"Then let's go."

The farm belonging to the Portuguese man and his draconic wife was on the eastern edge of Zimofa, just a little farther away from Chimoio. We climbed into the Land Rover and followed their truck along the dirt road. As we did so, we cut a circle around the fields where the horses were grazing. I kept a cursory eye out for some hole in the fence where the herd might have slipped through but, as I suspected, there was nothing.

"We're being fleeced."

Denzia looked at me, puzzled—while in back, the face of the groom who had summoned us here burst open with a big smile. "Yes!" he cried. "Madam, they are very cross."

At last, the vehicle in front of us slowed down and stopped, and I climbed out of the Land Rover. We were only a few acres distant from the paddocks on Zimofa, and the fields across which we looked were barren. I kicked my heels along the bank of the dirt road, glowering at the field. As far as I could tell, no crop had been planted here all season. The earth was turned and looked to have been plowed, but the only vegetation breaking through the surface was sprouts of scrub and buds of tough grass.

"Well?" the lady demanded.

"I think I've seen enough."

I had turned to climb back into the Land Rover, glad to be rid of these thieves and get on with my day, when I felt the woman's hand landing on my shoulder.

"What are you going to do about it?"

Shaking her off, I climbed into the driver's seat, motioning for Denzia and the groom to jump back in.

"Good God, woman!" I laughed. "There hasn't been a single soybean here all year! You're surely not trying to say the horses ate up every last scrap, right down to the roots?"

The woman was fuming, her nostrils wide. I kept my eyes fixed on her as I turned the Land Rover around and motored back up the road.

In the rearview mirror, the woman was engulfed in a cloud of red dust. Then, like some malevolent spirit, she simply disappeared.

At the riding school I was helping Albert and Never dip the horses, spraying them with solution to keep away ticks and lathering it up in their manes and the thick hair around their hooves, when Denzia rushed over.

"It isn't finished, madam."

I dragged the back of my hand across my brow, careful not to end up with the solution in my eyes.

"Miss Mandy, they're *here* . . ."

Sure enough, as I walked out of the stables the Portuguese man was waiting for me at the gates with a local Mozambican man I had not seen before at his side.

"I thought we'd had this discussion," I said, fully aware that the man would not understand.

The Mozambican man at his side translated, listened to the reply, and turned back to me.

"Maybe we should sit down."

In the corner of the riding school, a skeletal tree provided some shade. Denzia brought us chairs and we sat there, with the hot Chimoio wind sending up flurries of dust.

As the Portuguese man chattered on, the Mozambican translated.

"My friend here owns a business in town. Perhaps you know

him? He is a trader. His wife grows some crops on their land. A little wheat, some soybeans, the things a family needs to keep it alive." The Portuguese man began to chatter again, and the Mozambican duly listened. "He is, I'm afraid, quite adamant that something must be done. His wife planted twenty hectares of soybeans, which your horses have destroyed. These are not wealthy people. You must be fair . . ."

"Fair?" I exclaimed, outraged. "There wasn't a single soybean in that field, and he knows it!"

"You must be reasonable. This man's wife is an honorable lady. If she says she planted soybeans, she must have planted soybeans."

Inwardly, I fumed. I fancied I could even see smiles dancing on the corners of their lips as the pieces of their sting fell into place.

"What do you want from me?" I breathed.

The Portuguese man chattered.

"Payment," the Mozambican translated. "We want what is fair."

My mind darted back and forth, but I could see no way out. In Mozambique at that time, there was very little law and order as we know it, and we were at the mercy of the authorities. In the case of a local having her crop eaten, we would be held responsible and have to pay. There was no one who could arbitrate on our behalf, and sympathy from the authorities would lie with the Mozambican.

"You don't understand. I don't have money. I don't have anything to pay you, not if my horses had eaten all the soybeans in the world . . . I'm drowning in debt. Even if I had to pay you, I *couldn't*."

"There is one thing that you have."

The Mozambican man opened his arms, directing his gaze over my shoulder at where Brutus and Shere Khan, freshly dipped, nosed at bundles of dried grass.

"Your horses," he said. "If you cannot pay in the proper fashion, perhaps we should set a price in *horses*." The Mozambican man engaged in a rapid burst with his Portuguese friend. Smirking, he looked back. "I think we would set the price at two of your horses, in return for all twenty hectares of crop. We think that would be, as you say it, *fair*."

In silence, I stood. I nodded firmly at the two men and turned from them, just in time so that I did not betray myself with tears. I marched back into the stables where Albert and Never continued to dip the horses.

"What is it, madam?"

"Albert, I would like you to bring me . . ." My mind reeled. Of the horses who survived, there was not a single one I wanted to get rid of. There were too many memories circling each and every one of them. And yet . . .

I looked around me. Brutus eyed me back, with his permanently worried expression. He need not have worried; there was no way I could ever part with him. My eyes drifted on, to regal Shere Khan, and I pictured Pat's face purpling with rage when I told him she was gone. Then, onward I looked: Echo and Tequila, Slash with the white lightning across his brow, Philippe with his one sad eye.

"Which are the worst for riding?" I asked.

"Madam?"

"The horses we can't work with." I hated myself for saying the words; these were the horses that needed us most. But I could not part with Brutus, with Shere Khan, with Duchess or Duke, not the horses who might help me drag myself out of this financial mess so that we could finally go and join Pat. "Bring me Pink Daiquiri," I said, remembering her sunken back. "And"—my voice faltered—"Vaquero, too."

Thinking that Princess might calm me, I stopped in at her stall and steeled myself while Albert and Caetano set about the grim business. With one hand in my pocket, I fingered my phone, wondering how I could ever break this news to Pat.

When enough time had elapsed, I collected myself, put on my plainest poker face and left Princess behind. On the other side of the riding school, I could see the gangly, ill-shapen Vaquero standing in the pen, with Pink Daiquiri standing behind him, oblivious to the true intentions of the two men ogling them from the fence.

In short, sharp strides I marched across the yard and came between them.

"We'll take . . . *that* one," the Mozambican said, a fat finger thrust in Pink Daiquiri's direction. "And *that* one . . ."

His finger seemed to thrust in Pink Daiquiri's direction again, as if sparing Vaquero some hammer blow. Too late, I realized what was wrong. For Vaquero and Pink Daiquiri were not the only horses in the pen. Huddled close to Pink Daiquiri was her beautiful foal, Ramazotti. He seemed to be clinging to his mother's side.

I flashed a look sideways, searching for Albert, desperate to know how Ramazotti had found his way into the pen as well.

"There's been a mistake," I began, floundering for the words. "Ramazotti must have followed his mother. I didn't mean for . . ."

The Mozambican man rounded on me, his Portuguese keeper looming at his shoulder.

"No mistake," he announced. "We take *these* two."

I looked at them, speechless.

"We'll get our truck ready."

They had only taken two steps when I stopped them. "A truck?"

"How else did you think we would take the horses?"

"When you came here," I began, "you didn't come for horses . . ."

The Mozambican man muttered something in Portuguese and, together, the two men smiled. "It always pays to be prepared."

Pink Daiquiri and Ramazotti had no idea what was going on as they were roped up and led across the riding school into the darkness of a truck waiting by the side of the road. They did not look back, nor question who was taking them away to some unknown end. I supposed they trusted that they would be looked after, just the same as Pat and I had been looking after them for all this time.

As they drove away, the Portuguese man nodded to me from the cab of the truck. It was a look that sent shivers down my spine.

Vaquero's head appeared, snuffling in my armpit. I turned to see his strange, misshapen face, his protruding teeth and wandering eye. Putting a hand on his muzzle, I stroked him softly.

"I'm sorry," I whispered.

Vaquero looked up, his eye rolling. *You can't get rid of me that easily*, he seemed to be saying. *You're stuck with me for life.*

. . . .

It was some days before I could summon up the courage to tell Pat what had become of Pink Daiquiri and her beautiful foal. As I spoke to him, daylight paling into dusk, I could feel his anger reverberating down the phone. I held the phone away from my ear until he had calmed down, and I spent the rest of the night talking him down from returning to wreak his revenge. Pink Daiquiri and Ramazotti were lost to us, I said, along with Grey and Deja Vu—but the herd still needed us, and we still needed the herd.

"What's happening out there, Pat?"

Still evidently disgruntled, Pat switched the phone from ear to ear.

"I haven't had a ride in a few days, Mandy. The tourists are checking out. Most of the locals, too."

"Has something happened?"

"Not yet," Pat muttered, darkly. "Mandy, I'll have to call you back. We're taking the horses somewhere safe."

"Safe?"

"Well, as safe as can be. We don't know when it's going to strike . . ."

Now I was lost. Sensing something, I stood and wandered to the end of the long, empty corridor. My footsteps resounded all along the passageway, but they were only one of a hundred different signifiers that I was alone. Outside, a wind was whipping up the Chimoio backstreets. The trees at the fringe of the garden, behind the security gates, surged from left to right, and beneath them, the night guard hunched his shoulders. In the garden, just along the wall, Echo was tethered to one of the trees. I had brought him here several nights before, the grooms having found him stricken with a fever none of us could explain. None of the equine medicines that Pat had left me had worked until, fearing he was slipping away, I had forced him to drink a handful of dissolvable aspirin tablets that I kept on hand in case I ever got a migraine. Miraculously, in the morning, Echo seemed to have come out of his delirium, and now he was eagerly anticipating being returned to the herd.

"What's happening out there, Pat?"

"Mandy, haven't you seen the news? There's a cyclone out over the ocean." He paused, ominously. "It's heading right this way."

"Pat . . ."

Its name, Pat told me, was Cyclone Favio. It had formed in the western Indian Ocean, more than twelve hundred kilometers beyond Madagascar, and over the past days it had been moving southwest, missing the Reunion and Mauritius Islands by sheer good fortune. Tonight, it was entering the warmer waters of the Mozambique Channel, that part of the Indian Ocean between the coast of Mozambique and the vast island of Madagascar. Soon, forecasters predicted, it would bring its fury to the shore, tracking inland across Mozambique, into Zimbabwe, and beyond.

"Mandy, I've got to go. I don't want to take any chances with Lady and the rest."

Pat hung up and I stood alone in the empty house. The wind coasting through Chimoio seemed suddenly to be the harbinger of something much worse, the first tendrils of a storm massing some thousand kilometers away. I went to the door. A gust of wind whipped the dust into a miniature maelstrom in the garden.

We were in the path of the storm, but soon Vilanculos would be in its eye.

Chapter 14

IN VILANCULOS, the sky churned.

The guesthouse at which Pat and Jonathan sought shelter, deeming their own home too exposed, sat high upon the clifftops, overlooking the frenzied ocean. Gone were the perfect vistas of azure and gold; now, the sea beneath them roiled as the winds tore in from the ocean.

Inside, the guesthouse was empty, a cavernous hall where tables had once been laid for dinner, with a bar—now barren of all bottles—against one side and chairs stacked against the other. Outside, Pat and Jonathan cringed into the stirring gale as they brought all seven horses into view of the windows. The wind, already whipping branches and leaves overhead, was funneled away from the scrubby guesthouse yard—at least here there was some kind of shelter. The horses had all been fitted with halters, and Pat and Jonathan tied them, one after another, to the overhead picket, which ran the length of the restaurant.

Lady was the last to be tethered down. Putting his arms around her once more, Pat promised he would not be far, and he turned to follow Jonathan back into the guesthouse.

At the bar, the guesthouse owner, a blue-eyed Swiss man named Peter with a delightful grin, offered Pat a drink. If ever there was a time for Dutch courage, it was now, and gratefully they each slugged one back.

The wind moaned. Pat looked up. The guesthouse was capped with a timber A-frame onto which thatching had been tied, but already the thatch was lifting away, revealing slivers of shifting sky.

"How long do you think it will last?" Pat asked.

At the bar, Peter lifted his shoulders in dramatic jest. "You are not going anywhere today, my friend . . ."

Pat and Jonathan prowled the room, taking up a station, finally, at one of the shuttered windows. By prying the wooden slats open with his forefinger and thumb, Pat was able to keep a good eye on the horses roped outside. Black Magic strained furiously at her tether, and all of the horses kept shifting around, as if to attune themselves better to the wind. Perhaps the noise was fitful in their ears, for they did not seem to know from which direction the wind was coming. Pat drew the shutters open a little farther, daring to risk a glance into the sky. A great tuft of thatch arced overhead and he realized, for the first time, that the roof was being torn away.

He watched the thatch sail over, twisting in the current.

He looked, starkly, at Jonathan.

"It's coming the wrong way . . ."

"Pat?"

"The wind! They said it would come from over the ocean, but"—his eyes snapped back toward the horses—"it's coming from over the land . . ."

Jonathan's face was blank. Then, an instant later, he understood. "The horses . . ."

"We tethered them the wrong way," Pat breathed. "They'll take the cyclone full in the face . . ."

Pat stood and scrambled across the vast hall. Before he had gone halfway, there came a sudden splintering of wood, and he looked up to see the timber and thatch of the roof lifting away. For an instant it hovered there, as if suspended by some unseen hand. Then, the wind rampaged in. Trapped inside, the wind raged, spiraling upward, driving the thatch before it. One second the roof was there; the next, it was sailing away, revolving almost gracefully as it was borne up by the storm.

Exposed to the churning skies, Pat crouched away and made for the door.

"You can't go out there!" Peter cried—but Pat was already gone, Jonathan close behind, out into the storm.

In Chimoio, the wind gusted through the riding school. I stood with Albert and Denzia, watching the skies. At the edge of the paddock, Shere Khan stood tall, as if daring the storm to descend. One after another, the horses were being moved up to the stable stalls for shelter. I reached for my phone and dialed Pat's number.

The phone rang. I clutched it to my ear, but all I could hear was the ringing at the other end. Silence clicked in—only for the ringing to start again, broken, interrupted by whatever was happening up there in the sky.

With the phone pressed to one ear and my hand clamped around the other, I retreated inside the murky office. Slumped in a chair, I listened to the wind. The phone just rang, on and on.

Pat and Jonathan stepped into the gale. Doubled over so that it would not drive them back, they ran, bowlegged, to where Lady, Black Magic, Fleur, and the others were tethered. One after another, they unwound the lead ropes.

"Where?" Jonathan cried.

Pat looked around, holding Lady tight. He opened his mouth, but at that moment, the wind rolled through with the power of a breaking wave, robbing him of all breath.

Jonathan began to tug Black Magic across the scrub, closer to the guesthouse walls, as if he might tether her there. Pat clawed out, snatching at his arm.

"Cut them loose!"

"What!?"

"Let them loose . . ." Pat's eyes drifted upward. From somewhere, a tree had been torn up. It seemed to sail over them, eerily slow as the winds held it aloft. "What if we tied them in the path of . . ." Pat's hands slackened around Lady's lead rope. Then, he let it go. He stood, the wind pounding at him, and moved into the shelter of Lady's flank. There, he looked her in the eye. "Let Black Magic loose, Jonathan," Pat said. "Let them all loose. We can't stay out here long."

With all seven horses untied, Pat and Jonathan turned and, somehow, pushed back into the guesthouse. Exhausted, their skin prickling from head to foot, they retreated to their wall and slumped down to the cold stone.

Now, there was nothing to do but wait.

In Chimoio, I decided to try again. I dialed Pat's number and waited for the connection. One ring; then, a second. A third ring; then, a fourth. On the fifth, I was about to hang up, when—as if by black magic—Pat's mumbled hello reached my ears.

"Pat, are you there?"

I could hear what sounded like an engine growling in the background, but it was really the groan of wind in the speaker. Pat's voice, eerily calm, undercut the current.

"Mandy, what's it like where you are?"

I grinned. "Nothing compared to—"

I heard Pat mutter some curse. There was the sound of scrabbling, and then an almighty crunch, as of stone grinding against stone. A hundred thoughts charged, frenzied, through my mind.

"Pat?"

"It's okay, Mandy. It's the walls . . . The wind took the roof straightaway, but now . . ." He paused, shifting around. "It's taking the walls, too. They're . . . lifting."

As he described it to me, I tried to stay resolute. He said every time the wind roared up around the guesthouse, it strained at the walls. A deep fissure had appeared, running all the way around the hall, and soon that fissure began to deepen. Now, every time the wind came, the top half of the wall lifted, first by an inch, then by two, only to crash down again when the storm momentarily abated. Whenever it crashed down, dust exploded from the fissure, showering the spot where Pat and Jonathan crouched.

It had been two hours, and the storm was only just beginning to flex its muscles.

"We had to cut the horses loose," Pat said, in between gusts of wind. "They're out there now. I can see them through the crack in the wall . . ."

Every time the wall lifted, Pat squinted out. What he could see was nothing less than a miracle. Some ancient instinct, bred into our horses but dormant for countless generations, was holding them from panic. They seemed to have formed into a V, like a flock of flying geese, with Black Magic at its head, her rear end pointed into the wind. Somehow, the shape sliced through the wind, spreading it around them like the head of an icebreaker cutting through deep floes.

"Are they okay?"

"For now," Pat said, through gritted teeth. "They're switching it round every few minutes. Black Magic's shuffling into the V and Lady's taking her place . . ."

Four hundred fifty kilometers away, I marveled at it. These horses had never lived through a cyclone before, or any storm that came close to what they were going through now; this was ancient knowledge, bred into them by their forebears. That they could summon it up generations later was a mystery as wild and unbelievable as what was happening in the skies.

I heard the crash again as the wall around Pat smashed down. Then, there was perfect silence. "Pat?" I asked. "Pat?" I brought the phone from my ear. It was dead in my hands.

I dialed again, but this time there was no ringing, just a message in a language I did not understand, no doubt telling me that no connection could be made. I kneaded my hands in silent entreaty. Whatever was happening out there, I could only pray that Pat had the same fortitude as Black Magic, Lady, Fleur, Jade, Megan, Spicegirl, and Squib.

. . . .

"They're gone," Pat breathed.

"Gone?"

He turned to Jonathan. "They must have spooked . . ."

This time, when the wall lifted and the wind clawed in through the gaping crack, Black Magic, Lady, and the rest were nowhere to be seen. The yard outside the guesthouse, now bare in great patches where the wind had torn the scrub away, was empty of life. Pat crouched at the crack, glaring out. Then, with an enormous groan, the wall smashed back down. He reeled back.

"Come on . . ."

He took off, flailing his way across the cavernous hall, ignoring the cries of Peter, who was still propped up at the bar. The doors to the guesthouse were bolted, but the second Pat lifted the latch, the wind took them and opened the guesthouse to the swirling vortex outside. Suddenly, the wind was pounding at Pat's chest, curling around to propel him forward, tendrils seeming to snake around his legs.

Jonathan appeared at his side.

Pat took a step outside, clinging to the open door. When he let go, the wind thrust him forward. He braced himself, skidding across sand and scrub. When he lifted a foot, the wind closed its fist around him. He tried to take a step, but the step became a stride, and the stride became a great leap. In three bounds, borne by the wind, he had crossed the yard. Against the pummeling gusts, he turned his head to see Jonathan, eyes scrunched tight, following in the same weightless bounds.

"Where are they?" Jonathan asked, his voice barely audible.

They waited for a momentary respite and then set off again. No sooner had they taken a single step than the wind flurried up again. Pat grappled out for the bough of a tree, snatching at Jonathan with his other hand. Together, they clung on.

"We've got to go back . . ." Pat uttered, the breath snatched from his throat. Yet, when they tried to turn toward the guesthouse, its doors now ripped from their hinges and sailing somewhere overhead, they found that they could not move.

The wind was driving them, and it would not let them retreat.

Pat gave up, turning his head against the gusts so that he might fill his lungs. He closed his eyes, willed himself: *make a plan, make a plan, make a plan . . .*

"After the horses, then," he started.

Jonathan nodded. "After the horses, Pat."

They rode the wind along the track, releasing their grasp on the tree and letting the gale carry them on. Overhead, the trunks of uprooted trees sailed past, their slow rise and fall seemingly out of tune with the anger of the storm. Halfway along the track, lifted from the ground, Pat grabbed for another tree. Jonathan clung on at the opposite side of the track. Pausing only to gather their breath, they gazed up. A section of wall from some rondavel hut floated on.

They came along the track in stages, carried by the wind for meters at a time before snatching onto the semisecurity of whatever trees were left standing.

At last, they reached the stables where the horses were kept. Nobody was there. Nothing but the wind.

Pat and Jonathan clung to the trees that bordered the stables, seeking whatever shelter they could. Between gasps for air, they looked out onto the barrenness. On the far side of the stables, the fences were gone. One of the trees in the center had been uprooted; the only sign there had ever been anything there was the crater the wind had left behind when it tore the trunk into the sky.

Pat felt a vibrating in his pocket, went to pick up his phone, but as soon as he took his hand off the tree, he felt as if he might be ripped away.

"We have to move," he said.

"Where to?"

There was only one way to go: forward, deeper into the storm . . . wherever the wind might carry them.

They flew past the stables, up and over an intersection in the track. Some of the local huts still stood here, and Pat and Jonathan flew between them. There were no trails to follow in the sand, no signs of which way the horses might have fled. Somewhere along the way, the horses evaporated from Pat's thoughts. He found himself flung against the wall of a rondavel and heaved himself around it, dragging Jonathan into the scant shelter of its downwind side.

When he came out of his reverie, he saw that the door to the hut was gone, no doubt carried off into the storm. From inside, a group of terrified faces peered out. Their eyes urged him to move. He clawed out to take hold of the rondavel wall and, in that way, hauled himself inside, heaving Jonathan in after.

Lying on the earth in the middle of the rondavel, Pat looked up, through the missing roof, at the patchwork sky. Tree trunks and branches, pieces of wall, and household detritus all sailed past.

He turned against the spectacle and reached for his phone.

I was in the garden, arms around Echo, when the phone began to ring.

"Pat?"

"Hello, Mandy . . ."

The sound of the wind was duller now, but I could still hear it roaring around him.

"Where are you?"

"I lost them, Mandy. They spooked . . ."

"Are you okay?"

"Lady, Fleur, Black Magic . . . They're gone."

"Pat," I repeated, "are you hurt?"

"Damn it, Mandy, didn't you hear? I lost them all . . . I had to cut them loose. They took it as long as they could, and then they spooked. We followed, but we couldn't . . ."

"Stay where you are," I said, as if I was commanding a four-year-old Jay not to go wandering off into the Two Tree bush. "Are you listening to me, Pat?"

In reply, there was only the sound of the wind.

"Pat, are you listening?"

"I hear you, Mandy," he finally said.

"They might still be out there . . ."

"They might be in the ocean. They might be in the sky."

I found my hand squeezing the strands of Echo's mane. "So might you," I breathed.

I hung up and loosened my hold on Echo. The wind played its terrible percussion on the rooftops, but it seemed nothing but a gentle summer's breeze compared to what was happening around Pat.

Hours later, certain now that the storm had passed, Pat and Jonathan emerged from the rondavel to see a world carved apart. The other huts past which they had tumbled were gone completely, leaving no trace upon the land. They walked, in a daze, into stretches of barren scrub, the air curiously still all around them.

Hoping that the horses might now have gravitated back to their home, Pat and Jonathan picked their way back to the stables. Cashew nut trees, torn up by the roots, lay across the tracks, making them impassable. Pat and Jonathan clambered on, only to find the stable area barren.

"Where else?" Jonathan asked.

Unable to reply, Pat kicked wildly at a fallen trunk. He turned, was about to spit out a string of curses, when his phone chimed in his pocket. At last, there was signal again.

Moments later, he hung up and turned to Jonathan.

"They're out near the airstrip," he said.

It was five kilometers by the inland road, but not nearly so much by beach. "But how . . ."

Together, Pat and Jonathan hurried to the edge of the cliffs and scrambled down to the sand beneath. Though the tide was out, the sand was strewn with the flotsam the waves had disgorged. The head of a once-proud fishing dhow broke through the crust, half buried. Against all the odds, its mast still stood.

Like two wanderers at the end of the world, Pat and Jonathan picked their way through the wreckage and came by coast to the small village of Chibobobo. Here, few people moved. Those who had remained behind walked the empty streets, marveling at the gaping holes where houses used to be, the clear blue vaults of the sky.

Pat and Jonathan weaved toward the airstrip, clambering over the crude roadblocks of fallen trees, vivid reminders of the way the war vets still trapped Zimbabwean farmers in their homes. The airstrip was on the edge of town, a barren runway along which small passenger and cargo planes brought the outside world to Vilanculos. In the middle of the strip a small airliner with propellers on each wing sat skewed, as if pushed from its blocks by the force of the storm. Beneath its wings, there stood Lady and Black Magic. Pat began to run, vaulting the debris that had collected in the road, with Jonathan close behind. Soon, he could see Squib on the hidden side of the plane. Megan and Spicegirl stood together farther down the strip, with a lonely Fleur even farther along.

"Jade . . ." Pat uttered. "Where's Jade?"

He wheeled around, searching for the lost mare, only for a horse's head to loom suddenly in front of him. Reeling back, he saw that she was already being led. Jonathan stood at her side, Jade's lead rope in his hand.

"She doesn't have a scratch . . ."

Pat approached Black Magic and Lady cautiously, desperate that they should not spook and disappear off the end of the airstrip, out into the bush. By some strange mercy, there was not a mark on either of them. Pat ran his hands up and down them, searching for some unseen cut, but there was nothing.

He looked back over the ruin that had been wrought on Vilanculos.

"It looks like they got through it better than the rest of us."

Taking two lead ropes in either hand, with Jonathan gathering up the remaining three stragglers, Pat turned the horses toward Vilanculos. At his right shoulder, Lady strained at her throatlatch, tugging in the opposite direction.

At the end of the airstrip, they stopped. Ahead of them, the road was blocked by fallen trees, colored by debris swept in from the bush and up from the sea. Big pieces of thatch, torn from the roofs of homes, marked the path back to the coast.

It was going to be a long walk home.

In the days after the cyclone, Pat and I spoke every hour. The rondavel where he and Jonathan had been sleeping at night was destroyed, but they found a place to stay, an abandoned house surrounded by palm and cashew nut trees and the ocean only a stone's throw away, where they could live among the horses. In Chimoio, we gathered ourselves and returned to business. Piece by piece, dollar by dollar, we paid back what we had borrowed and inched closer to joining Pat.

It was to be a year before we could follow the road Pat had taken, a whole year before Vaquero, Princess, and I could go to the ocean and see what had become of my husband and the fragment of the herd with whom he was living. On the day that I went to the moneylender to pay off the final monies we owed, I felt like I was dreaming. I drove back through Chimoio's barren streets, feeling as if I were twenty years younger. With the windows wound down, I searched the radio for some music to buoy me on my way but found only snatches of songs amid all the static. It did not matter. There were 450 kilometers between me and Pat, but for the first time it seemed a simple skip and a jump away. We would be there by fall of night.

At the riding school, Albert had organized the grooms. Four great trucks were waiting. We could load six or seven horses into each, eight if they were smaller, but the insides were tight, and we would have to make many stops along the way. The roads were worn and rutted, not maintained by the government and left to fragment ever since the days of Mozambique's ruinous civil war. It would not be the most comfortable ride for the horses, but along the way, we would find water and grazing. It did not matter to me, and I doubted it mattered to Shere Khan, Princess, and the rest; we were leaving at last, going to find Pat.

Albert and the local grooms were leading the horses into each trailer.

Out on Zimofa Farm, the part of the herd living there had already been loaded. Others were loaded and parked around the school. Some trucks had come up from Vilanculos, where Pat had sourced them from other exiled Zimbabweans and South African entrepreneurs who were trying to forge lives on that part of the coast. Others we had leased in Chimoio itself. It was a ramshackle caravan of vehicles, but Albert had checked each of the engines, and we were confident they would, at least, get us to Pat. I did not care about the expense, even after everything I had been through to pay back the moneylender and wipe our slate clean. All I cared about was that we were finally leaving.

Princess, Shere Khan, and Duke were already aboard, and I stood, fussing over each of them as the rest of the herd joined them. At last, only Brutus, Vaquero, and Tequila were left in the field. I crossed the riding school to take hold of Tequila's rope and led him aboard.

"You won't be able to make a mad dash for the Bvumba now," I said, steering him up the ramp. "Sorry, Tequila—you're off to a new home."

After Tequila, Vaquero—his eye still rolling, his legs still gangly— followed. From the darkness, he looked back. It might have been my imagination, but I could have sworn he still remembered my attempts to foist him onto the Portuguese farmer. He seemed to have a wicked glint in his eyes.

Brutus was the last in, his face contorted in a particularly Brutus-esque expression of worry as we forced him aboard.

"Off to join Jade, Brutus," I said, as we hauled the ramp shut. "Don't look so frightened—she'll be glad to see you."

I walked one last time around the riding school. At last, I left the empty rooms and barren paddock behind and took my seat in the Land Rover. Albert was behind the wheel. We were to lead the convoy. It would be a long, slow crawl.

"Are we ready, Miss Mandy?"

I felt so relaxed in my seat, it seemed to reach up and envelop me. "Let's go."

. . . .

The road to Vilanculos was pitted with holes, and every time we reached a certain speed we had to slow again, weaving from one side of the road to the next. In stretches where the highway was flat, the Mozambican police lay in wait, eager to trap and elicit bribes from whatever motorists they could. Five times, they pulled us over to check documentation and receive healthy *tips*. Each time, too bent on Vilanculos to care, we left them grinning and applauding us from the side of the road as the convoy motored past.

That day was long. The sun baked. We stopped at intervals to feed and water the horses. Halfway there, having made sure they were watered and had enough maize still aboard to sustain them, we took the plunge. The road leveled out, the potholes became less frequent, and we sailed on, not intending to stop again.

At last, we could see the ocean. It hung on the horizon, a blue as perfect as the sky above. As soon as it appeared, my heart soared. It was a strange feeling that ran through me then, all up and down my heartstrings. Though I had never lived there before, I felt as if I was coming home.

In my pocket, my phone rang. On the other end of the line, Pat's voice kept breaking up.

"Are you near, Mandy?"

I looked up, the ocean growing larger in the windshield.

"Nearly . . ." I replied.

Soon we could smell the sea, hear the cries of seabirds as they flew in formation overhead. We left the main highway and followed a road of deep sand that wove its way through the sprawl of huts that surrounded the main road of Vilanculos. Leaving the town behind, we followed the line of the coast. Then, the sea was directly in front of us. Daylight was paling into dusk, but the ocean reflected and caught the last hints of sunlight, its gentle waves sparkling wherever they broke.

The convoy ground to a halt, and Jonathan met us at the side of the road. He looked different from the last time I had seen him, thinner, more drawn, but was still wearing his same irrepressible grin. Albert jumped out of the Land Rover to join him and together they organized the convoy to take the horses down to the stables.

"And Pat?" I asked, sliding into the driver's seat.

"He is at home, waiting," Jonathan replied.

"Home?"

"You will see . . ."

He pointed me down the road, and—now behind the wheel myself—I steered the Land Rover in the direction he described.

I came through more wood huts and faced the brilliant glare of the ocean. Down at the shore's edge, only meters from the line of lapping water, sat a little rondavel hut with concrete walls and a thatched roof, barely big enough to contain a single small room. At its side stood an outhouse made from local timber. A dilapidated trailer sat out front and, in front of that, there was my husband, bent over a saddle with his tools piled up at his side.

I parked the Land Rover and stepped out. A sharp incline dropped down to the rondavel, and I hurried down. Pat was shirtless and looked leaner than I had ever seen him before. When I got close, I realized exactly how lean; it was not only his cheekbones that looked more pronounced, but every bone in his body. My husband had once been broad and strong, but now he looked wiry, almost scrawny. I could see every line of his ribs, his eyes seemed to have retreated inside their sockets, and his hair was thin, with the grayness spreading across his whole pate.

He looked up. A smile twitched at the corner of his lips. Had it really been only a year? Could a year do this to a man? I was struck by a horrifying, absurd thought: here, framed by one of the most beautiful vistas in the world, Pat looked as if he had just stepped out of a concentration camp.

"Pat," I said, grinning, "you look terrible."

"Well, you know how it's been. Cyclones. Malaria. No clean water. And, on top of all that, I haven't *really* been eating . . ." He put down the saddle, stepped forward, and threw his arms around me. "Welcome home, Mandy, you're going to *love* it . . ."

Chapter 15

I CRASHED into the rondavel.

"Pat," I said, "Brutus has been *arrested*."

Pat looked up from mending a saddle.

"Arrested?"

"Yes."

"Brutus?"

"Yes."

"The *horse* Brutus, that little *pony* Brutus?"

"The very same."

Pat didn't know whether to throw his head back and laugh or lift his fists and rail at the gods.

"Only in Mozambique, Mandy."

"Come on, Pat, before they do something terrible . . ."

After the devastation of the cyclone, it had taken a long time for the tourists to return to Vilanculos. But return they had. I had been riding with some this morning, along the sweeping blue cove between the little rondavel where we had started living and the stables farther along the beach, when one of our local grooms had come floundering out of the long grass at the cliff's edge and flailed at me across the sand.

Underneath me, Lady seemed to want to shy away, but I kept her reined tight and listened to what the groom had to say.

"Chief Phophopho's waiting at the Archipelago Lodge," I explained. "Apparently, we've already ignored his summons twice."

"What?"

I could only shrug. "Somebody hasn't been passing on the message. Nobody wants to be the bearer of bad news in Africa . . ."

Pat and I hurried out of our little rondavel. The views from our step were perhaps the most beautiful I had ever seen—the pure white fringes of sand and calm, azure water, with the distant humps of islands marking the horizon—but there was no time to stop and admire them now, not when Brutus was in trouble.

The lodge, at which the chief was waiting, was perched on the cliff-tops between our home and the stables, and we made the short drive there in the Land Rover. Archipelago Lodge was a beautiful hotel with large wooden chalets featuring wide verandahs from which tourists could look over the serene and spectacularly beautiful bay. The owners, Jeff and Jane Reilley, encouraged horse riding, and most of their guests would take the opportunity to ride along the beaches. The lodge had been badly damaged in the cyclone, but builders had worked night and day to restore it.

At the very edge of the cliff, in the shade of palms that had somehow survived the cyclone, the local village chief, a tiny wizened man they called Phophopho, sat with his entourage of three younger men and an Italian woman, who I quickly realized was there to act as translator. As Pat and I tentatively approached, Chief Phophopho's big white eyes fell on me. He gestured that I should sit.

"What seems to be the problem?" I began.

The chief said something to which his entourage heartily agreed. I turned to the translator.

"First," the Italian woman explained, "we drink."

The old chief motioned and the barman appeared with glasses of wine, which he duly passed around. I lifted mine to drink, but the chief's eyes opened wide and I stopped. Around the table, he and the entourage drained their glasses. Then, after a little nod of instruction, Pat and I did the same.

"On to business," declared the translator. "You understand why you have been called to this meeting?"

"Actually," I said, "I haven't quite—"

The chief cut me off, speaking rapidly in his own language, Xitswa.

"Your creature—the big dog named Brutus—has been accused of theft. The women of the village reported seeing him in their maize, grazing it down to stubs. Do you deny it?"

I flashed a look at Pat.

"I know what happened here," he whispered. "I took them out to graze, roped them off so they wouldn't wander. It's those grooms—they fell asleep . . ."

It would not have been the first time. Watching a horse eat is not the most captivating activity, and between that and the fierce Mozambican sun, it was all too easy to drift off. I had caught the grooms at it once before, curled up in the shade of some baobab while Echo untied a knot and wandered off. Brutus, I supposed, had had enough of the tough yellow grass he was grazing and, taking advantage of the slumbering grooms, stepped daintily over the rope and off to tastier pastures.

"The big dog wantonly ignored the village women's cries. They banged tin pots, shooed him away, told him in no uncertain terms that the maize did not belong to him—but he heeded none of their warnings."

"Well, of course not," I began. "He's a horse."

"A thief is still a thief."

I whispered to Pat from the corner of my mouth, "Where *is* Brutus?"

"He was at the stables this morning."

"Looking well fed?"

"He didn't look as worried as usual . . ."

"He has been placed under arrest in absentia, awaiting his sentence," the Italian woman went on, translating Chief Phophopho's words. "If he cannot answer for himself, you must."

"Well," I began, "quite clearly he *can't* answer for himself."

Upon hearing the translation, the chief's face broke into a broad smile.

"Then perhaps," said the translator, "we should let the negotiations begin."

Remembering the last time somebody had accused our horses of theft and the bitter price they had exacted, I steeled myself. I still had no idea what had become of Pink Daiquiri and Ramazotti—but if Chief Phophopho was framing Brutus to take some of our horses for himself, he was in for a shock. I would not let it happen again.

I pitched across the table, angling myself to look the old chief in the eye. "What are you asking for?"

The old man smiled again.

"Everything has its cost," said the translator. "The chief would like you to pay for the villager's crops."

Suddenly, all the memories of Pink Daiquiri and Ramazotti evaporated. I laughed, long and loud. Perhaps it was the wine, perhaps it was the searing heat, perhaps it was just the ridiculous idea that Pat and I should be living here, on this beautiful stretch of coast, with barely enough money to rub two coins together—but it seemed laughter was all that I had.

The chief named his price. I looked, out of the corner of my eye, at Pat. He simply gave an enormous shrug.

"It's yours," I said.

Upon hearing the translation, the chief stood and threw his arms open wide.

"I'll go and get you your money," I said, turning to leave.

"No." The translator smiled, her face a tiny imitation of Chief Phophopho's big grin. "You must not go yet. First, we drink."

That night, still bewildered and wondering where the next tourists were coming from to pay for Brutus's adventure, Pat and I walked up to the stables. Roped up, Brutus was happily chewing on a bundle of dried grass. As I approached, he turned to face me. His face creased in exactly the same way it had when he was a tiny foal, as if pleading that he had done nothing wrong.

I scooped up a handful of horse cubes and ambled over to palm them into his mouth. Perplexed at first, he quickly gobbled them up.

"Brutus," I said, putting my arms around him and remembering the first time I ever saw him, huddled up to Jade on John Crawford's farm, "you are worth *every penny*."

As Jonathan and the grooms fanned out around the pasture, driving in stakes and raising a rope around its edges, Pat and I rode to the head of the column and gently brought the horses to a standstill. Beneath me, Vaquero seemed to be able to sense the lush grass in the field the grooms were roping off and urged me to take him there. In the year since Chimoio he had grown into himself, shedding some of the gangliness of his youth, and though his eye still wandered, and though his teeth still seemed too big for his jaws, there was something refined—almost *handsome*—about the dappled gray gelding he had become.

"Soon," I whispered, and I looked over to see Pat in Shere Khan's saddle, riding up the column of more than thirty of our best horses, checking to make sure that all was well.

Brutus's little adventure had taught us two things: first, that Brutus was not to be trusted when within sight of a stretch of lush maize; and, second, that grazing in our new part of the world was always going to be a problem. We had run out of grazing, and although we could buy maize from the market in Vilanculos, it was important to find fresh ground for the horses. So we divided the herd into two groups, bringing one group here, where we could leave the horses until the rains came and grazing improved.

We were thirty kilometers outside of Vilanculos, and it seemed too perfect to be true. At the bottom of the pasture, the grasses grew thick around the edges of a natural lake of crystal clear water. With enough water and grass here to nourish the herd for weeks on end, it seemed as if we had walked into a desert oasis.

In a fit of joy, a horse thundered past me and cantered into the middle of the field. On Fleur's back, there sat Kate. She lifted a hand and waved at me from the center of the field, then she drew Fleur back around and trotted back in my direction. Kate had graduated from the University of

Stellenbosch in South Africa and had been staying with us in Vilanculos while she planned her next move. To my shame, there was no room for her at the little rondavel that Pat and I now called home. Though it had one of the most perfect views on the planet, mere yards from the placid waters of the Bazaruto bay, our room was scarcely big enough for our two single beds, pushed together with a big mosquito net to cloak us, and the water basin out back. As Jay did when he came down from Gorongosa, Kate was staying in the kitchen area. She had been with us four months, but though she loved the horses and was quite brilliant at entertaining the tourists we took out for rides, I could tell that her heart wasn't in it. *Mozambleak*, she called it. *Vilanchaos*. She had her sights set on following Paul to London, and I could not blame her.

We shepherded the horses into the field and roped off the entrance. Bewildered at their good luck, the herd fanned out and instantly started to graze. Marquess and Fleur drifted down to the banks of the lake, while Shere Khan remained in the middle of the field, surveying the herd for a long time after they had all dropped their heads to eat, like the queen that she was.

"If only this was at our doorstep," Pat said.

We milled around the herd, and when we heard the noise of a truck drawing around beyond the rope, we set off to join it.

The last thing I saw as we climbed aboard to make the drive home was Vaquero, watching me with a mischievous glint in his eye, turning the grass between oversize teeth.

In Vilanculos, we rose with the dawn. Down at the stables, some of the local grooms were preparing horses for the day's ride. Duke and Black Magic were already saddled up when Pat and I arrived, with Fanta and Viper, the little purebred Arabian, waiting dutifully in the wings.

Today we rode down the coast, through rich coconut plantations, and to the local fishing village, where families of local Mozambicans had, from time immemorial, set out at dawn in their sailing dhows to cast their nets into the pristine waters of the bay. Our clients were a

South African couple and their daughter who were on a whistle-stop tour of the east African coast. As Kate helped them sort out chaps and riding hats, I checked the stirrups and girths of each horse and prepared to climb into Duke's saddle.

"There'll be fresh coconut waiting at the other side," Kate said to the couple's daughter, helping adjust her stirrup straps. The girl was in Lady's saddle, the preening little pony the perfect size for her. "And matapa. Have you tried matapa? It's made from cassava leaves. I'll let you in on a secret . . ." Kate paused, then she whispered into the girl's ear, "It's *disgusting* . . ."

The little girl was thrilled.

I had one foot in the stirrup and was about to swing my leg over when a car rumbled into the stable, through overhanging bush, and Jonathan stepped out. With a simple gesture of the hand, he got Pat's attention.

I was leading Duke on a little walk, waiting for Kate to saddle up and the tourists to be ready, when Pat called over.

"It's Echo," he said. "He's gone. You'll have to ride this one alone, Mandy. I'll go and find him."

"You know where he'll be?"

Pat grinned. "Halfway back to the Bvumba."

I shook my head. He had a very long way to go.

Hours later, Pat found Echo calmly walking along the side of the road with Evita and Jazzman at his side. Driving them back to the grazing land, he found two of the grooms asleep in the sun, and a length of rope lying coiled in the grass like a snake. Somebody, it seemed, had untied it from the tree around which it had been wound. The telltale teeth marks around the end told him the culprit had not been human.

Pat looked up, his eyes settling on Echo. The silvery horse looked almost smug, standing in the shadow of Shere Khan.

"Did you see him do it, Shere Khan?"

Shere Khan made no response, her nose held haughtily aloft.

"You two are too much trouble," Pat began, turning to Echo and Jazzman. "You can't stay here. I think we'll need a truck . . ."

That night I returned from the ride through the fishing village, belly full of fresh crab and cassava leaves, to find three horses back from the grazing fields. Echo, Jazzman, and Evita were tethered in the shade at the far end of the stable.

I brought Duke around as Kate and the grooms brought Black Magic, Lady, and the other horses we had been riding back in on lead ropes.

"They're too much trouble to leave in the grazing fields," Pat said, grinning as he put his arms around Echo. "This one unties the knots, so this one"—he thrust a thumb in Jazzman's direction—"can slip away."

"What about poor little Evita?" I said, swinging out of Duke's saddle.

"I don't know," said Pat. "I just don't trust her out there; she's so much like Brutus."

Brutus looked up, the creases deepening around his eyes.

At the start of the summer, just as the sun was flexing its muscles for months of searing heat, we drove out to the airport to wish Kate a fond farewell. She was bound for London. She would be able to see her brother and visit Granny Beryl in St. Ives—but, more than anything, she would be able to make a life for herself. Lifting her bags from the Land Rover was bittersweet. Pat and I stood at the edge of the airstrip as the tiny plane jerked awkwardly into the air. We watched as it dwindled and disappeared. Our children were grown and gone out into the world, and we had reached our final home.

We drove back along the bustling main street of Vilanculos, where the markets were overflowing and street hawkers mobbed us each time we stopped. At last, turning from the main highway, we wove our way through the local villages to reach the coast and our own little hut.

Jonathan was waiting in the garden, two of the beach dogs who roamed the sands basking in the sun at his feet.

"Pat," he began, "I think you'd better come."

· · · ·

In the stable, one of our local grooms, Luka, stood holding Vaquero and another small gelding.

"What are they doing here?"

"They are not good, boss," said Luka, summoning up his few words of English.

I did not have to get close to Vaquero to know that he was throwing a temperature. Pat ran a hand up and down his muzzle, but Vaquero simply let out a low, despondent snort. His eyes, usually a little wild and roaming, looked dark, discolored even, and his flanks had a sheen of sweat. I ran my hand down his haunch. When I brought it back, it was dripping wet.

The gelding at his side was much the same. His chest rose and fell heavily, a succession of rapid breaths.

Pat screwed up his eyes, as if weighing up the symptoms. "African horse sickness, perhaps?"

African horse sickness was endemic across southern Africa, and Vaquero was showing the classic symptoms of its most vicious strain. With his fever, the strange rattle he made when he breathed, and his downcast eyes and lack of engagement, it was little wonder that African horse sickness was on the tip of Pat's tongue.

Pat looked at the other horses contentedly waiting in the stable yard.

"Let's get them away from the herd," he began. "Come on, Vaquero, this way . . ."

It was only a short walk along the beach from the stables to our rondavel home, but rather than risk weakening Vaquero and the other gelding, we loaded them into a truck and took them along the back road, running parallel to the bay. Once we arrived at the rondavel, we opened up the back. Inside, Vaquero and the other gelding shifted uneasily. It seemed to take an age to coax them out.

Pat strode into the open kitchen area beside our hut and opened one of the fridges, powered by a noisy generator, that we kept there.

"One of those times you wish you were in Zimbabwe," he muttered, darkly, "with a vet on the other end of the phone . . ."

After rifling around, he produced a box of medication and returned to where Vaquero and the other gelding were standing. There was no treatment for African horse sickness, but we could deal with the symptoms. After administering shots to both horses, he went in search of antibiotics and, promising Vaquero he would be well again soon, gave him a good pat.

We sat with them through the afternoon, listening to the rasp of every breath, waiting for some sign that the medication might soothe their fevers. Vaquero looked at me with the same roaming eyes I remembered from that day in Chimoio when I had tried to trade him away. *You can't get rid of me that easily,* he seemed to have been saying. I found myself wishing he would say the same thing today.

The next morning, Vaquero and the gelding showed no signs of recovery. Pat stayed to nurse them, even though there was nothing he could do. I tried to push them from my mind as I took riders along the beach, north through sweeping red dunes and across an undulating expanse of crimson sand. In Duke's saddle, I led them on a canter along the sweeping bay, but it was late in the afternoon by the time we were trotting back toward the stable, up through the mangrove flats and sandy beach road.

When I arrived, it was to find the stable area empty but for a groom who indicated the next-door plot. Here in the plot, Pat tended to Marquess and Arizona; a little farther along, Jonathan was standing with Tequila's sister, Kahlua.

I rode Duke into the plot. Instantly, Pat looked up.

"It wasn't just Vaquero and the gelding. We had to bring Marquess and these others in from the fields, too. They have the same symptoms."

I pushed Duke a little farther but saw the caution in Pat's eyes and reined him in. That was why the rest of the herd had been roped off out in the bush; this plot was under quarantine now.

"Same symptoms?" I asked, looking at Marquess.

Pat nodded.

"That isn't all, Mandy. It's Vaquero." Pat stalled, his face a mask of stone. "Mandy, he's gone."

Long after midnight, starlight bathed the trees.

Pat and I drew the truck off the road and into the bush. Once we were far enough from the road, we killed the lights and stepped out. In front of us lay a great maw in the hard earth. A shovel was propped by its side.

When I had gotten back to the rondavel, Vaquero and the other gelding were lying, stiff and cold. Pat had covered them in sheets, but something compelled me to take a look. I stepped forward and lifted a corner, just enough that I could see Vaquero's head, his eyes still open, his tongue still lolling out. Pat said he had been the first to go. He simply took a deep breath, held it in his chest, and then he was gone. The other gelding followed only moments later, the two gone together to join that ancient herd in the sky.

"What *was* it?" I asked, knowing we had no answer. "We should have a vet here, Pat."

"We'll send for one. Fly one up from South Africa."

I beat a retreat from Vaquero's cold cadaver, unable to look at his glassy eyes staring. No longer would they roam around their orbits. No longer would they glimmer at me knowingly, as if sharing some mischievous joke.

"What are we going to do with him, Pat?"

"You're thinking of Grey, aren't you?"

Now we stood at an open grave in the dead of night, as Jonathan and Luka helped us lower Vaquero down to lie, his legs entangled with those of the gelding he had died alongside. There was no time for sentiment. There was no time to say any words or lament the loss. By the light of the stars, we poured the dirt over poor Vaquero and knew we would never see him again.

As we drove back to snatch a few hours' sleep before embarking on another day's riding, I told myself that, at least in death, Vaquero was safe. No local Mozambican would be there to dig up his body and butcher him for a fire.

I told myself all that, but it wasn't nearly enough to quell the ache in my gut.

In the days that followed, more and more horses came in, showing similar symptoms to Vaquero's. Soon, Marquess followed him into the ground. Then Arizona. Drummer Boy. Ratz. Roulette and Aurora. Sabi Star. Comet. At dusk, we walked through the stables and listened as the terrible rasp began in our horses' throats. Engulfing their lungs. Eyes drooped, sweat shimmered—and, one after another, the horses we had rescued from Mugabe's war began to die.

Pat stood with Shere Khan, while I ran my hand through Fleur's mane. November had turned into a cruel, scorching December. It had been three nights since the last death, but those nights had been fitful. The bush between our rondavel and the stable was now an unmarked grave-yard, haunted by the ghosts of our herd. When I closed my eyes, I could see the graves picked out across the backs of my eyes, like sparkling stars in a planetarium.

On the other side of Shere Khan, a figure crouched with his ear pressed up against California's chest. A little case was open at his side, with vials of blood placed carefully within.

"Any idea, Allan?"

Allan had arrived on the morning's plane, along with a family of French riders for whom we would have to paint on smiles and pre-tend our world was not falling apart. He was a tall South African with brown dreadlocks, who had been a veterinarian with his own prac-tice in Rustenburg. Now, as he crouched between Shere Khan and California, his face betrayed nothing. My insides churned; his, I knew, was a practiced face, designed to put his own clients at ease. I felt as if I could see straight through it to some yawning horror on the other side.

"We'll know more when we've done some tests. It isn't African horse sickness. I can promise you that."

He stood up, closed his case, and ran his hand along Shere Khan's mane.

"She really is a beautiful horse," he began. Shere Khan flicked her mane dismissively. "And she knows it, doesn't she?"

Allan flew back to Johannesburg the very next day, but it seemed an interminable wait for the laboratory results to come through. At last, as one dusk drew over Vilanculos in the deep of December, the phone rang.

"Tell me you have a cure," I began.

Allan's tone was somber. "I'd love nothing more, Mandy, but . . . I can't tell you what the cure is when I can't tell you what's wrong with your horses."

His voice trailed off, but I had no words to replace it.

"How many have died, Mandy?"

"Ten," I uttered.

"I'm sorry . . ."

He seemed broken too, but there was no way he could understand just how we felt.

"What can we do?" I breathed, not daring to dream there might be an answer.

"There are other things we could look for," Allan began, "but I'd need more samples . . ."

"We can do it," I cut in. "Pat can draw more blood . . ."

"Not blood," Alan interjected. "It has to be tissue."

"Tissue?"

"Mandy, we'd need a slice of brain."

All we could do was wait for another of our dearest horses to die.

Early in the morning, I was kneading the sleep from my eyes when Jonathan appeared, looking ragged and starved of sleep, to bring the news. With the steam from my tea beading on my face, I saw him whisper to Pat. Then he turned to walk back along the beach, the gentle susurration of waves behind him.

"Who is it, Pat?"

"Fleur," Pat breathed.

We brought her to the rondavel to die. There had been too much death in those stables. On the same grass where Vaquero had breathed his last, Fleur lay down. We brought her water, but by fall of night she was too weak to stand and drink. Instead, I lay with her head in my lap, listening to each stuttering breath, brushing back the sweat that beaded in her mane and trickled down her muzzle.

When death came, it came suddenly. She opened her eyes, seemed to be desperately searching for something; in that moment, I knew that she *understood*. Her forelegs gave tiny, almost imperceptible kicks; she breathed in, exhaled softly—and then Fleur was gone.

"She was so frightened," I breathed as I lifted her head from my lap and, my body numb, took Pat's hand to stand.

"So am I," Pat admitted.

It fell to Pat to conduct the grisly business. I could not bear to see it done. While he was readying Fleur's body, I headed for the airport to organize the tissue sample's delivery to Allan in South Africa. Yet, as I explained what we needed to the relevant authorities, their faces turned to stone: there was no way, I was told by the airline operator, that they could transport such a thing on their planes, not without a veterinary license, and that might take many months to receive. I left with tears in my eyes. There had to be another way.

When I got back to the rondavel, Pat's work was done. He was scrubbing his hands, though I could still see the red stains in the webbing of his fingers. We sat down and thought about our options. I can barely remember the moment it occurred to me, but there was a very simple way of getting the tissue sample into South Africa. A slice of brain matter was simply a slice of meat. We would put it inside a sandwich and ask one of our clients to deliver it to a wonderful lady named Meryl who kindly offered to rush the samples to the veterinary department. She would be waiting for our clients when they stepped off the plane on the other side.

Pat looked at me, his eyes glowing with the absurdity of it all.

"Only Africa would make us do a thing like that."

I couldn't help but laugh.

That night, we buried what was left of our beloved Fleur on the edge of a cliff under a baobab tree with a view of the sea. Back at the rondavel, I took down a chopping board and laid out two slices of bread. Like some mad scientist engaged in a midnight experiment, I cut two pieces of plastic film to the exact shape and size of the bread, and laid one on top of each slice. Then, I picked out the cold, gelatinous slices of Fleur's brain from the refrigerator and laid them on the plastic. Even after I had set them down, I thought I could feel a tingling on my fingers, and I hoped that Fleur might forgive us.

After laying another piece of plastic film on top of one slice of brain, I closed up the sandwich and wrapped it in yet more plastic, hoping that it might remain fresh throughout the short flight. Then I joined Pat outside the rondavel.

"Eleven dead already," I said. "He *has* to find something, Pat."

Pat nodded, refusing to give me any crude consolation. Then he left to see our most recent clients and their illicit sandwich off into the skies.

In December, Mozambique baked. Jay had come to Vilanculos to spend Christmas with us, but this year there would be no celebrations. We spent Christmas Day in the stables. In the evening, we left Jay to look over the horses while Pat and I joined our clients for a braai on the beach. I filled my plate with steak and the rich South African sausage we called *boerewors*, but it took me an hour to poke it down.

"You have to eat," Pat whispered to me, as the sounds of revelry crowded us from all sides.

"I'm not hungry."

"You look like a rake."

From somewhere, there came the sound of a guitar. People were dancing in the sand, and a chorus of voices rose to join the song.

I wanna be in the cavalry, if they send me off to war
I want a good steed under me, like my forefathers before
I want a good man when the bugles sound and I hear those cannons roar
I wanna be in the cavalry, if they send me off to war

Now that the party had started, the singing did not stop. The guitar was passed around and more songs poured into the night. Over the ocean, the starlight sparkled, and I could tell from the gleeful look in their eyes that our clients would remember this Christmas for the rest of their lives.

"Do you ever get bored of it?"

It took me a moment to register the question.

"Mandy," one of the clients asked, bouncing his exhausted daughter on his knee, "do you ever just wake up and realize how lucky you are, to be *here*, to have all of this . . . this *beauty*, all around you?"

I felt Pat's leg tense against mine underneath the table.

"Every morning," I said, through a painted smile. "Darling, it's like that every single time I wake up."

Early in the New Year, Pat picked up the phone, a call from pathologists at Onderstepoort Veterinary Institute. I had been bickering with Jay outside but heard him conversing in a low whisper. When he finally hung up, he came down the rondavel step and sank down to sit there, kneading the phone in his hands.

I broke from my argument with Jay. "Was it Allan?" I began.

Pat shook his head.

"It was Onderstepoort. They've found out what's killing the horses. We took them straight into it." He paused. "They're poisoned, Mandy. It was in their grazing. *Crotalaria* . . ."

"*Crotalaria?*"

"Sun hemp," Pat said, flinging his arms back. Realization seemed to be dawning. "It must have been out in the field, along that lake. They didn't know. They ate it. And now . . ."

Sun hemp had been introduced to Mozambique during the country's earliest days as a Portuguese colony, as part of an attempt to enrich nitrogen in the country's soils. Grown properly and harvested at the right time it is a wonderful plant, perfect as food for livestock; but when it is seeding, the plant is toxic. Horses are usually so intelligent and watchful. Instinct drives them away from toxic plants. Instinct drives them to graze on the rich grasses that they need. Instinct takes care of them where their owners cannot. But instinct cannot protect a horse forever. Perhaps the instincts of our own herd had somehow been scrambled by their long flight from home. Perhaps the sun hemp in the field seemed too good to turn down.

"What happens now, Pat?"

"You don't want to know."

Pat stood, strode toward the Land Rover. I hurried after.

"Pat, I want to . . ."

"They die, Mandy," Pat said, slamming his fists against the car door. "It stays in their system. There's no expunging it. There's no cure. It's already in them. It's already killing them, bit by bit. It bides its time and it festers and, when it's ready, it shuts them down." Pat's face was strained, even though he had checked his tears. "Every last one of those horses we took to graze in that field is going to die."

At least, now that we knew it was not a contagious disease, the horses could live as one herd again. Princess and Evita, Rebel and Philippe, Black Magic and Jade, even Lady and Duke, who had come all the way from Two Tree—we were now certain that they would survive, for they had never been near the poisoned land.

In the afternoon, we went riding with a British family based in

South Africa. As I tacked up Echo and Evita, I stroked their ears and told them how lucky they were. If Echo had not abetted Jazzman in his great escape by nimbly untying the knots in the rope, and Evita not followed them, we would have left them in the fields, and they too might have feasted on the sun hemp. Were it not for their mischievous ways, they might be dead already, under the sand with Vaquero, Fleur, and the rest.

I looked across the stable and saw Pat tacking up the regal Shere Khan. She looked down her long nose at him, as lofty and statuesque as ever. Yet I could see the look in Pat's eyes. Shere Khan had cantered in those fields. She had turned the grass in her teeth; she had kept her lofty eyes on the rest of her herd. She had been there throughout, and there seemed little hope that she had not eaten the poisonous vegetation like all of her friends.

We had taken more than thirty horses out to graze on the poisoned land. Almost all of them were already gone. When the twenty-ninth passed away, the new year was here and three months had already passed—but, Allan had told us, the *Crotalaria* poison could linger in a horse's system for six months or more, waiting for the cruelest moment to spring its deadly trap.

Shere Khan, the queen of the herd, was living on borrowed time.

I was standing on the beach, Brutus's lead rope in one hand and Lady's in the other, when I saw Pat urge Shere Khan into a gallop. Beyond him lay the sweeping azure sea; beneath him, the undulating golden sand. I thought I had never seen such a majestic sight, but, when he turned her toward me and reined her down, I saw that he was trembling.

"What is it, Pat?"

It took a moment for him to find the words. "I can feel it in her chest, Mandy. It's coming. It's already here."

Daylight lasted for long hours this deep into summer, and as the sun set in the west, somewhere over our old home in Zimbabwe, Pat and

I walked Shere Khan gently out of the stables. Behind us, Lady, Black Magic, Brutus, and the other survivors watched. I have always thought that they understood exactly what was happening that night; that this was the very last time they would see their queen in the living world.

We led Shere Khan slowly along the beach, listening to the gentle lap of waves at the water's edge. The light was soft, the palms swayed, a single sailing dhow bobbed out on the bay. Along the beach, we met Jay and, together—Pat holding Shere Khan's lead rope, knowing he would never ride her again—we came to our little rondavel.

Shere Khan's breathing was labored, but it was not until the morning came that we could fully hear the death rattle in her breast. Her tongue began to loll; a sheen of sweat shimmered across her beautiful hide, as if she had spent the day galloping through the fierce Mozambican heat; and by the middle of the next afternoon something had dimmed in her eyes. It was terrifying to see that knowing intelligence flicker and fade. Not once had we seen Shere Khan look so diminished. She was arrogant, confident, an imperious mare who knew she was more beautiful than anyone else—but now the knowing was gone from her eyes. She looked at us, but it was as if she were on the other side of a veil. Death was claiming her from the inside out.

We stayed with her through the long night.

"I'll never forget coming back to Biri after I'd been in England," I began, "and there she was. All those new horses you'd found . . . but she stood out, Pat. The most beautiful horse I'd seen."

But Pat just sat in silence, one hand on Shere Khan's trembling flank, her head propped in my lap.

In the morning, she was still with us. She took no water. She did not stand. We had clients to ride with this morning, but neither Pat nor I set out to meet them. In the rondavel, the phone rang and rang again. We let it go. There would be time enough for apologies later. This was our time now. This was Shere Khan's.

In the middle of the morning, Shere Khan's eyes rolled toward Pat. In that second, all of the old fire was there. Suddenly, she knew who she was. Suddenly, she understood that she was the queen, bigger, bolder, more intelligent, more beautiful than all the rest. She seemed to know where she should be—riding at the head of the herd, leading them on a thunderous gallop across these African sands.

But the moment was fleeting, and then the moment was gone. Shere Khan's chest rose, and then she exhaled. Then, eyes still open and gazing at the blue African skies, she was still.

I looked up. It had been a long time since I last saw my husband cry, but his hands were tangled in Shere Khan's ebony mane, and his tears flowed unchecked.

As soon as she was in the water, Black Magic performed an absurd belly flop and began to roll. A little farther along the beach, Brutus, seeing the preposterous fun Black Magic seemed to be having, attempted to do the same. Tentative at first—and still wearing his permanently worried expression—he only paddled. Then he too dropped down and rolled. I heaved on his lead rope, trying to encourage him to stand and come deeper into the water, but he steadfastly refused.

Along the shore, our other horses were coming in procession, their grooms on either side. At the head I saw Lady and Jade, Tequila and Echo tucked just behind, Philippe and Rebel on the edges, straining at their ropes to get to the water. At the end, Princess came with her daughter, Evita.

I saw the ghosts around them, too. There was Grey, cantering like a silvery streak; there was Deja Vu, whole again, her only scars the ones around her leg. There were Fleur and Marquess, who had come all the way from Two Tree together. I saw Arizona and California, plucked from a den of lions only to be led into the jaws of a crueler death. I saw Kahlua, trotting alongside her still-living brother, Tequila, as if they still belonged to the same herd. And, above them all, I saw Shere Khan, still a hand higher than the horses around her, still looking regally down her nose, still queen of her herd, even in that ethereal world.

One after another, we led the survivors into the water. Deep out, I sat on Brutus's back, while Pat clung to Black Magic's mane. The grooms led the herd around us, but Pat and I were suspended there, in the middle of the swirling azure waters.

We swam in circles, and when we turned, I saw a single horse's head bobbing toward us, with Jonathan trailing behind as if it were he who was wearing the halter and lead rope. Pat and I slowed down. Princess was coming to see us.

We waited for her to reach us. I put my hand on her muzzle and Pat put his arms around her, careful not to touch the sensitive flesh of her withers.

"Do you remember," Pat said, "the day you threw Resje and I chased you up through the Two Tree bush?"

If she remembered at all, it was part of a different world, like a false, distorted memory of childhood. I slipped from Brutus, kicked through the warm blue water, and rolled gently onto Princess's back. Sitting high, I gazed around at what was left of our herd, playing as the Mozambican sun beat down.

I looked up. On the beach, I fancied I could see Shere Khan and the ghostly herd watching. I turned to call Pat, but when I looked again, they were gone. Now, only memories cantered along that beach.

"What do you think, Princess? Are we home?"

She took off, as if making for shore.

Once, I had thought home was forever. Once, I had thought Crofton was where I would grow old and die, a place to which my children and, one day, my grandchildren could always come back. Now, home was different. Princess and I rose out of the ocean and stood sunning ourselves where, moments ago, the ghostly herd had stood. I thought I could hear the thunder of hoofbeats as Shere Khan led them on one final canter.

Home, I knew now, was wherever our herd still survived.

I turned and watched Pat and Black Magic, gleaming like ebony, rise out of azure sea.

Home was Pat, and here he was.

Epilogue

ZIMBABWE: YOU HAVE a lot to answer for.

February 2012 is the heart of a fierce Mozambican summer, but Jay and I are traveling west, through Chimoio and back over the Bvumba. I have been dreaming about writing a book about the story of our horses—but first, I know, I must see what has become of the country we used to love.

It is the first time I have crossed the border into Zimbabwe since we were forced to leave. It is after dark by the time we are through the checkpoint and traveling down the other side of the mountains. Mutare's streets are heavy with the scent of flowering trees along its roads, and a rush of nostalgia hits me. It is like an epiphany: for a while, we were happy here.

We spend the night with old friends, but in the morning we are gone west along the Harare road. Even the main highways are pitted with potholes now, and Jay must constantly slow and swerve to avoid smashing the car's chassis. Along the banks of the road, the telegraph poles are down, lying in tangled heaps, and the fields we pass, once rich, verdant farms, are either gone back to bush or planted with thin, straggly crops. Every ten kilometers we come to a checkpoint where police pull drivers over, ostensibly to fine them for dirty windshields or fractured mirrors, but really to ask for bribes; not even the police are paid in Zimbabwe now, and they must make their living on the country's roads like bandits of old.

Before we venture back "home," Jay and I head for Grasslands Agricultural Research Station at Marondera, one of the very first places Pat and I lived as a couple. The research station is wild and overgrown now, but on the outskirts of the local town lies a little graveyard. This, too, is overgrown, unkempt and untended, but we fight back the thistles and long grass and find a grave I have not seen in many years: the resting place of Nicholas, the baby we had to leave behind. We spend some time cleaning his grave and leave flowers to wilt in the harsh African sun. I do not know how long it will be before I will see him next, and as we head off, I am left with a feeling all too familiar: Zimbabwe has made me abandon him all over again.

In the afternoon, we reach Harare and spend the night at the home of my old friend Carol Johnson. Carol is widowed now and lives alone, with a dog named Scruffy, a Maltese poodle who walked in through her gate one day and never left. There is no electricity in her part of Harare—it seems that the only way to have a constant supply is to live near a minister— and she must buy her water privately. Jay, Carol, and I spend the day fortifying ourselves before setting out. We drive north from Banket on the Chinhoyi road. In the fields there is maize, tall and strong, and for a moment my heart soars: something, I think, has survived. Then Carol shakes her head. These are not Zimbabwean farmers, she tells me. These, Carol explains, are the Chinese. Since 2008, when the U.S. dollar was legalized, effectively ending the old Zimbabwean currency, Mugabe has been selling his country wholesale to investors from overseas, India and the Far East. Seeing the farms from which we were evicted going to waste, Mugabe sensed an opportunity to revitalize the ailing economy. Now, these lands are contracted out to mechanized Chinese farmers, the grain and other produce shipped thousands of miles to feed the starving mass of inland China.

After all of Mugabe's rhetoric about taking the farms from the hated white colonists, he has opened his arms and invited in a colonist of a different sort. Zimbabwe is being colonized economically. He has found yet another way to rape the land.

When we get there, Two Tree Hill farm is still and silent, its fields unfarmed, bush creeping down from the hills. Down at the dam, three black men wearing only rags see our car approaching and, fishing spears in hand, approach us and block the road. In the backseat, Carol and I listen as Jay engages them in Shona. For a moment, it is unbearably tense; I do not know what he is saying. Then, at last, the men begin to laugh. Jay draws the car around and we climb toward Crofton. I ask him how he explained who we were, that this is *our* land, that they are fishing the waters of *our* dam. He looks at me, perplexed. Of course, he said no such thing. He told them we were lost, looking for somewhere to fish. The dam, they said, is empty now. It was once so full of bream, but they have taken it all.

We reach Crofton, and Crofton isn't there.

The only part of the house left standing is a tiny corner of brick wall where Jay's bedroom used to be. We climb out of the car. Except for that small pile of bricks, you would not know that a house had ever stood here. You would not know that there was a garden where my children played, a paddock where our horses grazed, a corner where Kate used to hide with a Scottie pup whenever we had to sell one. I cannot even pick out the place where I lay down with Frisky as she died.

"There's still the mango tree," says Jay.

The fruit is unripe, but he reaches up and plucks one.

The road from Crofton to the farm has disappeared. There is a deep gulley and we are unable to drive the car down to River Ranch to see what remains of the farm we started from virgin bush. Would the tobacco barns and sheds still be intact, or would they have been dismantled like the homestead on Crofton? *Just as well*, I think. It would bring back too many painful memories.

We head back toward Chinhoyi, but we cannot get near Palmerston Estates. A village has grown up around the old farmstead and we are not welcome here. Instead, we drive on, taking the worn, uneven road up to Carol's old home at Anchorage Farm.

Carol, it turns out, was approached a season before by a young white man, the son of a farmer who was evicted ten years before. He had a proposition: Anchorage Farm was going to waste, unused by the war vets who occupied her; what if he were to lease the land from them, develop it for commercial agriculture again, and share a fraction of the profits with

Carol? Seeing it as a way of getting *something* out of the farm she had loved throughout her life, Carol accepted the proposition.

Now Anchorage Farm is slowly returning to full use. There are potatoes high in the barns and workers in the fields. The Anchorage farmhouse still stands, though its grounds are overgrown and nobody has tried to beat back the bush that has taken over. Inside, the house is just a shell, only one room inhabited by a settler and his wife, the others filled with goats whose mess covers the bare ground. At first, the war vet's wife is happy to show us inside. Even so, I feel a hundred eyes on me, the men at work in the barns and yards turning to stare at us, wondering who we are.

We wander from room to room, seeing the places where Carol used to host dinners, the room where my son Paul and her son Andy would play. None of it is familiar, and as we go from room to room, Carol begins to grow more jittery.

"Keep calm, Carol."

"I am calm," she insists—but she is not.

At last, as we step back out of the farmhouse, goats flocking out of our path, Carol turns to the woman.

"You know, this is my farm. You're living on my farm."

I am frozen, but the war vet's wife says nothing. It is only now that I realize: I am not the only one afraid. The war vet's wife looks suddenly bereft, unable to find the words. We are, both of us, trapped by this situation, standing on opposite sides of a chasm Mugabe himself has opened up.

"Yes, madam."

She has adopted the old words of servitude, even though it is she who now lives on this farm.

Jay and I steer Carol toward the car, eager to be off Anchorage before it is too late.

Carol, I understand now, is not the only one entering into pacts with the war vets. Across Zimbabwe, the younger white generation—those with the skills to use the land like their fathers—are leasing land from those who took it from us. To lease land back to farmers like Pat and me would be frowned upon, but to lease to the younger generation is somehow more palatable. They call these people the *Born Frees*, white Zimbabweans not tarnished with the same stink of the colonial, the stigma of having fought for Rhodesia in the bush war. That they enter into these pacts is perhaps understandable; but so too is the hate the farmers of old feel at seeing their farms taken by new hands. Farmer is being set against farmer while, just outside their lines of sight, the country is being sold to the Chinese. Mugabe has achieved his objective of remaining in power, but the cost has been so great. In the morning, we drive back toward Mutare to cross back into Mozambique, and neither Jay nor I can comprehend how quickly Africa's jewel has become a symbol of her ruin.

In Vilanculos, Pat is waiting. I will have to tell him the epiphany I have reached: Zimbabwe, like Rhodesia, is already gone. That little fire in my heart that I have always nursed, the hope that one day we might return, has finally been extinguished. You can never really go back home.

At our little rondavel by the sea, gazing out over azure waters with the archipelago hanging on the horizon, Pat is looking at photographs. Of the one hundred and four horses we brought over the mountains, we have only twenty-six left—but the herd must live on. Across the world, horses need rescuing. For us, the land invasions threw this into stark relief, but in every corner of the world the story is the same.

In the photographs, eight horses—bays and grays, geldings and mares, a small skewbald foal with inquisitive eyes and a startled expression—stand in a South African field. The farm on which they live is being sold for redevelopment, and they must find new homes. Our hope is that they can stay together, come north over another border, and join us here. One day, Africa willing, our herd will be strong again—and, in that way, we will all live, the horses repaying our faith in them, Pat and I repaying their faith in us.

Together, we walk along the beach and up to the stables. There is yet time for a moonlit ride. We saddle up our old friends Lady and Brutus and take to the clifftop road. From here, we can see for miles.

I will have to tell Pat about his home, but we look out over this beautiful, chaotic corner of the world that has harbored us, and my lips remain sealed.

There will be another night.

Acknowledgments

A big thank-you to Kate Kellaway, who wrote an inspirational article that caught the eye of our charismatic literary agent, Patrick Walsh, who in turn recklessly boarded a plane after reading Kate's article and journeyed all the way to Vilanculos, Mozambique, to persuade Pat and me to write this book. Patrick, thank you so much for everything. A very special thanks to the wonderful Rob Dinsdale, who worked tirelessly to help me put the story together. Rob's enthusiasm, hard work, and friendship are the reasons this book has taken form. Thank you to HarperCollins for publishing our book and a special mention to editors David Highfill, Kate Cassaday, Myles Archibald, and Jessica Williams for their dedication, encouragement, and kindness.

What happened in our country of Zimbabwe is heartbreaking—not only the displacement of her people and the fact that everything we loved and cherished was taken away from us, but the saddest thing of all, the consequences for the animals. There are so many people who have helped us and I would love to mention you all, but there is simply not enough space, so thank you to everyone for helping us make this impossible dream possible.

We would like to thank our incredible family—Paul and Sue, Rob and Lyn, Tristin and Tammy, Aunt Celia, Ant and Jules, Paul and Louise, Brendon, Jenny, Chelsea and Gareth, Anita, Tania and Andrew, Tim, Dave, Julie and Robert Cambray, and Granny Beryl—who questioned our sanity but were always there to support us. We would like to thank our old farming community in the Chinhoyi area, who did so much to help us. Charl and Tertia Geldenhuys, Pat and Carol Johnson, Les De Jager, Nick Swanepoel, Henry and Celia Rautenbach, Janey and Fred Wallis, CFU Chinhoyi, Rory and Lindy Hensman, Gary and Joe Hensman, Rob Gordon, Barnaby and Bev Pyper, and a very special mention for Gaydia Tiffin and her daughter Romaen, who did so much for us and the horses.

A big thank-you to the following people and organizations, who have all contributed in some way to the story of the horses: Robyn Dunne, who has gone beyond the call of duty; Rachel Ashman; Heather Armstrong; Sarah Cox, my equine godmother; Chris Tufnell, a most wonderful vet who flew out from Newbury, England, to help me with the horses; Wendy Hofstee; Neville and Edie Pearce; Ben Young; Donna Walker; Danni Holdsworth; Gemma Campling; Ian Hodgson; Christine, Andy, and Kate Johnson; Aimee Smith; Lisa Molera; Tanya Lumsden; Ahmed; Rosalyn Sclare; Wrenne Hiscott; Meryl Harrison; Mutare SPCA; Charlie Rodwell; Lyn James; Gerry Penford; Sue Elton; Hillcrest School; Vicky Bowen; Bridget and Keith Holland; the Dondeyne family; Murray Dawson; Ivor Keppler; Heather Trezona; Allan Hislop; Meryl Knox; Andrew Frodsham; Johan; Uli Meiners; Alex Lewis; Soraya and Peter; Beach Lodge; Richard Winkfield; Bill and Jane Clegg; Ann and Ralph Cheesman; George and Angie Lock; Sally Dilton-Hill and family; Chris and Sharon Maas; Des and Sally Bekker; Christo and Jan Kok; Steven Krynauw; Cathy Buckle; Julia Townsend; Olwen Law; Chris Aston; Jenny Gibson; Michael Moye; John Logan; Njerenje School; Armil; Mafua; the Malgahaes family; Kim, Billy, and Trevor Landry; Sally Bryson; Sicanda; Albert; Nomagugu Khupe; Jonathan Mazulu; Never; Mai Never; Bejai; Luka; Jeff and Jane Reilly; Brenda; Sandy and Snowy; Archipelago Lodge; Tracy and Grant; Nick Falk; Norman and Freda Higgs; Adele and Zoe; Ursula; Courtney; Michaela; Adi and Samara; and Casa Rex. Thank you to all of our wonderful clients and volunteers for some amazing photos. A very big thank-you to the community of Vilanculos for all their support and enthusiasm.

A very special thanks to Lucy Campbell Jones, whose loyalty and love got me through so many of the dark days.

A very big thank-you to our beautiful children, Paul, Jay, and Kate Retzlaff; and our grandchildren, Bella, Georgie, and Talia, who contributed so much to the book; and finally to my wonderful husband, Patrick, who never gave up.